Joan Didion

# Joan Didion

## Substance and Style

Kathleen M. Vandenberg

Cover image: Joan Didion in her Corvette Stingray, 1968. Photograph by Julian Wasser. Reprinted with permission.

Published by State University of New York Press, Albany

© 2021 State University of New York

All rights reserved

Printed in the United States of America

No part of this book may be used or reproduced in any manner whatsoever without written permission. No part of this book may be stored in a retrieval system or transmitted in any form or by any means including electronic, electrostatic, magnetic tape, mechanical, photocopying, recording, or otherwise without the prior permission in writing of the publisher.

For information, contact State University of New York Press, Albany, NY
www.sunypress.edu

**Library of Congress Cataloging-in-Publication Data**

Name: Vandenberg, Kathleen M., 1973– author.
Title: Joan Didion : substance and style / Kathleen M. Vandenberg.
Description: Albany : State University of New York Press, [2021] | Includes
   bibliographical references and index.
Identifiers: LCCN 2020024719 | ISBN 9781438481395 (hardcover : alk. paper) |
   ISBN 9781438481388 (pbk. : alk. paper) | ISBN 9781438481401 (ebook)
Subjects: LCSH: Didion, Joan—Criticism and interpretation. | Didion,
   Joan—Literary style.
Classification: LCC PS3554.I33 Z94 2021 | DDC 813/.54—dc23
LC record available at https://lccn.loc.gov/2020024719

10 9 8 7 6 5 4 3 2 1

*For Chris, Beckett, Dashiell, and Sidney,*
*who gave me the time, support, and space to write*
*And for Até, for 17 years, my constant keyboard companion*

# Contents

Acknowledgments — ix

Introduction: To Shift the Structure of a Sentence — 1

Chapter 1  Language and the Mechanism of Terror: *Salvador* — 29

Chapter 2  Preferred Narratives: New York City after the Central Park Jogger — 53

Chapter 3  Lifting the Curtain: The Rhetoric of Politics — 73

Chapter 4  *Terra Incognita*: On Loss and Memory — 103

Conclusion: What Remains — 133

Notes — 147

Bibliography — 163

Index — 169

# Acknowledgments

Cover photograph © Julian Wasser.

Some parts of the conclusion were originally published in *A Dark California: Essays on Dystopian Depictions in Popular Culture* © 2017. Edited by Katarzyna Nowak-McNeice and Agata Zarzycka. By permission of McFarland & Company, Inc., Box 611, Jefferson NC 28640. www.mcfarlandbooks.com.

An earlier draft of chapter 5 was published in *Prose Studies* 39, no. 1: 39–60 DOI: 10.1080/01440357.2017.1326451, as "Joan Didion's Memoirs: Substance & Style," by permission of Taylor & Francis Group, 3 Park Square, Milton Park, Abingdon, Oxon, OX14 4RN, UK. https://www.tandfonline.com/.

# Introduction

## *To Shift the Structure of a Sentence*

> We don't need more polemic about the superiority of the various old or new journalisms, nor more general paeans to Didion's keen eye, but a clearer and more detailed analysis of how writers like Didion incorporate the world in their texts. We need a greater appreciation for the sophisticated poetics of factual literature.
>
> —Mark Muggli, "The Poetics of Joan Didion's Journalism"

To be more than a casual reader of Joan Didion is to be familiar with a writer whose biography has likely commanded as much attention as her prose, if not more. Moving with ease between fiction and nonfiction, between novels, essays, reviews, and memoirs, she has been a consistently prolific writer, one who has not often been absent from the literary scene nor the public eye. Early extended critical works such as Mark Royden Winchell's 1980 *Joan Didion*, Katherine Usher Henderson's 1981 biography *Joan Didion*, and 1994's *The Critical Response to Joan Didion*, edited by Sharon Felton, as well as the far more recent *The Last Love Song: A Biography of Joan Didion* by Tracy Daugherty (2015), offer both comprehensive chronologies of her life as well as thoughtful analyses of the ways significant events in her childhood and early adulthood appear to have influenced her worldview as well as the thematic tendencies of her writing.[1]

The details of her life, many of them revealed in her own essays and interviews, have been extensively recorded and repeated—in these works and shorter responses—from her upbringing in Sacramento, her time at Berkeley, and her work with *Vogue* to her marriage to John Gregory Dunne in 1964 and her adoption of daughter Quintana Roo in 1966, as well as the subsequent deaths of both in recent years. As well, her slight size, reserved manner, apparent reticence, and tendency toward ill health have been detailed and dwelled upon, as has her marriage and her relationship to her daughter. These biographical details have been fleshed out with extended commentary on her eye for detail as well as her attention to décor, dress, and designer goods. Most often, such treatment of her biographical details has been offered in service of reviewing her latest work or initiating and sustaining a scholarly response to her oeuvre, making it clear that, for most critics, *who* Didion is or was is essential to understanding how and what she writes. Daugherty's biography, which is comprehensive and richly detailed, continues this trend. And yet, as essayist Katie Roiphe writes,

> even after reading every single word Didion has ever published, how much does one know about her? One knows what she packs on a trip to interview a subject, one knows about the jasmine she smells on the way home from the airport in Los Angeles, but one knows almost nothing about her family, say, or her marriage, or her daughter. The personal information she imparts is so stylized, so mannered, so controlled that it is no longer personal information. The "I" in her essays is an elegant silhouette of a woman. There is something shadowy about her, something peculiarly obscure, like the famous photograph of her hiding behind huge sunglasses. She is, in the end, a writer of enormous reserve.[2]

The prose of an author much admired, frequently imitated, and many times hailed as "American's greatest living writer," deserves and demands a much closer and more recent look than can be found in any extant reviews, articles, or biographies.[3] This is especially the case at this particular moment in history—the so-called "post-truth era." Former President Barack Obama recently bemoaned the fact that "too much of politics . . . seems to reject the very concept of objective truth."[4] His comments reflect a broader consensus that, with the election of President Trump in 2016, public opinion has seemed increasingly susceptible to emotional appeals, outright falsehoods, and "alternative facts."[5] As a recent *New York Times* article points out, "the past decade has seen a precipitous rise not just in anti-scientific thinking . . . but in all manner of reactionary obscurantism, from online conspiracy theories to the much-discussed death of expertise."[6]

But decades before there was collective and popular agreement that, in politics and the media, fictions and lies often trump facts and reality, Didion was writing critically (and dismissively) of the narratives spun by politicians, public figures, and cultural icons. Her critiques resonated because relatively few at the time (outside of scholars and conspiracy fans) questioned the authority and objectivity of the dominant institutions of the time: the government and the news media. Ironically, though, it is now the case that "with the rise of alternative facts . . . it has become clear that whether or not a statement is believed depends far less on its veracity than on the conditions of its "construction"—that is, who is making it, to whom it's being addressed and from which institutions it emerges and is made visible." French philosopher Bruno Latour believes that "a greater understanding of the circumstances out of which misinformation arises and the communities in which it takes root . . . will better equip us to combat it."[7]

It is exactly this "greater understanding" that Didion's social, cultural, and political critiques offer readers. She has, in both subject matter and approach, been amazingly prescient about the future of political and cultural discourse and the ways in which patterns of thinking and narratives of "fact" are rhetorically constructed, and grounded both in the past and in adherence to regional traditions and values. Back in the 1970s she was already perceiving, as Nathaniel Rich notes in his foreword to *South and West: From a Notebook*, that the past was not dead and that what she saw in the South—an embrace of tradition and clear divisions between races, a solidarity that grows stronger the more it faces the disapproval of the Northern elite—was the future. As he observes:

> Two decades into the new millennium . . . a plurality of the population has clung defiantly to the old way of life. They still believe in the viability of armed revolt. . . . They have resisted with mockery, then rage, the collapse of the old identity categories. . . . They have resisted new technology and scientific evidence of global ecological collapse. The force of this resistance has been strong enough to elect a president.[8]

Didion, he argues, saw this long before anyone else, saw beyond the dreams of the urban inhabitants of coastal cities among whom she lived and worked, and with whom she socialized.

She wrote then, and writes now, to undermine the power of ideological narratives, question our reliance on abstractions, and criticize the "magical thinking"[9] of politicians, the media, cultural icons, and the general public. If it can be said, as it is in *The New York Times*, that "our current post-truth moment is less a product of Latour's ideas than a validation of them," the same can be said Didion's writings.

The stories we are told, the stories we tell ourselves, she dissects and deconstructs, laying bare, with remarkable concision and precision, the rhetorical maneuvering of those who control the narratives of public and private discourse. As Chris Anderson notes, "she is profoundly metadiscursive in her writing, everywhere concerned not simply with the experiences she is trying to describe but with the language of those experiences—with the jargon, the rhetoric, the diction of individuals and groups and how that language reflects a point of view."[10] She has been insistent, across the decades, that we think critically and skeptically about language and its power to shape our perceptions of reality, and in this age of viral propaganda, social media memes, internet trolls, and fake news, her acute eye for rhetorical strategies is more relevant than ever.

This book analyzes her rhetorical craft, the technical ways her precise, densely packed, and exquisitely worded sentences pierce the illusory narratives dominating public discourse and establish new perspectives from which readers can understand reality. Frequently poetic in its fluidity, rhythms, and repetitions, her prose is no less powerful for being beautiful; it does not offer an escape into aesthetic experience, but instead demands that the reader see things her way, with her shrewd and incisive vision. She may be popularly viewed as shy, emotional to the point of being neurotic, and unnecessarily obsessed with the material minutiae of upper-class living, but in her prose she is, in fact, aggressively articulate, insistently rational, and concerned far less with detailing the domestic lives of the rich and famous than in dissecting the mythologies generated both by individuals and those in power.

Writing, Didion notes, is "an aggressive, even a hostile act. You can disguise its aggressiveness all you want with veils of subordinate clauses and qualifiers and tentative subjunctives, with ellipses and evasions—with the whole manner of intimating rather than claiming, of alluding, rather than stating."[11] Disguise it, she frequently does, but readers should take her at her word when she claims that she is a moralist, one who tends "to perceive things as right or wrong, in a very vivid way." Her self-described "strong West Coast ethic" may in fact dictate that she adopts a "strictly *laissez-faire* attitude"[12] when it comes to telling others what to do, but the result is that she persuades them with a style whose power is all the more potent for its subtlety. This is a controlled and deliberate subtlety; as she notes in a 2005 interview, usually her writing process involves "discovering what's on my mind and then hiding it."[13]

This book traces the major features of her style as it has evolved—in step with shifts in her life, experiences, and priorities—over the last four decades of her career, beginning with *Salvador* in 1983, when she moved away from an earlier focus on domestic and cultural concerns to study public, political, and international narratives. The chapters to follow offer close rhetorical analysis of her style, revealing that this move was accompanied by a grammatical and semantic shift in her prose as well the development of a voice that grew more skeptical, ironic, analytical, and certain during the last three decades of the twentieth century. The book ends by analyzing the memoirs she composed in the wake of great personal losses in order to foreground the beautiful power of her prose to move readers and invite their identification even as she circles back to a more tentative voice and the intimately personal concerns of her own life.

"Writing is the act of saying *I*, of imposing oneself upon other people," she notes in "Why I Write"; it is a way "of saying *listen to me, see it my way, change your mind*" [emphasis original] (5). Her wish to act rhetorically upon her readers is not just evident in her overt propositional claims or her inductive accumulating of evidence but in the very way she figures her language. Hers is a "sophisticated poetics;" she works on the level of syntax and diction to select, omit, rearrange, minimize and amplify, to persuade through style rather than merely with overt propositional claims or the laying out of detailed evidence. She does so, however, in a manner so controlled and elliptical that her irony, wit, and, often, disdain, are not apparent to the casual reader, nor, more crucially, as this book will argue, is the rhetorical potency of her style.

That she herself is, and has always been, aware of the importance of style, however, is without question. Here is a writer who, from her earliest days, revealed a keen awareness of how sentences work.[14] "All I know about grammar," she writes in "Why I Write," "is its infinite power. To shift the structure of a sentence alters the meaning of that sentence, as definitely and inflexibly as the position of a camera alters the meaning of the object photographed" (7). Even before the years she spent working at *Vogue* after winning its Prix de Paris in 1956 (a job where Associate Editor Allene Talmey would go over her brief captions and ruthlessly markup superfluous words and imprecise verbs) she was reflecting on the power of form over content.[15] In interviews and essays over the years, she has consistently emphasized her own attention to the control that sentences exert over content, spoken of the importance of the rhythms and echoes created at the level of syntax, and reflected on her own processes of revising and editing at the sentence level.

If shy or inarticulate in person, on paper she is a woman in control of her material down to the level of punctuation, which she manipulates for emphasis not grammatical correctness. Consider, for instance, the following exchange between Didion and Dunne and long-time friend Sara Davidson during an interview conducted by the latter in 1984:

> He said: Did you tell Sara the first line of *Angel Visits*? She shook her head, no. He said the line from memory: "*I have never seen Madame Bovary in the flesh but imagine my mother dancing.*"
> "Fantastic," I said. "Is there a comma after 'flesh'?"
> Joan: "Yes."
> John: "The first line, if you get it right, immediately sets the tone of the book."
> Joan said, "It might change." After a pause, "I may take the comma out."
> (The next morning she indeed decided. "There shouldn't be a comma.")[16]

The placing of a comma may or may not seem important to the reader, but for Didion, control over every aspect of her sentences is paramount; she sees the arrangement of sentences as doing "work," sees sentences themselves functioning as more than carriers of propositional meanings. Form is, for her, both separate from and complementary to (if done correctly) content. "The arrangement of words matters, and the arrangement you want can be found in the pictures in your mind," she writes, in one of the most-quoted passages in "Why I Write"; "The picture dictates the arrangement. The picture dictates whether this will be a sentence with or without clauses, a sentence that ends hard or a dying-fall sentence, long or short, active or passive" (7). Her ability not only to manipulate her sentences but to articulate the compositional choices she makes in order to do so reveal a writer in control of her craft at the most precise level.

This control, according to Didion, was learned at an early age, as she found herself drawn to the prose of writers like Hemingway, Conrad, and James. She found, for instance, Hemingway's arrangement of sentences "magnetic" and the sentences themselves "deceptively simple," "clear, clean," and "exciting." As she has commented on in several interviews, her response to this attraction was to start typing these sentences out herself, at which point she "could see how they worked."[17] She could, for instance, see "how a short sentence worked in a paragraph, how a long sentence worked. Where the commas worked. How every word had to matter."[18] Her attraction to Conrad's prose was similarly based on a sense of awe at his sentences, which to her "sounded wonderful." And James's sentences "with all those clauses" impressed upon her the importance of "keeping the options open, letting the sentence cover as much as it could."[19]

Her awareness of, and appreciation for, the variety and work of sentences and the importance of form is not merely, or even primarily, aesthetic. Rather, just as her awareness of scriptwriting and filmmaking enables her to understand the power of the camera's placement and movement in directing the audience's attention, her familiarity with the range of compositional choices available at the level of the punctuation, diction, and syntax permits her to craft her prose to achieve rhetorical ends. No sentence is composed carelessly; rewriting is an essential part of her composing process. Each book she writes, as she reveals in a 2006 interview, is retyped and marked up, from the beginning, each day, in order for her to get into the rhythm of her writing.[20] Furthermore, during the almost four decades of her marriage to John Dunne, they each read and edited everything the other wrote. What results from this process is sentences that are deliberately rhetorical in structure. Whether employing metaphors to make vivid and tangible what would otherwise be banal or abstract or depending on parenthetical asides to draw attention to her often-witty take on absurd situations, she maintains control over the composition of each sentence, keenly aware of the function of form.

Her awareness of the persuasive effects of her style is often evidenced in her interviews. On one occasion, justifying her use of repetition in *A Book of Common Prayer*, she remarked that "it seemed constantly necessary to remind the readers to make certain connections." She continues, "technically it's almost a chant. You could read it as an attempt to cast a spell or come to terms with certain contemporary demons."[21] Repetition—of sounds, words, phrases, and clauses—is one of the trademarks of Didion's style, but it is certainly not the only technique she employs to cast her spell on readers. Her familiarity with rhetorical figures enables her to craft sentences that alternately emphasize and marginalize key elements in her nonfiction. It allows her to create rapport with her readers and persuade them to accept her vision of events as fact.

All of which is to say that, for Didion and her readers, her style matters.[22] But this is too frequently overlooked in the many responses to her work, which remain heavily invested in "discovering" the "real" Joan Didion behind the oversized sunglasses and impenetrable gaze. The nature of Didion's work has been at least partially responsible for inviting this kind of attention. As one of the initial group of writers (among them Tom Wolfe, Norman Mailer, and Truman Capote) considered "New Journalists," Didion has spent decades composing essays that are at once personal and political, revealing and elliptical; she has built a body of nonfiction prose that appears to tell the world as much about Didion herself as it does about the subjects she covers, even if it does so obliquely at times. This is a woman who began a piece on Hawaii, "In the Islands," by describing an uneasy moment with her husband and daughter in the Royal Hawaiian Hotel in Honolulu, and writing "we are here on this island in the middle of the Pacific in lieu of filing for divorce."[23]

She continues, addressing the reader directly, as she often does in her earlier writings, and explains that she wants "you to know, as you read me, precisely who I am and where I am and what is on my mind. I want you to understand exactly what you are getting: you are getting a woman who for some time now has felt radically separated from most of the ideas that seem to interest other people."[24] Such personal revelations and ruminations are heavily scattered throughout her first two essay collections, 1969's *Slouching Towards Bethlehem* and 1979's *The White Album*, both of which established her as a serious and critically acclaimed author and remain among her best-known work. Their presence in these earlier writings established and influenced perceptions of Didion in the decades to come, with the effect that it is difficult to find a response to her work that is not heavily invested in trying to understand the author as much as her writing.

The other tendency of reviewers, the vast majority of whom write in glowing terms about her style, is to offer aesthetic assessments of her prose. Their work tends to view style as something added to thought, as superfluous, mere dressing, however beautiful, for the more substantial content it clothes. These tend to point to a number of striking phrases or evocative words and comment on their beauty, clarity, or sophistication, while reiterating the significance of her style.[25] Over the decades, a handful of adjectives have come to dominate these reviews—Didion's prose is described as "spare," "elliptical," "rhythmic," "incantatory," "long," and "striking." The responses of Michiko Kakutani, well-known *New York Times* book critic, who has written reviews of Didion's work over more than three decades as well as named her as a point of reference in dozens of other book reviews, alone demonstrate this tendency. Kakutani has closely traced the trajectory of Didion's writing since 1979; her reviews are always favorable and frequently use the same adjective to describe Didion's writing: "elliptical." The choice of adjective is not surprising—after all, Didion herself said of her novel *Play It as It Lays* that she "had . . . a technical intention . . . to write a novel so elliptical and fast that it would be over before you noticed it, a novel so fast that it would scarcely exist on the page at all" ("Why," 7)—but the number of times it is employed by Kakutani and others is striking.

Kakutani first writes about Didion in 1979's "Joan Didion: Staking Out California," her longest piece on Didion, a combination of profile, biography, and review in which she interviews Didion and assesses her body of work (both fiction and nonfiction) up until that point. This piece offers an example of both of the tendencies noted earlier—Kakutani focuses in great detail on the personal details of Didion's life before noting the aesthetic qualities of her prose. Within the first page of the article, after describing a visit with Didion in her Brentwood home, Kakutani notes that "novelist and poet James Dickey has called Didion the finest woman prose stylist writing in English today."[26] She continues with "and she has created, in her books one of the most devastating and distinctive portraits of modern America in be found in fiction and nonfiction." Kakutani then devotes a substantial portion of the rest of the article to noting such things as Didion's height and weight, the "carnation pink" of her girlhood bedroom, and her delight in domestic routines.

It is not until the penultimate page that she returns to Didion's prose, noting of *Play It as It Lays* that it is: "arranged in 84 staccato-paced takes" and "the elliptical prose is pared down, perfectly clean"[27] (after which she begins to summarize the novel's setting and plot). She mentions Didion's style once more near the end, observing that both *Play It as It Lays* and *A Book of Common Prayer* evidence Didion's reporter's eye, her ability to ground "the melodramatics of the plot in a precision of detail."[28] The reader of this article is never offered an explanation of how or where the prose is elliptical nor what is meant by "perfectly clean," and though it is implied that these are in fact positive qualities, Kakutani does not move beyond aesthetic assessment to analysis.

Such omissions are understandable, given the hybrid nature and purpose of the piece—but Kakutani's reliance on these same stock phrases across her handful of other Didion reviews, despite what one must assume is her growing familiarity with the writer over the decades, means the specifics of Didion's style remain opaque. For instance, her 1996 review of Didion's novel *The Last Thing He Wanted*, describes the work as a "dark, willfully elliptical novel that often reads like a thematic and stylistic distillation of Didion's work to date," an evaluation she does nothing to unpack, so that the reader is left unclear both as to what Didion's previous style was like and how it appears now that it is "distilled."[29] In 2005, more than twenty-five years since she first reviewed Didion's work, she composes a sympathetic and admiring review of *The Year of Magical Thinking*, within which she concludes that "the elliptical constructions and sometimes mannered prose of the author's recent fiction give way to the stunning candor and piercing details that distinguished her groundbreaking early books of essays."[30] This rather backhanded compliment fails to clarify in what ways Didion's previous prose was elliptical or mannered, and her next article, a 2011 review of *Blue Nights*, offers a similarly imprecise evaluation of *Blue Nights*. She writes that "whereas *Magical Thinking* was raw and jagged and immediate—the work of someone who prized order and control and found herself suddenly spinning into madness—'Blue Nights' is a more elliptical book."[31]

Other frequent reviewers of Didion's work display the same habits of praising Didion's style while remaining rather vague when it comes to analysis, in part because book reviews are obviously intended more to indicate, in a rather concise fashion, the reviewer's attitude toward the work reviewed than to parse in great detail the elements of writing responsible for this attitude. Thus, while many of the major reviews of her work contain high praise for her style, offering words and phrases the critics find especially enchanting, it is hard to get a sense from these reviews exactly why Didion's style is so distinctive or striking. For instance, fairly early on in 1979, well-known *New York Times* book critic John Leonard wrote of Didion's prose in *The White Album*, "[L]anguage is her seismograph and style her sanity. Nobody writes better English prose than Joan Didion. Try to rearrange one of her sentences, and you've realized that the sentence was inevitable, a hologram."[32]

Twenty-six years later, in reviewing *The Year of Magical Thinking* and noting that he's been "reading Didion ever since she started doing it for money . . . have reviewed most of her books since *Play It as It Lays*, and cannot pretend to objectivity," he notes that

> I've been trying for four decades to figure out why her sentences are better than mine or yours . . . something about cadence. They come at you, if not from ambush, then in gnomic haikus, icepick laser beams, or waves. Even the space on the page around these sentences is more interesting than could be expected, as if to square a sandbox for the Sphinx.[33]

A more recent piece, by Roiphe, comments on Didion's "use of *kind of* lulling, incantatory repetition," and her "long, oddly constructed sentences, with ridiculously complicated syntax . . . that are *weirdly beautiful, like tall and awkward teenagers*" [emphasis mine].³⁴ Roiphe's comments, like Leonard's and Kakutani's and so much of the popular response to Didion, are evaluative in nature rather than analytical—they praise aspects of her prose style or (less commonly) condemn others without articulating the stylistic choices she makes to produce such effects or analyzing the impact of those choices, with the result that for all the attention her style has received, there has been relatively little unpacking of her prose.

I begin this book by sifting through these responses, as well as her essays and interviews, in order to establish a background against which a new perspective on Didion's work may be added, a perspective possible only now that Didion, aged eighty-five at the time of this writing, has had the time to trace a substantial trajectory from the days of Haight-Ashbury to a post-9/11 world, from her own days as a young California writer just starting out, to an experienced critic who has honed her craft. With this book, I wish to argue that looking back over her career from this vantage point reveals the insistently and inherently rhetorical nature of her style. Her essays are not written as mere expressions of her own dissatisfaction with or distrust of the current culture or political situation, but are rather what she deems "calls to action." These calls become increasingly political in her later years, particularly in the time after she began writing under editor Bob Silvers in the early '80s, years that taught her that writing about politics had a "certain Sisyphean aspect," insofar as all efforts to define patterns or document inconsistencies seemed insufficient "to stop the stone that was our apprehension of politics from hurtling back downhill."³⁵

> Like Lily McClellan in *Run River*, she is "strikingly frail" (Didion is 5 feet 2, and weighs 95 pounds); like Maria in *Play It as It Lays*, she used to chain-smoke and wear chiffon scarves over her red hair; and like Charlotte in *A Book of Common Prayer*, she possesses "an extreme and volatile thinness . . . she was a woman . . . with a body that masqueraded as that of a young girl. There is a certain sadness in the face that indicates a susceptibility to what she calls "early morning dread"; even indoors, she wears oversized sunglasses to protect her light-sensitive eyes.³⁶

Kakutani's characterization of Didion during a 1979 visit both mirrors Didion's own frequent comments about her physical stature and sensitivities and anticipates decades' worth of commentary on these qualities. The secondary literature on Didion is replete with comments about her slight size, her reserve, her ill health, her at-times inarticulate conversational style. Consider Caitlin Flanagan's recollection of Didion's visit to her house in the early 1970s—only fourteen at the time, Flanagan recalls being struck by Didion's discomfort. She recently wrote of that evening:

> I can tell you this for certain: anything you have ever read by Didion about the shyness that plagued her in her youth, and about her inarticulateness in those days, in the face of even the most banal questions, was not a writer's exaggeration of a minor character trait for literary effect. The contemporary diagnosis for the young woman at our dinner table would be profound—crippling—social-anxiety disorder.[37]

Leonard, who provided the introduction for the 2006 Everyman Collection *Stories We Tell Ourselves in Order to Live*, observes of Didion that, over the years "she seemed sometimes so sensitive that whole decades hurt her feelings, and the prose on the page suggested Valéry's 'shiverings of an effaced leaf,' as if her next trick might be evaporation."[38] Having seen Didion speak in person once, on a book tour for *Political Fictions*, I too was struck by her size and fragility, which, while apparent in photos and television interviews, is quite a bit more obvious in person. What I am suggesting, however, is that her looks and frequent commentary on her health are too frequently seen as emblematic of her approach to life and writing, with the result that readers mistake her tentative social interactions as indicative of a similar uncertainty in her perspective or her prose. The fact that her nonfiction is largely to be found in the form of essays, a genre that embraces hesitance and ambiguity, has only added to the perception that Didion writes from the heart rather than the head, her work more personal than political.

Didion is quite open about her shyness, her tendency to be "neurotically inarticulate,"[39] noting in one interview that though she likes a lot of people, she doesn't "give the impression of being there" due to being "terribly inarticulate." "A sentence," she says, "doesn't occur to me as a whole thing unless I'm working."[40] In another interview, in response to the interviewer asking about "all this business of fragility," Didion concedes "I am not only small, I am too thin, I am pale, I do not look like a California person. It generally makes people think that I must be frail." But she then concludes "I'm not actually very frail. I'm very healthy. I eat a lot. I don't cry a lot."[41] For all her mention of migraines ("I was in fact as sick as I have ever been when I was writing 'Slouching Towards Bethlehem'; the pain kept me awake at night and so for twenty and twenty-one hours a day I drank gin-and-hot-water to blunt the aspirin and took Dexedrine to blunt the gin")[42]; depressions ("I cried until I was not even aware when I was crying and when I was not, cried in elevators and in taxis and in Chinese laundries, and when I went to the doctor he said only that I seemed to be depressed, and should see a 'specialist' ");[43] and psychiatric reports (one of her own is famously offered in "The White Album" as evidence of a moderately disabling period of doubt in the late sixties), Didion is neither tentative nor inarticulate in her essays. There is nothing uncertain and little emotional about her prose—these are not the incoherent and self-indulgent ramblings of an unstable woman. She is, in fact, on evidence, much as she observes admiringly of Georgia O'Keeffe, "simply hard, a straight shooter, a woman clean of received wisdom and open to what she sees."[44]

What Didion sees, appears, at a glance, to be inconsequential, tangential, even trivial. But such appearances are, like her assessment of Hemingway's sentences, "deceptively simple."[45] Her meticulous eye for detail, her insistence on juxtaposing the material with the abstract, is neither superficial nor merely poetic, but instead intensely rhetorical. For example, note the following description of a few events from the '60s:

> On the morning of John Kennedy's death in 1963 I was buying, at Ransohoff's in San Francisco, a short silk dress in which to be married. A few years later this dress of mine was ruined when, at a dinner party in Bel-Air, Roman Polanski accidentally spilled a glass of red wine on it. Sharon Tate was also a guest at this party, although she and Roman Polanski were not yet married. On July 27, 1970, I went to the Magnin-Hi Shop on the third floor of I. Magnin in Beverly Hills and picked out, at Linda Kasabian's request, the dress in which she began her testimony about the murders at Sharon Tate Polanski's house on Cielo Drive.[46]

One might be tempted to be struck, as many reviewers have been, by the ease with which she name drops, the dexterity with which she intertwines her shopping trips at luxury stores with some of the most significant events of that decade. Barbara Grizzuti Harrison, for example, writes of Didion's use of details and the specific passage above "these, and other assorted facts—such as the fact that Didion chose to buy the dress Linda Kasabian wore at the Manson trial at I. Magnin in Beverly Hills—put me more in mind of a neurasthenic Cher than of a writer who has been called America's finest woman prose stylist."[47] But the sentences preceding Didion's passage are crucial. In light of the tumultuous events of the '60s, and particularly the Manson murders, she writes, "all narrative was sentimental . . . all connections were equally meaningful, and equally senseless. Try these:" The readers are then invited to make the connections between the events presented, and experience for themselves the unnerving, sometimes awful, incoherence of those times.

The absence of transitional words suggesting causality as well as her reliance on declarative sentences create the impression that she is merely recording a series of events rather than attempting to impose her own interpretation of events on readers, but the intent is clearly rhetorical. At the end of the piece, she confesses that the events described and the fact that she and Polanski are godparents to the same child have not been made any more coherent to her through the process of writing. This is not offered as an expression of her personal inability to cope with the decade and is not to be understood as her recognition of her failure as a writer—it is offered, rather, as proof of the failure of narratives to resolve certain ambiguities inherent to reality.

The presence of celebrity names as well as the attention to luxury goods and references to a life lived among the rich and the famous, however, have proved a distraction to many of her reviewers, with the result that their focus turns either to imitating her attention to detail or ascribing to it a potency having nothing to do with persuasion. As an example of the first, one can consider the opening to Kakutani's "Joan Didion: Staking out California," which begins: "Didion is sitting in the den. The rooms of her house possess all the soothing order and elegance of a *Vogue* photo spread: sofas covered in floral chintz, lavender love seats the exact color of the potted orchids on the mantelpiece, porcelain elephant end tables, and dozens of framed pictures of family and friends."[48] As an example of the latter, there is Caitlin Flanagan's assertion that Didion's "attention—serious, thoughtful, and audaciously self-assured—to clothes and houses and flatware . . . accounts in large measure for the rapt interest women have always paid her work."[49] Flanagan may well be right about women being invested in such details, but this speaks more to the concerns of Didion's readers than to Didion's intent.

According to Didion, "we tell ourselves stories in order to live," and it was only during the turbulent years of the 1960s that she "began to doubt the premises of all the stories I had ever told myself."[50] She was, she explains in an interview with the *Paris Review*, a child "who tended to perceive the world in terms of things read about it." She began, she says, "with a literary idea of experience," and reflects that she still doesn't know "where all the lies are."[51] It is the "doubt," this suspicion of narratives that she begins to feel in the 1960s, that drives Didion's nonfiction, from her earliest more "personal" and cultural pieces to her later overtly political writing and her latest memoirs. In essay after essay, she questions abstractions, mocks attachment to transcendent ideals, and criticizes those, including herself, who use language as a form of "magical thinking." Frequently drawing on allusions to the world of script writing, movie production, and acting—a world familiar to her both through her personal connections to Hollywood "players" and her professional work with Dunne as a screenwriter on several pictures—she throws into relief the vast chasms between rhetoric and reality.

While it is not possible to locate the origins of her skepticism in any one biographical detail or any one essay, there is a good deal to suggest that her upbringing in the Sacramento Valley as a fifth-generation Californian played a large part in her initial interest in the gaps between reality and mythology. This was a childhood spent as a descendent of "a congeries of families, that has always been in the Sacramento Valley,"[52] families that not only passed down quilts, photographs, and flatware, but also stories, narratives about "crossings," abandonment, survival, resilience, and the frontier mentality. What has remained of all these for Didion, and in fact, grown stronger across the years, is not only the physical objects and their symbolic meanings, but a distrust in mythologies generated by those invested—historically, personally, financially, and politically—in a certain idea of California as a western Eden.

Relatively early on in her career, she remarks on her doubts regarding this vision, reflecting as a thirty-one-year-old that "it is hard to find California now, unsettling to wonder how much of it was merely imagined or improvised; melancholy to realize how much of anyone's memory is no true memory at all but only the traces of someone else's memory, stories handed down on the family network."[53] This distrust in memory and mythology, especially insofar as it related to her own understanding of the land of her childhood, only grows as she gets older and is able to see that land from a distance, both figuratively and literally. In *Where I Was From*, her 2003 collection of essays on her childhood and California, she reflects on a speech (entitled "Our California Heritage") she delivered at her eighth-grade graduation, noting that "such was the blinkering effects of the local dreamtime that it would be some years before I recognized that certain aspects of 'Our California Heritage' did not add up. . . . It was after this realization that I began trying to find the 'point' of California, to locate some message in its history."[54] As many critics have commented, so much of what she writes about California signifies change, loss, and disillusionment, and these are themes she returns to repeatedly across the trajectory of her nonfiction writing.

The California imagination, Didion comes to realize, is derived from the claiming of the landscape and "the romance of emigration, the radical abandonment of established attachments," and remains insistently invested in the symbolic to the exclusion of the merely literal.[55] Didion's repeated description of her attempts to penetrate the myth of California is offered less to highlight her own personal failure to decipher the California code than to exemplify the ultimate opacity of any mythology and to undermine attempts to turn the literal into the symbolic. Her gradual disillusionment with the mythology of California reflects a larger disenchantment with mythologies of any type. While her initial writings mostly concern mythologies related to place (California and New York for the most part, though also Hawaii, and, later, Miami and Central America), she later widens her focus to include political, public, and personal mythologies.

According to Didion, these mythologies, with their attendant abstractions, ideologies, and platitudes, became impossible for her to ignore or accept at some point in her early thirties. At that time, she writes, she began to feel like she had lost the plot, missed her cues, and mislaid the script. "In what would probably be the middle of my life," she reflects, "I wanted still to believe in the narrative and in the narrative's intelligibility, but to know that one could change the scene with every cut was to begin to perceive the experience as rather more electrical than ethical."[56] Her distrust in narrative and rejection of her previous "essentially romantic ethic"[57] came about in large part due to her self-described "outsider" status—a status that permitted her to turn her critical gaze on the mythologies constructed by others "to fill the void."[58] As she writes in her essay about Michael Laski, "General Secretary of the Central Committee of the Communist Party U.S.A.": "I am comfortable with the Michael Laskis of this world, with those who live outside rather than in, those in whom the sense of dread is so acute that they turn to extreme and doomed commitments."[59]

She continues to emphasize her outsider status throughout her body of work, repeatedly highlighting—ironically, dismissively, condescendingly—the means by which others simplistically resort to narratives to confront and resolve their dread. She describes, for instance, the way Hollywood insiders, in confronting serious social issues such as racism, turn to the conventions of film to cope with disturbing ambiguities: "[W]hat we are talking about here," she remarks, "is faith in a dramatic convention. Things 'happen' in motion pictures. There is always a resolution, always a strong cause-effect dramatic line, and to perceive the world in those terms is to assume an ending for every social scenario."[60]

Narratives are often heavily dependent on abstractions and ideals, and these too she dismantles coolly, as she does the language used to communicate them. Her ironic use of quotation marks has been much noted; these are frequently employed in service of undermining the rhetoric she observes being used by individuals and groups committed to one or another dream or ideology.[61] In describing her trip to cover the national congress of the United States Junior Chamber of Commerce in Santa Monica, for instance, she writes that she supposes she went out there "in search of the abstraction lately called 'Middle America,'" and ends up describing people who exemplify the beliefs of many in small cities and towns across America insofar as they embrace business success as a "transcendent ideal." Ultimately, the abstractions and ideals she analyzes are upheld in language parroted and unexamined, often to the great detriment of those who employ it.

There is, for instance, the Haight-Ashbury movement, which she refuses to idealize or romanticize, seeing it as composed of "children" who are "less in rebellion against the society than ignorant of it, able only to feed back certain of its most publicized self-doubts, *Vietnam, Saran-Wrap, diet pills, the Bomb.*" These children are avidly anti-intellectual, she says, "their only proficient vocabulary is in the society's platitudes," and this disturbs her, committed, as she is "to the idea that the ability to think for one's self depends upon one's mastery of the language."[62] Feminists come in for the same kind of scorn; she describes the literature of the movement as beginning to "reflect the thinking of women who did not really understand the movement's ideological base." From her perspective, these women are therefore all too ready to be moved by "half-truths" that, when repeated "authenticated themselves," preventing women from asking what she sees as obvious and yet essential questions regarding their own autonomy. Failure to ask these questions, on either their part or on the part of those observing the movement, means being complicit with these arguments, arguments she sees as existing at a "spooky level" insofar as they "had only the most tenuous and unfortunate relationship to the actual condition of being a woman."[63] It is these "tenuous and unfortunate relationships" between rhetoric and reality that increasingly became the focus of Didion's writing, even as she continued to write novels throughout the seventies and eighties.

While the political strains of Didion's writings were apparent even in these early essays, she did not see herself as primarily a political writer until much later in her career, when she began, in the 1980s and '90s, turning her attention almost exclusively toward various forms of nonfiction, including not only reportage but critical essays and memoirs. *Salvador* (1983), *Miami* (1987), *After Henry* (2001), *Political Fictions* (2001), and *Where I Was From* (2003) followed years of writing novels and reviews (primarily for *The New York Review of Books*, for which she began writing in 1973), and have not yet received the amount of scholarly attention that her two earliest collections of essays as well as her fiction had, though certainly many of them have been extensively reviewed by the popular press. In 2006, Didion, raised in a family of Republican conservatives, and later registered as a Democrat[64] (though far from a passionate one—she votes sporadically), described her shift to reporting on political subjects in an interview for the *Paris Review*.

She was, as she explains, already planning on a trip to El Salvador with Dunne in 1982 when her editor at *The New York Review of Books*, Bob Silvers, indicated he'd be interested in having one of them write something about their journey. As Dunne was at work on a novel, Didion started writing a piece, one that ended up being very long and very much a travel piece. Silvers guided Didion's editing of the piece, and especially its resolution, until it evolved into a commentary on the fluid and violent political situation in El Salvador. While the evolution of this one work was guided by an editor, Didion is quick to note, in the same interview, that the end result represents her point of view, her "taking of sides" in regard to the political situation. More importantly, she explains that her movement from more personal writing to political writing was a deliberate one, prompted both by boredom and by her feeling that she had no way to deal with the increasingly strong and emotional responses generated by her more personal pieces. *Salvador* was received with both great praise and no small share of criticism, most of the latter generated by the fact that many thought she had no place weighing in on a subject so far outside of her expertise. The fact that she was in El Salvador for only two weeks only heightened this criticism.

For Didion, though, it was precisely because she was an outsider, and therefore not party to the "American effort," which seemed to her to be a "dreamwork devised to obscure any intelligence that might trouble the dreamer"[65] that what she had to write about El Salvador was of value. Such outsider status allowed her to realize that the rhetoric generated by political processes was mere surface, that "words didn't have any actual meaning, that they described a negotiation more than they described an idea," and that the subsequent "lack of specificity" is "an obscuring device."[66] For her, her outsider status is essential to her perspective as a critic, for both ideological and practical purposes. In terms of the latter, for instance, she observes that part of what made her coverage of the Central Park Jogger case unique is that she was often unable to obtain press and police passes, which led her to other approaches, primarily ones that emphasized her critical distance from the popular coverage. Much of her writing for *Political Fictions* was done without traveling to Washington or interviewing her subjects, as other reporters did.

As she notes in "A Foreword," in *Political Fictions*, when Silvers asked her to write some pieces about the 1988 presidential campaign, rather than file for press passes and hit the campaign trail immediately, she procrastinated before finally showing up without Secret Service clearance or any firm sense of what it was she was going to cover or write.[67] Watching the politicians and the reporters covering them without the pressure of having to file a story herself every day allowed Didion the opportunity, as she says, "to realize that there was actually less there than met the eye . . . I had no idea that these things [rallies, speeches, "candid" shots of the candidates] were as Kabuki-like as they were. They just went through these motions—this was a set that kept getting struck three or four times a day. The difference between the way things looked standing there and the way they looked on television the next night . . . it was instructive."[68] More and more, as she continued to write about politics, she focused on the use of language as "an obscuring device,"[69] on the construction of political narratives as little more than stagecraft for elaborately plotted "films" dutifully captured by the complicit media and consumed uncritically by a public eager to take comfort in the rationalizations offered by familiar narrative tropes.

While Didion herself points to these moments as revelations, it is clear, in looking over her previous body of nonfiction work, as I have done very briefly above, that her suspicion of narrative, her understanding of the artificial construction of most public discourse, and her refusal to embrace the magical thinking of those around her was apparent in her very earliest essays and remained consistent features in her work across the decades. One need only look at her essay "Good Citizens," from *The White Album* to observe her early efforts to pull back the curtain on the theatrics of politics. Employing understatement and dry wit, she describes a news crew directing Nancy Reagan to do "precisely what she would ordinarily be doing on a Tuesday morning at home," which in this case, as suggested by the news crew, might involve picking flowers in the garden. Recording the dialogue that follows this prompt without inserting her own commentary, she allows the absurdity of the situation to reveal itself:

> "Fine," the newsman said. "Just fine. Now I'll ask a question, and if you could just be nipping a bud as you answer it . . ." "Nipping a bud," Nancy Reagan repeated, taking her place in front of the rhododendron bush. "Let's have a dry run," the cameraman said. The newsman looked at him. "In other words, by a dry run you mean you want her to fake nipping the bud." "Fake the nip, yeah," the cameraman said. "Fake the nip."[70]

Didion is a skilled and powerful rhetorician, and the scholarly response to her writing does evidence awareness of the rhetorical potency of her prose. It is in this body of work that one finds the most extensive analysis of her style, with scholars from a multitude of disciplines (Literature, Composition, Trauma Studies, Women's Studies, and Communications among them) attending to how her sentences work to, among other things, invite identification, induce cooperation, and amplify her concerns. While it is a small body of work, it suggests a strong starting point for productive further analysis of Didion's style.[71]

One of the earliest scholarly publications on Didion's work is Katherine Usher Henderson's 1981 *Joan Didion*, a monograph that offers a biography of Didion as well as commentary on three of her novels (*Play It as It Lays*, *Run River*, and *A Book of Common Prayer*) as well as *Slouching Towards Bethlehem* and *The White Album*. In this work, Henderson devotes four pages to analysis of Didion's style; while this treatment is brief, it is illuminating. She herself notes that Didion's style has been much acclaimed but little analyzed before beginning a precise listing of some of Didion's more frequent rhetorical techniques, including parallelism (sometimes with antithesis) and the combining of long sentences with short. Henderson employs short excerpts from Didion's essays to demonstrate how the first of these techniques, parallelism, allows her to organize ideas, while her deliberate omission of it in some cases where it is expected emphasizes the final clauses in a series. In pointing to the mix of sentence lengths, Henderson demonstrates how Didion controls rhythm and cadence (with the longer sentences expressing an almost breathless speed, and the shorter establishing "sharp emphasis"). She then makes brief points about Didion's use of alliteration, incongruity, metaphor, and allusion before concluding that

> Didion's style is difficult because it is so various in its use of rhetorical and stylistic devices. It ranges widely in diction, using both simple and esoteric words; in sentence structure, using long and short sentences, loosely and tightly coordinated ones; in tone, from mocking irony to straightforward praise or blame; in manner, from the most intimate to the rather formal.[72]

Despite her acknowledgment of these difficulties, Henderson is clear in her evaluation—she finds Didion's prose economical, graceful, and effective. Were her analysis more comprehensive, it would have done much to provide a firm starting point for further analysis of style in Didion's subsequent nonfiction.

As it is, there was little subsequent scholarly treatment of Didion's style across the '80s—the next work focused on her style comes from Mark Muggli in 1987. In "The Poetics of Joan Didion's Journalism," he calls for more attention to her style in order to respond to what he sees as an overemphasis on the voices, personalities, and roles of literary journalists rather than their texts, an overemphasis he sees as occurring because the journalism texts students study describe subject matter but do not suggest how to analyze textual elements.[73] What he calls "Didion's rhetoric of fact," however, is best approached, he argues, by close literary analysis.[74] His argument echoes that of Chris Anderson, who points out that literary nonfiction is a necessarily hybrid type of text, a site where "the methodologies and concern" of literary criticism and rhetoric and composition "come together in unique and provocative ways."[75]

Muggli's analysis, in the end, however, is more literary criticism than rhetorical criticism, though no less insightful for being so. He engages a rhetorical perspective primarily to explore Didion's use of tropes, in particular metonymy and metaphor, with an extended focus on her use of "emblems," which he defines as "an extreme form of metaphor."[76] He details how passages from her work that are full of concrete details and vivid images are not to be confused as being important in themselves as illustrations or representations of actual historical moments but rather are significant insofar as they are evocative and emblematic of "a large world of meaning beyond the confines of the particular story."[77]

For instance, he looks closely at "On the Morning After the Sixties," an essay in the *White Album*, and picks a passage from the beginning when Didion, in explaining the fairly ambivalent attitudes toward adulthood that she and others felt in Berkeley in the fifties, recalls that she saw "a woman picking daffodils in the rain one day when I was walking the hills [and] a teacher who drank too much one night and revealed his fright and bitterness."[78] Muggli points out that these details, these vivid images, move beyond being realistic, beyond even being symbolic, to become emblematic of "the pain that is another core of all adult life, of existence itself,"[79] though he is careful to note that there is a delicate boundary between symbol and emblem. The latter, he believes, achieves an almost intangible intensity through the stylistic choices Didion makes on the level of the sentence—her repetition of words and the rhythm of her sentences.

Although in this instance Muggli brings the sentence into focus, his analysis of texts such as "The White Album" and *Salvador* is not largely concerned with the particulars of syntax and diction. However, his careful unpacking of Didion's use of major tropes does point the way toward a more serious consideration of Didion's style insofar as it painstakingly explores the role figuration plays in generating, rather than merely ornamenting (or distracting from) Didion's persuasive nonfiction. While he is certainly aware of those who take issue with Didion's reporting methods, seeing in her figuration and subjectivity only incompleteness and inaccuracy, he concludes by asserting the power and sophistication of her prose and calling for a more studied appreciation of her poetics.[80]

The most recent, significant, and sustained work done on Didion's style can be found in Anderson's 1987 book *Style as Argument: Contemporary American Nonfiction*, in which he analyzes Didion along with Tom Wolfe, Truman Capote, and Norman Mailer. Anderson is a composition instructor, and his goal, in part, is to encourage an appreciation of nonfiction as both a literary and rhetorical genre in order to invigorate the teaching of writing. In emphasizing the rhetorical nature of these literary journalists, Anderson takes the work of style seriously, and his analysis of Didion's style is the most extensive stylistic analysis of her prose undertaken to this point. As the title of his work suggests, he sees style, or form, as itself an argument, and his analysis of Didion recognizes not just her critiques of political rhetoric (her "metadiscursive commentary on the challenge of language in American culture")[81] but the ways in which these critiques are given rhetorical force and expression through her style. His work, therefore, closely attends to the stylistic devices she employs, and he is able to construct a "grammar" of her style that outlines how particular devices produce specific effects.[82]

In particular, he focuses on how Didion employs anecdotes, artifact, and details in place of abstractions in a "rhetoric of concreteness" or "particularity;" withholds interpretation and commentary at every level of language in a "rhetoric of gaps," encouraging the readers to engage in active interpretation of her work; and employs a "rhetoric of process," in combination with her rhetoric of particularity, to create presence.[83] Of these strategies, he thinks her "rhetoric of particularity" is the most central to her prose, involving as it does her habit of isolating details that evoke and signify. He analyzes, for instance, how in "On Morality," instead of abstractly considering the theme assigned to her by *The American Scholar*, "what can be considered moral in America," she finds herself drawn to particular images: a miner guarding the corpse of an accident victim from desert coyotes; a rescue diver extending his search for a corpse to the point where he is exhausted and incoherent; the flickering of some unknown light in the depths of desert watering hole in which he dives. While he does not extend on this analysis in the way Muggli does in terms of tracing the boundaries between metaphor and metonymy, symbol and emblem, his is a careful consideration of how her diction allows her to frame images in concrete ways.

To demonstrate how the "rhetoric of gaps" occurs through her deliberate withholding of interpretation and commentary at the level of the sentence, he analyzes "On Going Home," from *Slouching Towards Bethlehem*. In the passage below, he notes, she moves from discussing how the postwar generation found the notion of home irrelevant to describing a contest for topless dancers, without providing any connection between the two in the form of transitional words or phrases:

> The question of whether or not you could go home again was a very real part of the sentimental and largely literary baggage with which we left home in the fifties; I suspect that it is irrelevant to the children born of the fragmentation after World War II. A few weeks ago in a San Francisco bar I saw a pretty young girl on crystal take off her clothes and dance for the cash prize in an "amateur-topless" contest. There was no particular sense of moment about this, none of the effect of romantic degradation, of "dark journey," for which my generation strived so assiduously.[84]

He finds the movement between the two topics "abrupt and dislocating," but he understands it as Didion's method of prompting the reader to do the work of regrouping and comparing the information in order to come to the realization that the anecdote is meant to illustrate the assertion it follows. The details of the anecdote, he also notes, are often either metonymic, insofar as they prompt a chain of association in the reader's mind, such that the reader ends up with a more comprehensive impression of the anecdote, or synecdochic, insofar as they symbolize larger meanings.[85] In both cases, her use of these tropes leads to the reader's active collaboration in the meaning of her argument.

This active collaboration mirrors, to some extent, how Didion writes metadiscursively, reflecting on her own process of thinking and composing. Anderson details how, through the "rhetoric of process," she sometimes offers simultaneous interpretations, other times records her modification and qualification of previous statements, and frequently does not synthesize contradictory assertions. All of these choices produce prose that is self-aware and highly meditative, creating, as they do, the impression of a writer exploring through her writing and confronting ambiguities that are not necessarily resolvable.

Anderson's attention, then, is both to what Didion "does" on the sentence level—her use of the tropes of metonymy and synecdoche as well as the schemes of asyndeton, polysyndeton, parallelism, parenthesis, cumulative sentences and appositives, in addition to her employment of qualifiers and repeated predicates—and how these choices construct her arguments and rhetorically position her readers to see things from her point of view. He therefore offers a far more insightful and detailed analysis of her stylistic choices than others, and it is this analysis that allows him to see that "there is more to her prose than 'mere" style and readability, certainly more than the stylish resonances of her nearly perfect sentences."[86] The depth and intelligence of his analysis exhibit how productive a serious approach to Didion's style can be, while its relative brevity (one chapter in a larger work on key New Journalists and style as argument), and its almost three-decades old publication date (predating, as it does, a significant portion of Didion's nonfiction oeuvre, most notably: *Salvador* (*1983*); *After Henry* (1992); *Political Fictions* (2001); *Where I Was From* (2006); *The Year of Magical Thinking* (2005); *Blue Nights* (2011); and *South and West: From a Notebook* (2017)) suggests a need for a more extended and updated analysis of her style.

Chapter 1, "Language and the Mechanism of Terror: *Salvador*," focuses on Didion's first extended work of political criticism, *Salvador*, written during and after her two-week visit to the embattled country in the summer of 1982. At just over one hundred pages, this piece manages to convey to the readers—in vivid, concrete, and concise prose—the ways in which terror became, during the El Salvadorian civil war, "the given of the place."[87] Shifting, grammatically and semantically, the focus from the personal, domestic, and cultural concerns that had consumed much of her attention in her previous nonfiction to the political, military, and international affairs impacting a country with which she was utterly unfamiliar, Didion evidences an ability to use words cinematically and persuasively, impressing upon readers the ways in which political rhetoric can initiate, perpetuate, and obscure violence. Distant, ironic, and analytical, Didion moves past the confessional, emotional, tentative, authorial voice often employed in her earlier nonfiction to argue—forcefully and insistently—that all is not as it seems.

Chapter 2, "Preferred Narratives: New York City after the Central Park Jogger" offers a stylistic analysis of "Sentimental Journeys" (the last and longest piece in *After Henry*), analyzing it in the context of the other nine chapters of that work. Just as California is a place steeped in mythologies, New York City was once, to Didion, a girl raised in the West, not merely a city but instead "an infinitely romantic notion, the mysterious nexus of all love and money and power, the shining and perishable dream itself."[88] Over the years she spent living there, however, it became to her a "city rapidly vanishing into the chasm between its actual life and its preferred narratives."[89] In this essay, she turns a critical eye on what she sees as New York City's "sentimentality," and deconstructs the stories "the city tells itself to rationalize its class contradictions."[90] Focusing on how Didion dismantles the rhetorical illusions permeating the city's response to tragedies in the 1980s, I examine how she employs figures to amplify the cognitive dissonances resolved by these narratives as well as foreground the power of sentimentality to subvert reason. Choices she makes in regard to diction, voice, tense, and punctuation are examined as critically important to her ability to emphasize the tensions between ideology and reality implicit in the city's mythologies.

Chapter 3, "Lifting the Curtain: The Rhetoric of Politics": Most of the extended critical treatments of Didion's work, having been written in the '80s and '90s, predate her more sustained and focused engagement with politics, which began in 1983 with *Salvador* and saw its fullest expression in 2001's *Political Fictions*, a collection of pieces she had written in the '90s. This collection highlights Didion's eye for the absurd as well as her understated and ironic manner of throwing into clear relief the conflict between "the empirical and the theoretical" so often at play in politics. Emphasizing her position as an outsider to the political process, Didion focuses on the fictive elements of political narratives that enable political players to maintain illusions and obscure issues. As well, she directs her skeptical gaze at the media, whose collusion in sustaining these public narratives is laid bare by her precisely worded, meticulously arranged prose. Skeptical, ironic, and understated, Didion often reveals her keen sense of humor as she works subtly to persuade readers to adopt her vision of the political process. By the end of this work, this chapter argues, her audience is likely to identify with her frustration with domestic politics, about which there remains, despite her efforts to understand it, "something resistant, recondite, some occult irreconcilability."[91]

Chapter 4, "*Terra Incognita*: On Loss and Memory" looks at Didion's latest two nonfiction books, *The Year of Magical Thinking* and *Blue Nights*. Both of these books, and particularly the first, have received much critical acclaim from reviewers and readers alike, with the first winning the National Book Award for nonfiction. There is also a growing body of scholarly responses, though these have been primarily concerned with their function as trauma memoirs. Written after the sudden death of her husband (*TYMT*) and the illness and subsequent premature passing of her only daughter (*BN*), these works reflect a mature writer in the process of confronting the dissolution of personal mythologies that have sustained her over the years. She has observed that in writing both books she was less certain about what she wanted to accomplish, less deliberate in her initial composing process.

Working from a place of doubt rather than her characteristic certainty, she struggled, for instance, to write *Blue Nights*, unsure of what it was she wanted to say or where it was she wanted the book to go—she explained to a friend that she "didn't know what to do with it,"[92] with the result that the book is looser and more unstructured than previous works.[93] Turning her unflinching eye on her own life, past and present, a life that has increasingly become "terra incognita," Didion achieves resonance more through omission than accumulation, more through implication than explication. Frequently addressing the readers, even as she stylistically holds them at arms' length, she achieves an emotional connection with them all the more remarkable for her reserve. In these works, this chapter argues, Didion's ability to invite the readers' identification reaches its zenith, as she figuratively places before their eyes tableaus that evoke emotion rather than argue for it. Although they have been called "spare," "elliptical," and "pared down," these works are composed of sentences as long and complicated as they have ever been. And just as many of her sentences delay resolution until their inevitable ends, prolonged by parenthetical asides, repetition, and repeated modification, so too does the emotional impact of these works build subtly and linger long after the final pages.

The close readings in these chapters are undertaken to demonstrate, comprehensively, how style is her formal means of achieving persuasion—how, with it, she, among other things, makes her arguments present and memorable, foregrounds and emphasizes her major claims, and creates rapport with her readers. The works analyzed have received far less scholarly attention than her earliest nonfiction (most notably *Slouching Towards Bethlehem* and *The White Album*) and were produced after Didion had begun to focus more explicitly on the rhetoric of narratives and the cognitive dissonances resolved by the public, politicians, and individuals by turning to such narratives. Appearing moderately late in the long trajectory of her writing career, they also reflect the increasing sophistication of her style, while still evidencing the characteristic patterns of her earliest nonfiction prose.

CHAPTER 1

## Language and the Mechanism of Terror

### *Salvador*

Much has been written about Didion's work in the 1960s and '70s, the years during which she composed the pieces that would be later published in her most celebrated essay collections *Slouching Towards Bethlehem* in 1968 and *The White Album* in 1979. These are also the years in which she published her first three novels—*Run River* in 1963, *Play It as It Lays* in 1970, and *A Book of Common Prayer* in 1977—though critical reception of these was never as favorable as it was for her nonfiction. As her output increased and she began to receive widespread recognition, it remained the case that it was Didion herself who interested readers, possibly even more than her work. As Louis Menand writes, there was interest in both her nonfiction and fiction:

> Mainly, though, everyone was fascinated by the authorial persona, the hypersensitive neurasthenic who drove a Corvette Sting Ray, the frail gamine with the migraine headaches and the dark glasses and the searchlight mind, the writer who seemed to know in her bones what readers were afraid to face, which is that the center no longer holds, the falcon cannot hear the falconer, the story line is broken.[1]

Part of this was driven by the fact that these decades saw Didion and Dunne at the center of Hollywood life—with Dunne's brother Nick, a Hollywood producer, putting them in touch with some of the biggest names of the decades in music, film, and writing. What Didion has already written about her life during these years, in *Slouching* and *The White Album*, Daugherty does a fine job of fleshing out in his biography in thorough detail, with vivid descriptions of the dinners, parties, and deals that kept the Didion/Dunnes at the intersection of Los Angeles life. Her daughter Quintana was, as a teenager, best friends with Susan Traylor, who was dating, and would later marry, Bob Dylan's son Jesse; Harrison Ford worked as a contractor on their Malibu home in the '70s (and thirty years later would pilot Didion to California in his private plane when Quintana was unexpectedly hospitalized in the ICU). They frequently hosted dinner parties (such as one for Tom Wolfe upon the publication of *The Electric Kool-Aid Acid Test*; Janis Joplin was in attendance). Didion—a fashionable, photogenic, enigmatic figure, her slim body adorned in Lily Pulitzer shifts—would throw herself into cooking elaborate meals; alcohol flowed freely. They lived for a time down the street from the Mamas and Papas; Dennis Hopper and Natalie Wood were friends, as was Warren Beatty.

These same decades, which saw the rise of the counterculture, the civil rights movement, and the women's movement, marked a turning point for literature and journalists—these were the years when Gay Talese, Tom Wolfe, John McPhee, and Truman Capote, among others, were pushing back against more traditional "objective" journalism and publishing pieces in *Esquire*, *The New Yorker*, *The Atlantic*, and *Harper's* that took a more literary approach to the stories being covered. New Journalism, as it later came to be called, represented a new approach to reporting, one in which the techniques of fiction (e.g., use of a narrator, scene setting, the inclusion of dialogue) were employed in writing about nonfiction subject matter.[2] Wolfe perhaps put it best, describing it as "really stylish reporting" with an "esthetic dimension."[3] It was an approach to writing that married the subjective with the objective, allowing, for the first time, the voice and personality of the writer to intrude significantly upon the telling of the story.

Such reporting was still dependent on conventional journalistic methods—research, interviews, data checking, fact finding—and it was still expected that everything in a piece would be based in fact, but New Journalists shifted the focus of such writing from mere reporting to storytelling. Thus, a writer such as Capote spent a considerable amount of time fleshing out his characters and setting the scene for the true-life murders of the Clutter family in his groundbreaking book *In Cold Blood*, and Hunter S. Thompson created "Gonzo" journalism, involving himself in the stories he wrote, living the experiences of his subjects (as he famously did by riding with the Hell's Angels for more than a year) and becoming a character in the subsequent pieces he produced.

And Didion spent 1970, in part, by taking a road trip with Dunne through Louisiana, Mississippi, and Alabama and jotting down observations in her notebooks, which have only recently been published as *South and West: From a Notebook*. In these, her approach is clearly both "traditional" and literary. Her talent at constructing sharply evocative images that dissolve, as through a stereopticon, seamlessly into one another, produce vivid three-dimensional pictures.[4] Some of the sentences contained within these notes are rich with prepositional phrases (uninterrupted by commas) that layer her imagery, giving it depth. In Biloxi, in June 1970, she sees, and thus the reader does as well, that "[i]n the sawdust under the awning a small girl sat, stringing the pop tops from beer cans into a necklace."[5] In the same month, she stops in Winfield, Alabama, where she sees that "[a]t the little concrete pool between the motel and the creek, two teenage girls in two-piece bathing suits were laying in the sun on the stained pavement" (75). In each sentence the reader is given the close-up, the medium shot, the long shot, flawlessly edited together.

Some imagery is also given dimension by her characteristic mix of sentence types, whose fluent rhythm owes more to poetic form than journalistic traditions. Short declarative sentences often establish a backdrop, a series of these sentences uninterrupted by coordinating conjunctions, emphatic but matter-of-fact. She writes, of the Deep South: "Everything seems to go to seed along the Gulf: walls stain, windows rust. Curtains mildew. Wood warps. Air conditioners cease to function" (30). Alternately she pens sentences that rise and fall rhythmically to convey scenery rich with tactile details: "There was occasional rain and an overcast sky and the raw piney woods" (40).

Long, lyrical, sentences—accumulating details through coordination and repeated modification, weighty with metaphors, made fluid through alliteration or anaphora—frequently travel across the pages of this work. Based in fact, but steeped in imagery, these have an aesthetic dimension unlike the traditional prose of reporters. Quite often, as with the scenes mentioned below, rather than reflect back to the reader, as if in a seventeenth-century Claude glass, settings and worlds harmonized and colors softened, her sentences capture the raw, dark, edges of places. In their concrete, sensory detail they are so tactile as to border on haptic communication. "In New Orleans in June," she observes, "the air is heavy with sex and death, not violent death but death by decay, overripeness, rotting, death by drowning, suffocation, fever of unknown etiology" (5). The metaphoric heaviness of the atmosphere is echoed in the repetition of the harsh "d" sound: "death" (four times), "decay," "drowning." After visiting the Garden District, she reflects that "[w]hat I saw that night was a world so rich and complex and I was almost disoriented, a world complete unto itself, a world of smooth surfaces broken occasionally by a flash of eccentricity so deep that it numbed any attempt at interpretation" (15). The anaphoric use of "world" stiches together, seamlessly, the literal and the figurative, and carries the reader forward to the uncertainty that concludes the sentence.

These protracted sentences are frequently interrupted by brief, fragmentary sentences that demand attention. While fragments are commonly considered to be, as Constance Hale puts it, "adrift, without clear direction or function,"[6] Didion's fragments are sharp-eyed and rooted in the visible and tactile: "A black woman sitting on her front porch on the backseat from a car. Cannibalized rusting automobiles everywhere, in ditches, the kudzu taking over. White wild flowers, red dirt. The pines here are getting lower, bushier. Polled Herefords" (42). And on the road from Meridian to Tuscaloosa: "Dixie Gas stations, all over, with Confederate flags and grill work. Boys working on the road between Cuba and Demopolis. Making measurements with fishing poles" (62). And then she writes, a few sentences later, "I think I never saw water that appeared to be running in any part of the South. A sense of water moccasins" (62–63).

While, as Michael Arlen was quick to point out as early as 1972, there was not much new about New Journalism (he notes that there had been "a vein of personal journalism in English and American writing for a very long time"), it was the case, as he argues, that New Journalists "considerably expanded the possibilities of journalism."[7] In describing the parameters of this genre, one of its foremost practitioners, Gay Talese, explains:

> The new journalism, though often reading like fiction, is not fiction. It is, or should be, as reliable as the most reliable reportage although it seeks a larger truth than is possible through the mere compilation of verifiable facts, the use of direct quotations, and adherence to the rigid organizational style of the older form. The new journalism allows, demands in fact, a more imaginative approach to reporting, and it permits the writer to inject himself into the narrative if he wishes.[8]

Didion had been writing in this genre for years (though she herself did not claim to be a New Journalist and saw few similarities between the leading male writers in the genre and herself) while continuing to work on her novels as well as screenplays with Dunne. She only really began to turn her attention to politics in the early '80s. She began writing for *The New York Review of Books* in 1973, under Silvers, who would be hugely influential in shifting the trajectory of her writing.[9] Initially, her reviews for the publication centered on literature and celebrity, with her shift to coverage of political rhetoric occurring in 1982. With this shift in focus, there was a marked change in Didion's style. Where before, in the pieces collected in *Slouching* and *White Album*, her complicated nostalgia for a mythic California and the cultural narratives that sustained early generations of her family and informed her childhood inevitably produced prose both reflective and introspective, her political essays—from *Salvador* through to *Fixed Ideas*—reflect a writer far more disenchanted and insistent. While there remains what Ellen Friedman calls "an obsessive nostalgia" for things lost,[10] there is a growing interest in language—its uses, misuses, and abuses.

Several of her stylistic strategies—increasing use of anaphora, expletives, parentheticals, and hedges in particular—seem to arise from a determined effort to avoid the language through which "fixed ideas" and "political fictions" are communicated. While old stylistic patterns remain—an affection for long, cumulative, and complex sentences, a talent for striking metaphors, a tendency toward anastrophe, irony, and understatement—Didion recedes from the center of her narratives, emphasizing her "outsider" status in order to secure her position as an objective and unbiased critic. Personal details—such as the packing list in "The White Album," with which longtime fans are intimately familiar, or the meals she and her then eleven-year-old daughter share in "On the Road,"—are much less frequently noted. If one could be said to have developed a sense of "Joan Didion" the writer from her first two essay collections, it is fair to say that in these political pieces, she would remain a quite shadowy and unformed presence to those unfamiliar with her writing or reputation.

Didion offered varying accounts for her trip to *Salvador*, but it is clear that she approached the country and the topic from a place of intellectual and professional curiosity rather than any deeply personal interest in the country's affairs or passionate opinion about the direction in which the country seemed headed. The casual, almost offhand way in which she describes her decision to travel to a country seized by unthinkable violence is striking—in a 2003 interview with *Guardian* writer Jemima Hunt, she offers that "[t]he decision to go to El Salvador came one morning at the breakfast table. I was reading the newspaper and it just didn't make sense."[11]

In another interview, in 2006 with Hilton Als, she indicates that her motivation to write the book came from Silvers, who, upon hearing that Didion and Dunne were traveling to San Salvador, asked if one or the other would write something about it.[12] In any case, in June 1982, she and Dunne, accompanied by Christopher Dickey, then Central American Bureau chief for *The Washington Post*,[13] traveled to El Salvador, a country then marking its fourth year of an explosive and extremely violent civil war that would eventually end only in 1991, nine years after her visit.[14]

When Didion landed at the El Salvador International Airport the country was in the midst of chaos—it is almost impossible to overstate how unpredictable, unstable, and dangerous El Salvador was at the time. Visitors were not wholly protected from the terror infusing the place, and, indeed, some of the most widely publicized and horrific acts of violence against both visitors and citizens occurred shortly before her visit. She arrived "approximately a year and a half after four American church women were murdered there; approximately six months after all the residents of the village of El Mozote were massacred by the Salvadoran army's Atlacatl Battalion (trained by the United States military); and shortly after the ARENA party's Roberto D'Aubuisson, who had been implicated in the assassination of Archbishop Romero, was elected president of El Salvador's constituent assembly."[15] Neither at the time of Didion's visit, nor for many years afterward, was there clarity on who orchestrated or perpetrated these acts, though there were certainly many rumors (and strong indications) that U.S.-backed death squads were responsible for great numbers of the killings.

Economic and military aid from the United States—whose presence and support is frequently signaled in Didion's work via reference to American brands and cars—was predicated on the notion that El Salvador was an ally in its Cold War fight against communism, and included training the government-supported soldiers whose opponents "then-President Ronald Reagan identified as Cuban-backed guerrillas."[16] The involvement of the United States in the civil war complicated the efforts of many U.S. reporters to uncover and report on the violence taking place there. In the case of El Mozote, there was initially a complete denial that a massacre had even taken place, and even when the United States conceded that it had occurred, there were years of denial over the number of victims. In a sign of just how difficult it was to identify perpetrators of these and other acts of torture and terror and bring them to justice, consider that it was not until 2002 (twenty years after Didion's visit) that two retired Salvadoran generals, now permanent U.S. residents, were found legally responsible for the torture that had occurred during the war.[17]

The book that resulted from Didion's two-week sojourn, *Salvador*, has been described as "pamphlet-sized"[18]—it is a slim volume, just one hundred pages, an impossibly short work within which to describe comprehensively her time there, much less explicate the complexities of the ongoing civil war of which she only saw glimpses. In speaking with Als, she claims of *Salvador* that its "through-line" was "always pretty clear: I went somewhere, this is what I saw. Very simple, like a travel piece." But it is clear that in the actual composing of the work—the editing and revisions that follow her initial experiences and note taking; the sophistication of her sentences—she adopts a particular point of view and works to persuade readers of it as much through her arrangement of material as through any explicit claims.[19] Susan Braudy—who interviewed Didion for *Ms. Magazine* forty years ago and recently reviewed *South and West* (2017)—notes that she thinks Didion, can, in her descriptions of her thinking and writing, be "disingenuous," a point with which I concur. As Braudy observes, Didion's "process is not simply inductive. Along with her genius for recording detail, she's an intellectual."[20]

Just as the screenplays she and Dunne co-authored involved setting scenes and directing action, so to do her nonfiction narratives direct readers to see things her way, to dream her "dreams." As Leonard Wilcox notes, "What is implicit in her often disjointed and oblique narratives is the absolute necessity for the individual, whether reader, 'witness' or 'analysand,' to experience the process of reconstruction of the past in order to understand and learn from it."[21] Such direction occurs—in this work as in her earlier nonfiction—through a focus on the concrete, an emphasis on the empirical: the bodies littering the El Salvadoran landscape and the language issued in official reports, dispatches, and speeches are the tangible evidence of a terror unchecked. What becomes clear in this slim volume, perhaps more so than in any of her nonfiction up until this point, is that, contrary to popular perception, Didion does not write to express but to persuade. Her emphasis—always and already—is on composing as a means to comprehend, the rearranging of words and sentences the method by which she makes clear—to her readers and herself—what is "really" happening. Here is a writer focused not on promoting ideology but on exposing the differences between "grammars," her own and those she critiques as obfuscating and illusory.

While in her earlier works she alludes to therapeutic motives for writing ("I write entirely to find out what I am thinking"),[22] this work is politically, not personally, focused. While her personal safety seems to be quite frequently challenged during her two weeks, her dispassionate accounting of these instances ensures she acts as emblem not empath. A lack of action verbs, and the presence of frequent nominalizations, irony, and sarcasm keep the camera trained on the absurdity and horror of El Salvador, her refusal to play up "reaction shots" a sign that she means to move the reader cognitively rather than emotionally. In her interview with Als, she notes that she had become bored by the writing she had done up until that point and had found it limiting. But also, she offered, she was finding the "very strong response from readers . . . depressing;" she did not want, in her words, "to become Miss Lonelyhearts."[23]

It is hard to imagine the author, as constructed in this work, as the same writer over whom fans, particularly female fans, have swooned for decades, hard to understand how so much of what is projected on her so thoroughly misses the mark.[24] "It's a common mistake, in assessing Didion's work, to interpret her sensibility as a reflection of the times—to imagine, as Daugherty puts it, that she has 'always spoken for us,' " Menand writes. "That's certainly not the way she has presented herself. In a column she started writing for *Life* in 1969, she introduced herself as 'a woman who for some time now has felt radically separated from most of the ideas that seem to interest other people.' She's not like us. She's weird. That's why we want to read her."[25]

And, indeed, Didion is frequently at pains to cast herself as apart from the "herd," immune to the seduction of the common and the facile—note her later scorn in *Fixed Ideas*[26] for conventions of post-9/11 rhetoric, which excoriated anyone (Chomsky, Sontag) who dared to question the accepted storylines. In *Salvador*, it is abundantly clear that Didion does not trade on her celebrity or exploit her readers' apparent fascination with getting to know the "real Joan Didion"—hers is not a rhetoric of identification. In striking contrast to both her earlier and later nonfiction, she seldom uses "we" in this work,[27] setting up a distance between herself and the reader, the better to reinforce a point hinted at throughout the book and made explicit in its final pages, when she describes realizing that "the texture of life in such a situation is essentially untranslatable."[28]

She inserts herself into the narrative only insofar as her presence in El Salvador is necessary for making certain visuals clear to the reader, her stringing together of vignettes given a cohesiveness and credibility by her movements from air to land, from site to site. The voice she creates, the self she composes, marks her attempts to walk a very fine line; she is at once criticizing the "objective" and official language of political entities (military leaders, ambassadors, embassy staff) and its attendant narratives and composing her own story of what is happening in El Salvador. This story, on one hand, is the story of America's responsibility for (and evasion of responsibility for) a considerable amount of the violence and terror of the place; this story, on the other hand, is about the unreliability and violence of language. "Language as it is now used in El Salvador," she observes near the end of her work, "is the language of advertising, of persuasion, the product being one or another of the *soluciónes* crafted in Washington or Panama or Mexico, which is part of the place's pervasive obscenity" (65).

As is typical of the New Journalists, Didion—in *Salvador* as in all her other nonfiction—dwells on the particular, the tangible, the describable. Wolfe, in describing the "essential difference" between New Journalism and traditional reporting, claims that "the basic unit of reporting [is] no longer the datum or piece of information but the scene."[29] The scenes Didion describes work to contextualize and anchor her inferences; they mark her attempt to convey the "texture of life in such a situation" (103). Working inductively, she edits together firsthand observations with long shots to make the case for the failures of the political language on which, and through which, foreign policy is enacted and understood.

Her writing, like that of all the New Journalists,[30] depends heavily on the techniques of fictional writing, but also on incredible amounts of research and attention to detail, so that vivid descriptions of "body dumps" presumably viewed firsthand are set against excerpts from official reports. For instance, in the first chapter of *Salvador*, she quotes, at length, a previously classified January 15, 1982, memo drafted by the political section at the embassy in San Salvador (it describes the existence of death squads and considers the likelihood that American-backed security forces constitute at least some of their members). Then, without comment on it, she writes, "Vultures of course suggest the presence of a body. A knot of children on the street suggests the presence of a body" (19). Even as she is working to uncover the fictions of El Salvador she is carefully composing a narrative of her own, understating her presence to keep attention on the story, always flitting around the edges of grisly scenes in order to keep the readers' gaze focused on the "facts on the ground"; she is always at once present and absent.

She achieves this paradoxical status in part through her use (and elision) of deictic terms, and in part by employing present tense to describe El Salvador and past tense to describe her experiences there. While, throughout the book, she frequently identifies her location (and thereby clearly establishes her credibility as a firsthand witness), she almost never employs the spatial deictic term *here* and rarely uses personal deictic terms such as *I* or *me* when writing in the present tense. Just as she does not employ any first-person pronouns until seven pages into the book—she remains, in the pages that follow, at a remove from the country through which she moves and on which she reports. Rather than write, for instance, that "the dead and pieces of the dead turn up *here* everywhere, every day," she writes, "The dead and pieces of the dead turn up in El Salvador everywhere, every day, as taken for granted as in a nightmare, or a horror movie" (19). The deictic term *here* would be appropriate, given that she describes going to Puerta del Diablo, a notorious body dump, and richly details the setting (e.g., "foliage thick and slick with moisture"; "a steady buzz, I believe of cicadas" [20]). But she does not employ it, instead downplaying her proximity to bodies. Additionally, she reverts to passive constructions that allow her to absent herself from the scene. "Body dumps are seen in El Salvador as a kind of visitors' must-do, difficult but worth the trip" (20), she writes, rather than locate herself at the site.

Shortly thereafter, she describes the difficulties of getting down the sides of the dump in order to see bodies, but does not employ a deictic term to indicate that it is in fact something she ever did herself. The reader learns that "[t]he way down is hard. Slabs of stone, slippery with moss, are set into the vertiginous cliff, and it is down this cliff that one begins the descent to the bodies, or what is left of the bodies, pecked and maggoty masses of flesh, bone, hair" (21). It is difficult to conclude whether she writes this way in order to pass off as firsthand experience what has been in fact gathered secondhand, or if she herself has actually viewed the bodies at the bottom of the ravine, in all their macabre permutations, and is choosing to adopt a dispassionate, reportorial tone. The effect, however, is that the reader receives no psychological cues on how to respond—with no "cut" to a reaction shot of Didion, it is left to the reader to decide how to assimilate and respond to the evidence of extreme violence.

It remains a place apart, "a country that cracks Americans" (92–93), and it may well be that Didion finds El Salvador so untranslatable (it is, after all, a "place [that] brings everything into question" [35]), that deictic terms fixing her firmly in the *here* of El Salvador, experiencing things personally, are impossible to use effectively. Deictic terms only "work," if readers can be assumed to understand the context for them; while their semantic meaning is fixed, their denotational meaning is dependent on situation. It is telling that she does not use first person to describe her arrival in El Salvador, minimizing her presence as the country grows to meet the descending plane. It is only in the ending pages, which describe her last night in the country and her morning departure, that she foregrounds her presence, deictically using "I" and active voice to gesture to herself and her location: "I was picked up . . . I was seized by the conviction . . . I sat without moving . . . I averted my eyes" (106). Only as El Salvador recedes beneath her does she move herself to the center of the text.

Her refusal, both implicit and explicit, to align herself fully with the country in an act of sympathetic identification seems at least partially responsible for some of the criticism of her motivations and credibility. Whether or not Didion was qualified to write about El Salvador has been much debated; many were critical of the brevity of her stay as well as her lack of experience in political reporting. Although Daugherty admires her style, he notes that her approach to foreign places had typically been to "describe the *surface* of a place so thoroughly that its *depths* were exposed, like polishing wood until its grain came through" (italics original). Such a focus, he observes, puts her at risk of seeming "culturally uninformed," superficial and condescending.[31] Noël Valis also points to Didion's lack of familiarity with the country, noting that "Didion's understanding of El Salvador's history is relatively weak and her appraisal of the weight of history insufficient,"[32] a point one can imagine she might not debate.

She freely admitted that she had not much thought about politics—domestic or international—until working on her novel *The Book of Common Prayer*, which required her to read about Central America. And it was not until she actually traveled to Salvador, as she acknowledges in the interview with Als, that she began to see the connections between American domestic policies and the political affairs of countries with which she had little familiarity or in which she had little interest. Even with the publication of *Salvador*, her interest lies less in the particular affairs of that country than in the way political language operates to obfuscate and obscure, the way in which "the lack of specificity is specific in itself . . . an obscuring device."[33] The words used in political discourse, she says she realized with her trip to El Salvador, don't "have any actual meaning . . . they [describe] a negotiation more than they [describe] an idea."[34]

That words in El Salvador can be meaningless (as indicated by her frequent use of ironic quotation marks), obfuscating, and arbitrary complicates any attempt by Didion to compose a credible account of the situation. When one can no longer confidently link signifier to signified, when one's response to seeing the corpse of a young man lying alongside a road "with a clean bullet-hole drilled neatly between his eyes . . . his genitals covered with a leafy branch," is to note that the body is "the least equivocal fact of the day" (45), one has truly confronted the slipperiness of language. Recovering or establishing signification *through* language presents the writer with a formidable task.[35]

It would be tempting for a writer in this situation, especially one well practiced in referencing the personal to illuminate the universal, to turn attention then from *logos*—from language and logic—to *pathos*—the emotional appeal. This, Didion does not do. Despite the grotesque details scattered throughout the book—the eyes pecked clean by vultures, the dried blood on the church floor, the tufts of hair clinging to rotting skulls—despite the terror whose signs are present everywhere—the bullet holes in the Sheraton wall, the metallic clicks she hears up and down a dark street upon opening her purse, the corpses that litter the landscape—her voice remains calm, dispassionate, detached, even ironic. Hers is an attitude that mimics, to a great degree, what she understands to be attitude of those she profiles—their numbed response her own. After spending a day with Irish and American priests and nuns living in Gotera, she describes sitting with bottles of Pilsner beer "in the sedative half-light" and talking "in a desultory way about nothing in particular, about the situation but no solutions" (47). "These were people not much given to solutions, to abstracts: their lives were grounded in the specific" (47). What follows this assessment is four sentences, anaphorically listing these gruesome specifics: a morning funeral for a parishioner dead of a cerebral hemorrhage, the death of two children that week from intestinal illness, a lack of medicine in squatter camps whose members numbered twelve thousand, an absence of water clean of "bacteria and amoebae and worms" (47). Like these temporary residents of El Salvador, she stays "grounded in the specifics," muting any emotional reaction.

The Didion that appears "in" these sentences is thus understated, ironic, and reserved; she steps behind her sentences much the same as the director stands behind the camera, always present but visible to the viewer only through impression. The voice that emerges is of a writer determined to make clear the abuses of language that enable the violence (and its denial) while establishing the credibility of her own composition. Valis notes that critics have read Didion's reserve as disengagement, her refusal to make explicit arguments a sign of her inexperience in political analysis. "By viewing El Salvador as ultimately unexplainable and uninterpretable [some critics say] Didion resorts to a facile, quasi-colonialist narrative, distancing herself in this manner from the Salvadorans themselves"[36] And it is the case that she risks appearing to, as John McClure accuses her, write off El Salvador as unknowable, as culturally inferior, as "Other," a tiny country whose reality only provides her a chance to indulge her "penchant for, indeed her obsession with, the quintessentially modernist experiences of disorientation, horror, and radical dissolution."[37] Her work, he charges, "declares El Salvador a realm so debased as to be beyond civilized comprehension, let alone redemption."[38] Mark Falcoff reaches a similar conclusion, reading dismay and condescension in her tone and accusing Didion of "writ[ing] off an entire country, along with [her] own national values."[39]

But Valis reads Didion's tone differently, seeing in it a refusal to be sentimental, which would, in his eyes, constitute "an entirely inadequate response to a situation of extremity like El Salvador in the 1980s." He interprets her irony as a strategy meant to counteract appearing "too fascinated with horror itself," her detachment a "centripetal movement of verbal embodiment" offering "a moral counterpoint" to her descriptions of the "centrifugal, metonymic effects of body parts."[40] The bodies of El Salvador, littering the landscape, filling the "body dumps," logged at the mortuaries ("the man in charge had opened his log to show us the morning's entries, seven bodies, all male, none identified, none believed older than twenty-five. Six had been certified dead by *arma de fuego*, firearms, and the seventh, who had also been shot, of shock" [103]) challenge comprehension and defy easy explanation and simplistic solutions.

*New York Times* correspondent Warren Hoge, who frequently reported from El Salvador, recalls time spent "staring down at a culvert piled with a morning's grisly harvest of corpses," and concludes that "in a country so small the sheer number of such deaths meant that killing had to have become the daily occupation of many Salvadorians." These numbers meant, he speculates, "that there were hearths where a father bounced his baby on his knee and asked what was for dinner and spread his arm wide in his favorite chair to stretch from his body the rigors of just another day spent torturing, mutilating, and killing people." "If that's the reality," he notes, "then what's the solution? Or is there one?"[41] For Didion, the reader can easily conclude, there is not, and any suggestion that she is the one to uncover, definitively, "*la verdad*" (67) is fallacious.

As Daugherty observes, Didion did not see herself as an investigative reporter[42]—this work is not meant to be a definitive report on the civil war in El Salvador. Instead, the reader find in this book-length essay long sentences in which images materialize and are edited together to direct and hold the reader's attention. Writing, she concedes in her interview with Als

> is hostile in that you're trying to make somebody see something the way you see it, trying to impose your idea, your picture. It's hostile to try to wrench around someone else's mind that way. Quite often you want to tell somebody your dream, your

nightmare. Well, nobody wants to hear about someone else's dream, good or bad; nobody wants to walk around with it. The writer is always tricking the reader into listening to the dream.

The "montages" that coalesce under Didion's direction "[trick] the reader into listening to the dream"[43] rather than demand attention and acceptance. These montages work to amplify[44] her ideas and emphasize their significance in order to make the things she sees present in the mind of the reader.[45]

Any serious reader of Didion can appreciate how integral to her approach amplification is throughout her body of nonfiction work, work that frequently results from her efforts to use the essay as a means of exploring and making sense of the places she inhabits, the people with whom her life intersects, the times in which she lives, and the personal, cultural, and political narratives she encounters.[46] The essay (and particularly the New Journalistic essay) is a genre uniquely suited to amplification, as it derives its power not from the careful and logical laying out of demonstrative arguments grounded in the facts or data of a scholarly argument but rather in the studied reflection on the facts of the world as perceived through the personal or lived experience.[47] Amplification, centered as it is, "around a point of view, attitude, or proposition," expressed and elaborated on through "reexamination, reinforcement, reconsideration, and refinement" until "its nature is completely described and its nuances are revealed" finds its natural home in the essay,[48] although this aspect of her style is often perceived as meaningless repetition by those who misunderstand the rhetorical function of her prose style. A great deal of her persuasion is effected through the act of selection—the details that are foregrounded as well as those that are omitted act upon the reader's perception of reality. A great deal of her persuasion is also effected through other figures of speech and syntactical dexterity—repetition and the cumulative sentence, synecdoche, parenthesis, polysyndeton, and anaphora—all are employed in her efforts to move the reader to her point of view.[49]

In the cinematic opening to *Salvador* Didion describes what greets the traveler upon landing at the new El Salvador International Airport—she begins with an establishing shot, one that is quickly undermined by the end of the sentence. She writes:

> The three-year-old El Salvador International Airport is glassy and white and splendidly isolated, conceived during the waning of the Molina "National Transformation" as convenient less to the capital (San Salvador is forty miles away, until recently a

drive of several hours) than to a central hallucination of the Molina and Romero regimes, the projected beach resorts, the Hyatt, the Pacific Paradise, tennis, gold, water-skiing, condos, Costa del Sol; the visionary invention of a tourist industry in yet another republic where the leading natural cause of death is gastrointestinal infection. (13)

The central theme of this book—that idealized narratives are employed by various sources to manipulate public perception of disturbing realities, that the rhetoric of El Salvador is at odds with the reality—is conjured up initially in a single image, a single sentence, one as metaphorical as it is literal. This sentence asks the reader to move from the literal to the figural, from the physical to the cognitive, from the denotative to the connotative, from an airport literally inconveniently located in relation to the capital, to one "located" in a hallucination. One is asked to "enter" figuratively into the reality of Salvador through the image of the airport as one would literally enter the country from the air through an airport.

The image of the beautiful new airport juxtaposed against the data on gastrointestinal infection acts synecdochally, rather than merely descriptively, highlighting the contradiction between the regime's rhetoric and the people's reality. In one sentence, she moves from terms with positive connotations, terms that emphasize the ideology, the newness, purity, and beauty of the government project: "three-year-old," "glassy," "white," "splendidly isolated," "conceived," to terms that denote reality: "natural," "death," and "gastrointestinal infection."

In much the same way that one's perception of an area would literally change as one descended in flight upon a new space and details came into focus, so too, she suggests with this opening passage, does the idealized rhetoric of El Salvador, as represented by this airport, fall apart as one works through the idealized to the real. "In the general absence of tourists these hotels have since been abandoned, ghost resorts on the empty Pacific beaches," she continues after the opening sentence, "and to land at this airport built to service them is to plunge directly into a state in which no ground is solid, no depth of field reliable, no perception so definite that it might not dissolve into its reverse" (13). Her use of asyndeton speeds the pace of the sentence, so that the reader, who is directed first to consider a literal landing ("to land at this airport") is quickly and efficiently pulled into a figurative landing, plunging "directly into a state," a state that now refers to a cognitive condition rather than an actual area.

Her subsequent use of anaphora—the repeated "no"s—amplifies her rejection of the previous rhetoric; there is no one reliable perspective or presentation of the facts on which one can rely, to the point where anything can become its opposite "dissolve[ing] into its reverse." This last phrase of her opening paragraph is not accidental—it describes exactly what occurs in her first sentence, as the idealized rhetoric of the Molina regime, "splendid" and "white," dissolves into its ugly and horrifying reverse—huge numbers of the population dying from diarrhea. She then continues:

> The only logic is that of acquiescence. Immigration is negotiated in a thicket of automatic weapons, but by whose authority the weapons are brandished (Army or National Guard or National Police or Customs Police or Treasury Police or one of a continuing proliferation of other shadowy and overlapping forces) is a blurred point. Eye contact is avoided. Documents are scrutinized upside down. Once clear of the airport, on the new highway that slices through green hills rendered phosphorescent by the cloud cover of the tropical rainy season, one sees mainly underfed cattle and mongrel dogs and armored vehicles, vans and trucks and Cherokee Chiefs fitted with reinforced steel and bulletproof Plexiglas an inch thick. (13–14)

Here, Didion employs hypotyposis as she enlarges on and emphasizes the first statement: "The only logic is that of acquiescence."[50] The "truth" of her first statement is not so much proven as explored and articulated in the sentences that follow, with the result that a scene unfolds before the readers' eyes.

In this scene, hypotyposis establishes some elements as a foreground against which other elements of a situation fade in importance to the point that the audience does not regard them as important. This figure is particularly useful for taking subjects removed from the audience through distance, time, or familiarity, and making them seem more real. In so selecting some elements to amplify, Didion endows them with "presence," which is crucial to persuasion insofar as "the thing that is present to the consciousness assumes . . . an importance" that items not selected do not have.[51] In this passage, in the process of narrating arrival and entry into El Salvador, Didion focuses the reader solely on images of terror and implied violence—automatic weapons, faceless authorities, neglected animals, and armored vehicles. These are brought to the foreground not only by their inclusion but also by the juxtaposition of this inclusion with omissions—she does not reference herself or her feelings (employing, instead, the third person singular "one"), name those handling the weapons, documents, and cars (relying on passive construction to mask agency—"Documents are scrutinized"), or distill her focus by detailing the many mundane things related to air travel but not specific to El Salvador (i.e., disembarking, finding baggage, arranging transportation).

As a result of her choices, the readers are inserted into the scene she has constructed and invited to experience it as if through their own eyes, rather than mediated through Didion's. The scene consequently becomes more vivid, the "phosphorescent" green hills seeming close in time and space rather than located in some distant, unknowable country. A good metaphor, Aristotle asserts "sets the scene before our eyes; for events ought to be seen in progress rather than in prospect,"[52] and here Didion's use of metaphor does just that—soldiers (or guards or police) with guns are transformed into a "thicket of automatic weapons" to be negotiated, so that the reader is compelled to visualize the difficulties that would attend navigation through a densely wooded area composed of guns rather than trees.

The violent connotations conjured by this thicket are transported outside the airport where a seemingly beautiful setting of new roads and green hills is disrupted by a highway metaphorically described as "slicing" through it and revealing starved animals and armored vehicles. All of these elements—the weapons, the roads, the animals, and the armored vehicles—are intended to act synecdochically insofar as they, as only very small parts of El Salvador, are meant to represent the country as a whole. They are a microcosm, rendered in concrete details, meant to represent the macrocosm of El Salvador, a country whose politics at the time were not well understood by the American public, and whose daily violence often went untraceable, unreported, and unpunished.

In employing hypostasis, metaphor, and synecdoche to make this distant land present to her American audience, Didion sets before their eyes a reality she finds deeply problematic. She further draws their eyes to this reality by employing anastrophe, a deviation in word order that "surprises expectation" and thus effectively draws attention.[53] She writes, "Immigration is negotiated in a thicket of automatic weapons, but by whose authority the weapons are brandished (Army or National Guard or National Police or Customs Police or Treasury Police or one of a continuing proliferation of other shadowy and overlapping forces) is a blurred point." Here, rather than write "It is not known who authorizes the weapons," she employs passive construction to note "by whose authority the weapons are brandished," before concluding the clause two lines down with "is a blurred point," with the result that the reader's attention is uncomfortably sustained throughout the long sentence in anticipation of the completion of the thought.

    She further amplifies the audience's discomfort by using polysyndeton and parenthesis. Polysyndeton, the repeated use of conjunctions, slows the rhythm of a sentence, which focuses the readers' attention on each of the elements in that sentence and suggests that each is significant and equally probable. She employs polysyndeton twice—the first instance occurs in a parenthetical aside disrupting the syntax of the sentence and thus drawing attention to itself; she writes, "Immigration is negotiated in a thicket of automatic weapons, but by whose authority the weapons are brandished (Army or National Guard or National Police or Customs Police or Treasury Police or one of a continuing proliferation of other shadowy and overlapping forces) is a blurred point." The passive construction of the first half of the sentence establishes both propositionally and stylistically that the source of terror in El Salvador is uncertain; this uncertainty is then emphasized by her repeated use of *or*, which, in concert with the parenthesis, invites the reader to slow down and consider the many possible sources of terror in El Salvador while simultaneously suggesting that all are equally probable and thus certainty is impossible. This suggestion is heightened by the fact that she moves, in the course of this sentence, from concrete proper names to the general and abstract phrase "proliferation of other shadowy and overlapping forces," a movement from precision to confusion that stylistically represents the "blurred point" with which she concludes.

    In the last half of the last sentence in the passage, she again employs polysyndeton, this time using *and* rather than *or* to give the impression of a long list of elements roughly equivalent in importance. As one drives into El Salvador, she writes, "one sees mainly underfed cattle and mongrel dogs and armored vehicles, vans and trucks and Cherokee Chiefs fitted with reinforced steel and bulletproof Plexiglas an inch thick." These four "and"s join together cattle, dogs, and armored vehicles to suggest that no aspect of El Salvador is spared the terror that is "the given of the place,"[54] while the manner of their joining mirrors the experience one would have looking out the window of a traveling vehicle and viewing a continuous succession of images flowing into one another. In so laying this scene before her reader's eyes and, through stylistic amplification, highlighting the features she finds most disturbing while peripheralizing those that might distract,

Didion implies, through form, her attitude toward El Salvador rather than making it explicit through reflection and proposition.

There are, scattered throughout the work, frequent moments in which Didion does reflect on the situation in which she finds herself, but such reflections are tightly controlled, often contained in relatively short sentences that bear the weight of the accumulating details that precede them. She ends chapter 1, which began with her landing in El Salvador, by describing an evening on the porch of a restaurant in Escalón, having moved the reader in the course of the chapter from an establishing shot of the whole country to a tightly framed scene on the ground. As she and Dunne eat, she becomes aware of "two human shadows," one sitting in a darkened Cherokee Chief, one "crouched between the pumps of the Esso station next door, carrying a rifle." Alone, with only the light from the candle on their table for illumination, they "continu[e] talking, carefully." She concludes "nothing came of this, but I did not forget the sensation of having been in a single instant demoralized, undone, humiliated by fear, which is what I meant when I said that I came to understand in El Salvador the mechanism of terror" (26).

The slow unfolding of this sentence suggests Didion had experienced and then processed the moment calmly, coolly, and in a controlled fashion. She evidences restraint by inserting "in El Salvador" between "to understand" and "the mechanism" and by inserting "in a single instance" between "having been" and "demoralized," which delays the impact of the passive action.[55] Nothing about the way this sentence unfolds suggest that she is "undone"—it is as carefully composed as she is, from the repeated modifications of "demoralized" to the long relative clause "which is what I meant when I said that I" preceding the completion of her thought. This sentence is also, to use Kakutani's favored adjective, elliptical, depending, as it does, on the reader to recall that five pages earlier Didion had concluded a visit to a body dump by noting she had come "to understand, in a way I had not understood before, the exact mechanism of terror." In neither instance does Didion explicitly define "the exact mechanism" of terror, relying instead on the readers to infer its meaning when presented—in concise and vivid detail—with the things she has witnessed.

Similar stylistic strategies are at work in two other key passages in the text, both of which describe moments of personal terror yet keep the emotion, and the reader, at arm's length. In the final chapter of the book she describes visiting a morgue with her husband and an unnamed American newspaper reporter to see firsthand the bodies of slain young men. As they wait in their car to leave afterward—surrounded by "a number of wrecked or impounded cars, many of them shot up, upholstery chewed by bullets, windshield shattered, thick pastes of congealed blood on pearlized hoods" (103)—three men in uniform, one of whom is blocking their way with his motorcycle, a G-3 in his lap, stare silently without making eye contact or responding to the driver's request to move. The situation is resolved when the driver manages to maneuver out of the space without hitting the motorcycle, while Didion sits in the car and silently studies her hands. "Nothing more happened," she reflects, "and what did happen had been a common enough kind of incident in El Salvador, a pointless confrontation with aimless authority, but I have heard of no *solución* that precisely addresses this local vocation for terror" (104). She offers no solution of her own, only this spare description of her own stillness and silence in a moment in which she has no real control, in a place that operates outside of logic.

"To persist in so distinctly fluid a situation required a personality of considerable resistance" (89), Didion observes, as the work reaches its final pages. Her description of her final hours in the country mark the first instance in which she hints that hers is not such a personality. After only two weeks she finds herself "seized by the conviction" that her ride to the airport is not taking the most direct way to the airport, that the driver is not in fact an embassy guard. "I boarded the plane without looking back, and sat rigid until the plane left the ground. I did not fasten my seat belt. I did not lean back" (106). These terse sentences, spare and direct, are the closest Didion comes to conveying her own personal terror, and they are as composed and still as her frozen upright figure as it is lifted away from "heart of darkness" alluded to in the Conrad quote that acts as epigraph to the work. "This flight from San Salvador to Belize to Miami took place at the end of June 1982," she reports in the next paragraph.

She then concludes the book with the following sentence, a sentence that mimics yet reverses the first sentence of the book, moving from the reality of the tangible and reportable to the political rhetoric that renders such reality meaningless and impotent:

> In the week that I am completing this report, at the end of October 1982, the offices in the Hotel Camino Real in San Salvador of the Associated Press, United Press International, Television News, NBC News, CBS News, and the ABC News were raided and searched by members of the El Salvador National Police carrying submachine guns; fifteen leaders of legally rec-

ognized political and labor groups opposing the government of El Salvador were disappeared in San Salvador;[56] Deane Hinton said that he was "reasonably certain" that these disappearances had not been conducted under Salvadoran government orders; the Salvadoran Ministry of Defense announced that eight of the fifteen disappeared citizens were in fact in government custody; and the State Department announced that the Reagan administration believed that it had "turned the corner" in its campaign for political stability in Central America. (107–108)

In one sentence, Didion works inductively, piling up evidence while at the same time exhibiting, through sentence structure, just how easily "the truth" can dissolve into its reverse. The fluidity of the sentence—its seamless transition from evidence to obfuscating interpretation—is achieved through its additive structure. In eschewing subordination and the abstract reasoning it permits, she emphasizes the complete superficiality of such rhetoric while signaling her own refusal to be drawn in and manipulated by it. She herself is entirely absent in final passage, as she is in the initial passage of the book, receding so that the reader is left with the images that accumulate across the lines of the page.

*Salvador* was met, both upon its publication and over the decades that followed, with both praise and criticism, much of the latter fairly predictable—given audiences' familiarity with Didion and her writing at the time and since—in its evaluations and concerns. Frequently charged with being elitist and neurotic for, in her earlier works, things such as obsessing over the presence or absence of "pastry marble," or describing keepers of private notebooks such as herself as "lonely and resistant rearrangers of things, anxious malcontents, children afflicted apparently at birth with some presentiment of loss,"[57] she does not escape similar criticism with this book.[58] Bruce Bawer, writing for the *Hudson Review*, dismisses Didion as a "two-week tourist" and argues that her work "can feel less like an act of compassion than of condescension and exploitation, a work in which the author looks down, godlike, upon the mortals as they squabble ridiculously."[59]

George Eder, characterizing Didion as "strident," is dismissive of her efforts, advising that "those who seek the facts behind the Salvador situation would do better to listen to the reasoned views of Dr. Jeane Jordon Kirkpatrick. . . . On the other hand, those who seek a delightful and even poetical prose style, those who prefer fiction to fact, will do well to stick to Didion-Dunne."[60] McClure contends that her cynicism and "particular modernist sensibility"⁶¹ cause her to "write off" El Salvador, and invite "her readers to see the official terror in El Salvador as a sign of a general cultural inferiority, rather than a function of long-term, systematic oppression of the majority in the service of local and foreign interests" (112). While he credits her for being at times "powerfully illuminating" (110) and sharply denouncing U.S. policy, and acknowledges that her experience of El Salvador might be accurately represented, he argues that hers is not the only possible experience of the place and time and accuses her of a "secret sympathy" with the goals of "official terrorism" (114).

But, on the whole, this work was well received by critics, with reviewers acknowledging the difficult task facing Didion and marveling at her ability, as neither a politician nor political reporter, to make present to audiences the terror of the place. Christopher Lehmann-Haupt notes "that it is difficult to deny that everything she writes grows out of close observation of the social and political landscape of El Salvador. And it is quite impossible to deny the artistic brilliance of her reportage. She brings the country to life so that it ends up invading our flesh. To get rid of it then is as simple as shaking off leeches."⁶² That she is able to impress upon the reader the incomprehensibility of El Salvador at the time in a manner that is, in point of fact, comprehensible, is largely due to her talent in constructing sentences that argue as much through form as through content, rather than through any "cult of personality," any reliance on her popular appeal to, in particular, female readers.

Although *Salvador* predates Didion and Dunne's move to New York by five years, it is clear from this work as well as from her novels *A Book of Common Prayer* (1977) and *Democracy* (1984), that the late 1970s and early 1980s mark a time when Didion began to turn her attention from the local (California history, politics, and culture), the personal (her ancestors, her marriage, her small child), and the emblematic (the Bevatron on the hill, the water works, the governor's mansion) to domestic and foreign political affairs and the systems of power and language through which those affairs are managed and communicated. In her earlier nonfiction (which, arguably, until the publication of *The Year of Magical Thinking* in 2005, provoked most of the critical and popular writing that exists in response to her work), Didion's presence in her essays seemed essential to their appeal (friend and fellow New Journalist Dan Wakefield observes that "the reader comes to admire what can only be called the *character* of this observer at work"),⁶³ as did her mourning for lost rites, rituals, and assumptions, and her tendency to assume a set of shared values with her audience. She appealed in part because she was comfortable speaking for those who found themselves passing through the same tumultuous days and years of the late 1950s and 1960s, a time of profound changes to the culture and the family.

Those who read her (though it is almost certain they had never, as children, been invited to play in the large halls of the Governor's Mansion in Sacramento) were assumed to be, through the timing of their births, like Didion, "born into the last generation to carry the burden of 'home,' to find in family life the source of all tension and drama."[64] She appealed, too, because she seemed so open, at least on paper, to revealing raw, intimate moments that spoke to frailty and suffering. Braudy seemed to speak for many fans of Didion when she recently wrote, "I believed—believe—that Didion is best as a subjective journalist. She's a beacon to women writers because she records what previously felt unsayable in heart-wrenching particulars."[65] One can imagine she is referring to passages describing domestic moments, such as when Didion writes, in the essay "In the Islands," of the tension between herself and her husband: "I avoid his eyes, and brush the baby's hair."[66]

This concern for the local, the personal, and the emblematic, though never entirely absent from the nonfiction she writes in the '80s and '90s, largely recedes as her attention turns to power, politics, and global affairs. So too does she largely shift from introspection, from reflection on the seismic shifts in history and culture that undermine her sense of certainty and shatter her nerves, to assured criticism of political systems and political rhetoric. She, in some sense, moves from a sustained engagement with the breakdown of "old orders," in order to train her critic's eye on the establishment and perpetuation of the "new orders"—the political parties and insiders and deals responsible for the narratives that determine national and global realities as well as the news business that covers them.

The training for her political analysis, she reveals in a 2001 C-SPAN conversation with Frank Rich, occurred in her years as an English major at Berkeley, when she learned to approach fiction through the lens of New Criticism. *Reading* fiction, she reflected, had influenced her far more than writing it. The textual analysis she engaged in with works like *The Golden Bough* taught her how to read imagery, "to make discoveries," and could be used productively, she realized, to approach "reading the newspaper or reading current events."[67] The language of politics, as the title of *Political Fictions* makes explicit, makes use of the same literary devices a young Didion had been trained to find within the texts of canonical fiction, and recognizing and deciphering these devices takes her beyond, or behind, the text, the fictions.

Attention to language and the fictions composed by it largely moved her, for two decades, away from a domestic focus. As Daugherty puts it, whereas in Didion's recent fiction,

> [T]he house in which the couple will or will not live happily ever after is a given. The later Didion, intent upon cracking official fables, insists the *real* narratives are these: who owns the land on which the house was built; who built the house and when; who sold the house to whom; when, why, and for how much; who, ultimately benefited from the sale, where did the proceeds actually go, for what purposes was the house used?[68]

These concerns with larger structures of power and production, while moderately apparent in her earlier essays on, for instance, the economic inequalities on evidence in the fin-de-siècle mansions of Newport, Rhode Island ("The Seacoast of Despair"), and Hollywood politics ("Good Citizens"), are only fully realized for the first time in *Salvador*, and the rhythms of her prose evidence this shift. Her sentences are increasingly insistent, anaphoric, and repetitive in structure and sound even as they accumulate and modify ideas whose resolution is delayed until their emphatic endings.[69] She had once noted, derisively, that talk of politics in Hollywood relies on "borrowed rhetoric by which political ideas are reduced to choices between the good (equality is good) and the bad (genocide is bad)," which "tends to make even the most casual political small talk resemble a rally."[70] It is precisely this kind of polarized and simplistic language she avoids in her prose of the next two decades.

CHAPTER 2

## Preferred Narratives

## New York City after the Central Park Jogger

In 1992 Didion published *After Henry*, her first collection of essays in thirteen years (the last had been *The White Album* in 1979). These essays are, in many ways, a continuation of the type of reportage she had begun to do with *Salvador* in 1983 and *Miami* in 1987—in them she turns a critical eye on invented narratives, sentimental mythologies, and political posturing. After the opening essay, a reflection on the passing of her longtime editor Henry Robbins, the work is divided into three parts, each devoted to places that have attained mythic status in the minds of Americans: Washington, D.C., California, and New York. Most of the essays, written primarily in the late '80s and early '90s, are to be found in the section devoted to California, Didion's place of birth and a state whose history and mythologies occupy a great deal of her oeuvre. However, it is in the first section, on Washington, that she establishes the themes that subsequently run through the remainder of the collection and find their fullest expression in the single essay comprising the final part of the collection on New York, "Sentimental Journeys." It is thus useful to consider the nature of Didion's rhetorical analysis in the essays preceding it.

With "In the Realm of the Fisher King," the sole essay in Part Two of the collection, Didion, ironic and amused, pokes holes in the artifice and theater of Ronald Reagan's presidency, one which she portrays as centered on a president who was, in many ways, physically and mentally, not present. "In the absence of an actual president," she begins one sentence, "speechwriters like Peggy Noonan "invented an ideal one."[1] This invented president, according to Didion, ran an administration more fond of image, appearances, and rhetoric than reality, one in which, for instance, merely "talking tough" was considered the "favored foreign policy."[2] Didion portrays the Reagans themselves as comical figures who viewed their roles as president and first lady as part of a production put on by a studio system that would see to their needs and direct their performances.

On this particular "movie set," their clothes were to be understood as "wardrobes," and these, together with their housing, travel, and furnishing, were merely "production expense[s]." In service of dismantling the rhetoric of this "production," Didion relates an account of the couple taking part in an Episcopalian church service during Reagan's campaign, an act that required an aide who scouted the "correct location," and negotiated the terms of the service with the minister beforehand, and a couple willing to "perform" the ritual of Holy Communion regardless of their unfamiliarity with the practice. Despite fumbling with the communion wafer (Nancy Regan accidentally drops it in the wine, and her husband, instructed to do what she does, drops his in deliberately), the president leaves the service upbeat, the overall "performance" a success. Didion attributes this self-satisfaction to Reagan's focus on "the story, the high concept" or "the big picture." In this case, the big picture "was of the candidate going to church on Sunday morning, the details obsessing the wife and the aide—what church, what to do with the wafer—remained outside the frame."[3] In the rendering of this anecdote, Didion establishes one of her fundamental criticisms of the political world, namely, its slavish devotion to the rhetorical act of constructing productions, pseudo-events that frame reality in such a way that any elements that do not fit are simply not acknowledged, much less addressed.

Criticism of this tendency toward artifice and misdirection, as well as the public's hunger for such theatrics, runs through Part Three of *After Henry*, which sees Didion's attention focused on California "stories." She begins by considering the story composed by "California girl" Patricia Hearst, which, with its unresolved questions and ambiguous central character, could not serve as the type of idealizing narrative the public was willing to digest. In her telling, the rejection of Patricia Hearst was, at its heart, a rejection of her "story" as she chose to tell it. Didion ends the essay by juxtaposing this rejection against the eagerness of Californians to embrace the self-mythologizing narrative, the "local opera," of Jim Jones (before, of course, that narrative reached its grisly end). Another essay in this section covers the case of a murdered road-show promoter, which she portrays as a particularly compelling piece of theater with "principals" and a "cameo role . . . played by Robert Evans."[4] And in the final essay, she lays bare the "invention" of Los Angeles, "the most idealized of American cities, and the least accidental," by "the *Los Angeles Times* and by its owners."[5]

In all of these essays in Parts Two and Three, then, Didion's concern with the rhetorical posturing of politicians, prosecutors, and the media, as well as her insistence on deconstructing the mythologizing that permeates political and public life, are clear, and thus the reader begins Part Four with the expectation that what is to follow is less a story than a story about the stories people tell. By Didion's own account, it was only a year or so after returning to New York, following an almost twenty-five-year absence, that she realized how incomprehensible the city had become to her and how unengaged she was with it. This realization prompted her interest in reporting on it, though what she ended up doing, she notes, was not so much reporting as "coming at a situation from a lot of angles."[6] This "situation" involved the brutal rape and beating of a twenty-nine-year-old woman in New York's Central Park, and it is worth noting that Didion's interest in the case was, in a very real sense, purely rhetorical; writing about it, for her, was only a means to an end, an opportunity to penetrate the New York she had returned to after so many years.

"We know her story, and some of us, although not all of us, which was to become one of the story's several equivocal aspects, know her name." With this sentence, Didion begins the essay "Sentimental Journeys," a work that appears, superficially, to be about the highly publicized assault and rape of the "Central Park Jogger" in 1989, but is, more precisely, a critique of the stories New York City "tells itself to rationalize its class contradictions."[7] Such stories need not be constructed through words; Didion points to Central Park, the scene of the attack, as an instance of an embodied narrative, an "essay in democracy," a place pitched as a sort of social experiment where those of all social classes would be drawn together to mingle peaceably. This vision or "preferred narrative," she argues, "worked to veil actual conflict, to cloud the extent to which the condition of being rich was predicated upon the continued neediness of a working class."[8] Narratives, whether verbal or embodied, are therefore, according to Didion, a type of magical thinking.

This type of thinking was at work, Didion notes, when people began rejecting the notion that they should not, in light of the attack, run alone in Central Park at night. Their resistance, Didion notes, was "interesting, suggesting as it did that the city's not inconsiderable problems could be solved by the willingness of its citizens to hold or draw some line, to 'say no'; in other words that a reliance on certain magical gestures could affect the city's fate" (702). What Didion deems "magical thinking" and "magical gestures," is, at its essence, metaphorical thinking, and it is Didion's argument that this same type of thinking is what allows citizens of New York to understand one thing—the current conditions of their lives in the city—in terms of another, the brutalization of the jogger. Their reliance on this metaphorical thinking, Didion argues throughout the essay, is so conceptually systematic that, as metaphorical constructs tend to do, it blinds them to any facts that are inconsistent with their version of truth.

It is to the city's great discredit, Didion suggests, that its response to its considerable problems is a narrative that symbolically violates a woman already brutalized. She writes of the jogger: "[S]he was wrenched, even as she hung between death and life and later between insentience and sentience, into New York's ideal sister, daughter, Bacharach bride: a young woman of conventional middle-class privilege and promise whose situation was such that many people tended to overlook the fact that the state's case against the accused was not invulnerable" (688). Following her metaphorical use of the word *wrenched*, Didion inserts a parenthetical aside that introduces a moment of stasis in the sentence, a pause before the completion of her thought. The interrupting clause, with its pair of antithetical phrases ("death and life"/ "insentience and sentience") suggests stillness, a stillness that is then disturbed by the return to the original sentence much as the victim's suspended state terminates in her transformation to idealized symbol. Within the parenthetical, Didion resists the conventional ordering of the antithetical pairs (which would typically be written as "life and death"/ "sentience and insentience") and thus foregrounds the extreme vulnerability of the jogger, who was initially near death and in a coma for weeks. This stylistic emphasis on her vulnerability makes her subsequent treatment by "New York" (which Didion describes using personification, suggesting the degree of identification between people and the city) appear all the more striking.

While the essay appears to be, at points, a critique of the prosecutor's case (and therefore a critique of New York's rush to embrace the guilt of the accused), Didion's primary interest is less in the facts of the actual case than in the way those "facts" are coopted by the city to serve its own ends. Certainly, portions of the essay could be read as a defense of the minors found guilty of attacking the jogger in Central Park,[9] or, at the very least, as indictments of the system that started with a presumption of guilt and speedily affirmed this presumption with convictions. Such a reading, however, would overlook the essential point of this essay, which is to persuade readers that New York has a long history of engaging in rhetorical narratives that contribute to its appealing mythos while concealing its less palatable realities. According to Didion, these realities include the ever-widening gap between the rich and the working class; the tensions between whites and blacks; the "minimal level of comfort and opportunity its citizens have come to accept" (705); the "essential criminality" (713) of a city that works "on little deals, payoffs, accommodations, *baksheesh*, arrangements that circumvent the direct exchange of goods and services and prevent what would be, in a competitive economy, the normal ascendance of the superior product" (705); and the "absence of civility" (708) that accompanies this criminality. In order to make this point, she delineates the narrative conventions that make possible the construction of a public myth out of one violent event of many occurring in New York City around that same time period.

There is no doubt that the attack on the jogger was, in its savage brutality, shocking in the extreme. The twenty-nine-year-old woman was found naked, her skull crushed, and her vagina filled with twigs and dirt. She had lost 75 percent of her blood and had to be placed in a medically induced coma for weeks to ensure her survival (685–86). However, were this attack "merely" extremely violent, there is little chance it would have held the public attention for long—the jogger would not have become, in Didion's words, "unwilling and unwitting, a sacrificial player in the sentimental narrative that is New York public life" (686). There were, after all, "3,254 other rapes" reported that very same year, including one in which a woman was nearly decapitated, and another in which a woman was sodomized before being thrown down a four-story air shaft (686).

Yet these latter stories, involving, as they did, "lower"-class black women, failed to capture the headlines, and, certainly, the intense and sustained attention of New Yorkers in the way the jogger's attack did. According to Didion, the fact that the jogger's accused attackers were markedly different than she—black males who lived in public housing and federally subsidized apartment complexes—made this particular crime "newsworthy," made it a "story" that could be used to provide a scapegoat through which the city could expunge its guilt. Scapegoats have historically been made of those at the margins of society, have traditionally been constructed through an emphasis on their perceived differences from the rest of society, their punishment or expulsion a way for a culture to symbolically rid itself of what plagues it while reaffirming its own essential goodness. Scapegoating myths, which have, throughout history, operated independently of any verifiable guilt, have long provided comforting narratives for those facing seemingly irresolvable conflicts. Such myths, which in New York City's case often provide a "sentimental reading of class differences and human suffering, a reading that promises both resolution and retribution," offer, according to Didion, the promise of a sort of analgesic or opiate, "a built-in source of natural morphine working to blur the edges of real and to a great extent insoluble problems" (705).

In choosing to unpack the enigma of New York by focusing on the case of the Central Park jogger, Didion sees it synecdochally; for her, what narratives spring forth in the wake of this brutal attack represent a long and larger history of similar narratives and anticipate future narratives. Those in control of the narratives (the prosecutors, the police, the press) remain, necessarily, at a distance from their central "characters," from whose lives they select and enlarge upon details that support their preferred story lines. In this case, this selection of, and emphasis on, certain details to the exclusion of others is a rhetorical act that distorts, flattens, and idealizes the victim and thus ensures she "fits" the conventions of their redemptive narratives. In collusion with the city officials and the media, according to Didion, are the multitude of wealthy, predominantly white, upper-class citizens whose own desire to resolve any cognitive dissonance created by their participation in an economic and political system that creates the class differences leads them to embrace narratives that obscure this participation.[10] Focusing on this one case permits her to sustain an extended critique of all of these narratives yet remain grounded in the particulars necessary for convincing her readers that such rhetoric is at work. The result is a relatively concise (compared to *Salvador* and *Miami*, works similar in their attention to the dangers of idealized narratives) but no less potent deconstruction of the mythologizing impulses that define New York's conception of itself.

In undertaking this deconstruction, Didion engages in a stylistic construction of ethos that emphasizes her insider status as a New Yorker while it simultaneously highlights her position outside of the dominant narratives she critiques. In beginning the first sentence of the essay with the first person plural pronoun "We," Didion establishes herself immediately as a New York insider, an identity crucial to appealing to her audience of New York readers and to establishing her credibility as someone "in the know." Privy to details of the case not widely shared, intimately familiar with the geographical details of New York's terrain, and well acquainted with the "economic and historical groundwork" of New York, the "civic and commercial arrangements, deals, negotiations, gimmes and getmes, graft and grift, pipe, topsoil, concrete, garbage" (726), Didion displays, here and throughout the essay, her obvious familiarity with key political figures and the machinations of the media, as well as her ability to reference key New York historical, political, and economic events. In alluding casually, and without further explanation, to things such as "Jim Buck's dog trainers," "Henry Kravis's Bentley," and "Saint Laurent" (699),[11] she clearly signals that she is "of" New York, and, more precisely, of the class of "the more privileged white, citizens of New York" (711) upon whom she turns her critical eye.

Having established herself as a New Yorker, Didion, paradoxically, also works to construct herself as an outsider, one who is able to maintain the critical distance necessary to recognize the media and city's narratives for what they are: sentimental renderings promising cathartic resolution, stories designed to blur, to obscure, to placate, and to sell. In her role as outsider, she performs the work of rhetorical critic, analyzing the rhetoric employed by the city's political elite and, in doing so, undermining the self-serving narratives such rhetoric creates. At the same time that her use of "We" in the first sentence establishes her as someone with whom the audience can identify, the repeated use, in the same sentence, of the pronoun "her," without the presence of an antecedent, heightens the impression that she is in possession of privileged information that her audience may not have. Because the readers may or may not know about whom Didion is speaking, may or may not know to which story she is referring, much less what its other "equivocal aspects" may be, and thus may or may not be named by the "We" with which this essay begins, they are also rhetorically positioned as potential outsiders and thus dependent on Didion for information.

Anderson has written of Didion that her "characteristic strategy is to reflect on contemporary life from the standpoint of her own experience or to engage in autobiographical narrative, which ultimately leads to commentary on the social problems of the time." The result, he proposes, is that her reportage is lent the qualities of "reflective/exploratory writing."[12] This is true of much of her earlier writing (and in fact Anderson made this point in 1987) as well as her latest memoirs, but in in this particular essay Didion is far more removed from her readers. Even as she evidences her familiarity with New York, she makes little explicit reference to her own personal experiences as a New Yorker, and offers far less evidence of a writer grappling with uncertainty or irreducible ambiguity as her earlier works do. The tone of many of her earliest pieces is often tentative, and their structure sometimes seems quite loose or spontaneous, an apparent reflection of a mind exploring rather than arriving. In these works, she often writes, as Anderson puts it, by employing a "rhetoric of process,"[13] one that displays her own experience of using writing to work through ideas.

Whether describing hanging out with hippies while they drop acid in *Slouching Towards Bethlehem* or detailing the significance of California's relationship with water in *The White Album*, she is present in many earlier works both as a "character" within the experience and as a writer working through the significance of those experiences. She appears available to her readers, her private thoughts seemingly presented without design or artful intervention. The essayistic form has frequently been understood to be especially appropriate for showcasing this type of ethos, for displaying the progress of a writer engaging in a process of discovery, a process that is understood to be as interesting as, or perhaps even more interesting, than any conclusions at which the essayist might arrive. Many essayists value the essayistic form precisely because it avoids fact, certitude, and conclusion in favor of the more open-ended and meditative "display of a mind engaging ideas."[14] However, in this piece, her conclusions—repeated throughout the essay for emphasis—are clear, and the structure of the essay, which seems, at times, meandering but is meticulously plotted, is designed to lead the reader through to these conclusions. Her voice—ironic, sarcastic, understated, insistent, and certain—is carefully constructed through her use of quotation marks, parenthesis, litotes, hedges, expletive constructions, and passive voice.

This is a voice that is established early in the essay. Four paragraphs in, following an introduction that graphically describes the crime and highlights some of the headlines generated by it, Didion observes:

> Later it would be recalled that 3,254 other rapes were reported that year, including one the following week involving the near decapitation of a black woman in Fort Tryon Park and one two weeks later involving a black woman in Brooklyn who was robbed, raped, sodomized, and thrown down an air shaft of a four-story building, but the point was rhetorical, since crimes are universally understood to be news to the extent that they offer, however erroneously, a story, a lesson, a high concept. (686)

Didion's use of passive voice in this passage is typical of much of her writing in this essay; she begins with "later it would be recalled," the passive construction allowing her to suggest people other than herself have actually recollected and recounted this exact series of incidents, when it is highly unlikely that these specific facts were selected and recalled in exactly this same fashion by anyone other than her. Her use of the expletive construction "it would be" furthers this ambiguity, as the "it" is a dummy pronoun with no clear antecedent—she does not locate the recollection in a defined source. In constructing these arguments in the passive voice, Didion puts forth her argument clearly but makes it appear as though what she is stating is merely accepted fact—that others have already done these calculations and come to the same (implied, rhetorical) conclusions.[15]

The conclusions follow from her juxtaposition of the rape of the (white) Central Park jogger against both the total number of rapes in New York that year (which implies that the rape of the jogger was not isolated and therefore is undeserving of special notice) as well as similarly horrific rapes of black women (which implies that the special notice has been granted to her due to her race). Observing that "the" (rather than "her") point of all this information is "rhetorical" she follows with the passively constructed "but crimes are universally understood to be news to the extent that they offer, however erroneously, a story, a lesson, a high concept." In writing "the" rather than "my" point, she suggests the objective status of this point, and the succeeding "crimes are universally understood" is similarly presented as objective fact. While appearing objective, she is, of course, being ironic, as she obviously does not believe her readers to understand this, hence the need for her observation in the first place. This irony, however, is so understated as to go unnoticed in all but the closest reading.

Didion ends the first part of the passage with asyndeton, apposition, and tricolon: "a story, a lesson, a high concept," the latter two words seamlessly emphasizing and modifying the first and so amplifying her point that narratives are often rhetorical rather than objective, as the omission of coordinating conjunctions lends a persuasive rhythm to this most significant portion of the sentence. She then relies on exemplification to amplify her point as the passage continues, and she turns to another New York crime narrative—this one also concerning a young, white, upper-class woman:

> In the 1986 Central Park death of Jennifer Levin, then eighteen, at the hands of Robert Chambers, then nineteen, the "story," extrapolated more or less from thin air but left largely uncorrected, had to do not with people living wretchedly and marginally on the underside of where they wanted to be, not with the Dreiserian pursuit of "respectability" that marked the revealed details (Robert Chambers's mother was a private-duty nurse who worked twelve-hour night shifts to enroll her son in private schools and the Knickerbocker Greys), but with "preppies," and the familiar "too much too soon." (687)

Once again, Didion relies on the passive voice ("the 'story,' extrapolated more or less from thin air but left largely uncorrected") to imply that her subjective interpretation of events is objectively true and thus presents herself as a neutral observer. She then parenthetically inserts details emphasizing what she sees as the reality of situation while employing quotation marks to undermine the conclusions drawn by others ("preppies," "too much too soon").

The combination of parenthesis and quotation marks signals graphically, to the careful reader, that, despite the constructed appearance of neutrality, Didion is once again being ironic. The quotation marks both emphasize the fictional nature of the narrative (the "story") and suggest certain words and phrases are so clichéd as to speak to the superficiality of the narratives they support ("preppies" and "too much too soon"). The parenthetical, which might on the face of it seem to be tangential due to its interpolation as an aside, is actually highlighted by the fact that it does not fit the syntax of the sentence in which it falls. Parenthesis allows the reader a chance to hear the writer's voice editorializing, with the result that this particular sentence is more emotionally charged than those around it.[16] As a consequence of these stylistic choices, and the ones noted above, Didion's voice remains, paradoxically, both forceful and understated.

Her rhetorical use of understatement to achieve persuasive force is on evidence throughout the essay, but is particularly obvious in a section in which she deals with the subject introduced by the very first sentence of the essay: the refusal of the prosecutors and (most) of the press to officially name the victim (whose name was known to many, including several who repeated it on air). This is a refusal Didion finds problematic, both because she believes it stigmatizes the victim further by suggesting she should somehow be ashamed of her attack and because she believes it allows the city to coopt the victim in service to their narratives—in anonymity the victim can be "readily abstracted, and her situation, readily made to stand for that of the city itself" (689). In contrast, the names of the alleged perpetrators had been released by the police and the press long before any of them were even indicted, this despite the fact that some were juveniles. This release was justified, the police said, "because of the seriousness of the incident" (693).

In criticizing this rationale, Didion writes: "[T]here seemed a debatable point here, the question of whether 'the seriousness of the incident' might not have in fact seemed a compelling reason to avoid any appearance of a rush to judgment by preserving the anonymity of a juvenile suspect" (693–94). Here the use of the words *seemed* and *might*, hedge words, allows her to appear as if she is carefully qualifying her argument and not overstating her case, even while her use of quotations marks signals her rejection of the use of this phrase to justify unethical procedural decisions.

Were this her only use of the word *seemed* in this section, a reader might make no more note of it. But she continues on to use it six more times in the short paragraph that follows, and it becomes clear that the word, in conjunction with other stylistic choices, allows Didion to employ understatement to rhetorical effect. "There were, early on," she continues,

> certain aspects of this case that seemed not well handled by the police and prosecutors, and others that seemed not well handled by the press. It would seem to have been tactically unwise, since New York state law requires that a parent or guardian be present when children under sixteen are questioned, for police to continue the interrogation of Yusef Salaam, then fifteen, on the grounds that his Transit Authority bus pass said he was sixteen, while his mother was kept waiting outside. It would seem to have been unwise for Linda Fairstein, the assistant district attorney in charge of Manhattan sex crimes, to ignore, at the precinct house, the mother's assertion that the son was fifteen, and later to suggest, in court, that the boy's age had been unclear to her because the mother had used the word "minor." It would also seem to have been unwise for Linda Fairstein to tell David Nocenti, the assistant U.S. Attorney who was paired with Yusef Salaam in a "Big Brother" program and who had come to the precinct house at the mother's request, that he had "no legal standing" there and that she would file a complaint with his supervisors. (694)

In terms of content, this passage clearly provides evidence that those involved in prosecuting the case acted unwisely in a number of different ways, and thus Didion's use of an expletive construction ("There were") at the beginning of the passage appropriately suggests certainty about the version of events to follow. Rather, however, than begin each of the following sentences with the assured "There were," she chooses to employ the conditional "It would seem," which implies that she is merely speculating about the nature of the decisions described. She then offers a series of sentences in which thoughts are expressed through the denial of their opposites (phrases such as "seemed not well handled" and "seem to have been tactically unwise"). In expressing her points in this fashion, Didion employs litotes, or extreme understatement, in order to emphasize, in an ironic fashion, the numerous failures of the police and prosecutors in regards to the case. This use of understatement also works to suggest that readers are free to draw their own conclusions, though of course the detailed list of repeated missteps, taking up, as it does, three-fourths of a page, leaves little doubt that mistakes were made.

Within the passage, Didion also uses anaphora to circle repeatedly back to the subject of her argument and intensify the sense of accumulating evidence. She does the same in the passage below, where she describes multiple instances in which the victim was transformed, through the language of the press and the mayor's office, into a symbol of the city. Here, Didion employs anaphora to emphasize how repetitive and insistent these attempts at transformation were:

> She would be Lady Courage to the *New York Post*, she would be A Profile in Courage to the *Daily News* and *New York Newsday*. She would become for Anna Quindlen in *The New York Times* the figure of "New York Rising above the dirt, the New Yorker who has known the best, and the worst, and has stayed on, living somewhere in the middle." She would become for David Dinkins . . . the emblem of his apparently fragile hopes for the city itself. (689)

Didion ends the paragraph in which this passage is located with the following: "[I]t was precisely in this conflation of victim and city, this confusion of personal woe with public distress, that the crime's 'story' would be found, its lesson, its encouraging promise of narrative resolution" (689). In putting "story" in quotation marks, Didion again emphasizes her ironic distance from the city's rhetoric. Her use of passive voice works here, as elsewhere, to allow her to argue that something has happened without requiring her to actually identify a responsible party or point to an actual moment. Passive voice also ensures that "the crime's 'story'" becomes the object of the sentence, receiving the action of the verb, *found*, a word suggesting the accidental rather than essential connection between actual events and their narrative translations and thus highlighting her point that narratives have little to do with reality.

Her double employment of "this," acts as a cohesive device, referring back to, while emphasizing, the list of ways the city has rhetorically constructed the jogger, and thus creating a causal connection between the assortment of quotes and the construction of a narrative. These rhetorical actions are also emphasized by apposition—apposing "this conflation of victim and city," with "this confusion of personal woe with public distress" Didion both repeats and renames what she sees happening: the jogger being treated figuratively by a self-serving city. She employs anaphora and apposition again at the end of the sentence—"its lesson, its encouraging promise of narrative resolution"—not only to rename "story" but to elaborate on the function of the "story." The rhythmic pattern created by this double use of anaphora is heightened by her use of alliteration at the beginning of the sentence in the words "conflation" and "confusion" as well as "personal" and "public." Cumulatively, these three figures create a formal pattern, a rhythm that subtly invites the readers' collaboration in her critique of the city's rhetoric.

Reviewers have observed of her writing that her rhythms and intonation are "intimately familiar,"[17] and that her rhythm "can feel like a snare, something one can't escape from, a spell, a seduction."[18] Rhythm and repetition—created, many times, through the use of anaphora, alliteration, and asyndeton, often in combination with parallel structure—are critical to her ability to perform a sort of rhetorical enchantment in this essay as in her other writing. Many of her works, this one included, contain references to the "magical" powers of rhetoric, to "magical assumptions," "magical gestures," and "magical ability," as well as to chanting, spells, superstition, and the occult, and she has noted in the past that her use of repetition is often chant-like, "an attempt to cast a spell."[19] It is obvious in this work that she deliberately depends on sound, along with sense, to move her readers. The result of her awareness of and sensitivity to the potential of language to aurally seduce is passages patterned so as to emphasize and reinforce, to enchant the reader with sound.

"The insistent sentimentalization of experience, which is to say the encouragement of such reliance, is not new in New York," writes Didion. She continues, relying on asyndeton to provide the passage a rhythm not unlike that of the city that never sleeps:

> A preference for broad strokes, for the distortion and flattening of character and the reduction of events to narrative, has been for well over a hundred years the heart of the way the city presents itself: Lady Liberty, huddled masses, tickertape parades, heroes, gutters, bright lights, broken hearts, 8 million stories in

the naked city; 8 million stories and all the same story, each devised to obscure not only the city's actual tensions of race and class but also, more significantly, the civic and commercial arrangements that rendered those tensions irreconcilable. (702)

Had Didion used natural word order for this very long declarative and cumulative sentence, she might have begun it by writing: "The city has a preference for presenting itself in broad strokes." Instead, inverting the natural word order, Didion begins with "a preference for broad strokes," delaying the subject of the sentence, and, in so doing, foregrounding her assertion that New York is given to generalizing in the service of creating self-serving mythologies. This initial phrase is further amended through apposition, allowing her to emphasize and define the nature of this generalization, which she does using isocolon. The "broad strokes" occur through "the distortion and flattening of character" and "the reduction of events to narrative," according to these parallel phrases, whose similarity in length and corresponding structure create a pleasing rhythm that aurally reinforces the substance of her claims.

Following this, she continues with the predicate of the sentence "has been for well over a hundred years the heart of the way the city presents itself," before further amplifying her claim through enumeration. What follows is a list of evocative and familiar images of New York, a blend of its best (Lady Liberty, bright lights) and worst (gutters, broken hearts), the pace of the list unbroken by coordinating conjunctions, her intent less to emphasize any individual image than to create a quickly accumulating sense of the city's iconic images, a verbal montage of its most evocative elements. As the list of items nears its end, the rhythm is climactically intensified, first by alliteration (bright lights, broken hearts) and then by anaphora (8 million stories, 8 million stories), and lastly, as the climax reaches its peak, by epanalepsis (8 million *stories* and all the same *stories*), until it is broken as she concludes the sentence by elaborating on the function of these "stories."

Each, she notes, using the passive voice is "devised to obscure not only the city's actual tensions of race and class but also, more significantly, the civic and commercial arrangements that rendered those tensions irreconcilable." In employing *correctio* to amend the first part of this final phrase—the story obscures "*not only* the city's actual tensions of race and class *but also* . . . the civic and commercial arrangements that rendered those tensions irreconcilable"—she is able to lay out a rather complex argument in very concise terms. As well, *correctio* allows her to keep the two actions within the same sentence, the proximity in space suggesting the relationship claimed in the content.

This was a city where anger and fear, in the days after the brutal rape, escalated quickly, and Didion captures the rhythms of its intensification by employing climax in combination with anadiplosis at crucial moments in the piece, such as this passage, where she describes the inevitable convictions of the defendants:

> So fixed were the emotions provoked by this case that the idea that there could have been, for even one juror, even a moment's doubt in the state's case, let alone the kind of doubt that could be sustained over ten days, seemed, to many in the city bewildering, almost unthinkable: the attack on the jogger had by then passed into narrative, and the narrative was about confrontation, about what Governor Cuomo had called "the ultimate shriek of alarm" about what was wrong with the city and about its solution. What was wrong with the city had been identified, and its names were Raymond Santana, Yusef Salaam, Antron McCray, Kharey Wise, Kevin Richardson, and Steve Lopez. (696)

After employing exergasia ("bewildering" is repeated and reworded as "almost unthinkable") to amplify how resistant "many in the city" were to ideas in conflict with their preferred narrative, Didion climactically creates a sense of rising urgency. Within just one sentence, the "attack on the jogger" becomes a "narrative," the "narrative" becomes a "confrontation," and the confrontation becomes "'the ultimate shriek of alarm'" that enlarges to become everything that "was wrong with the city and its solution." The long sentence ends at this climatic high. The next sentence is short and begins by repeating that final phrase of the preceding sentence, "What was wrong with the city," this use of anadiplosis allowing Didion to suggest the ease with which the built-up emotions of the city were seamlessly transferred into the conviction of the defendants. The repetition of the phrase marks the point at which the rhythm built up through climax deescalates, and the brevity of the second sentence suggests the speed at which this occurs, just as the city's own anger is quickly and cathartically released by selection of suitable "scapegoats" to its many problems.

And indeed, as Didion notes, several pages later, with the conviction of the first of these three defendants, "this particular narrative had achieved full resolution, or catharsis," and, subsequently, when the fourth and fifth defendants later came to trial, the city had largely lost interest in the case, its attention transferred to the economy, which had "come center stage in the city's new and yet familiar narrative work: a work in which the vital yet beleaguered city would or would not weather yet another 'crisis' (the answer was a resounding yes); a work, or a dreamwork, that emphasized not only the cyclical nature of such 'crises' but the regenerative power of the city's 'contrasts' "(726).

Didion's use of "center stage" reminds the reader, yet again, of the fictive and theatrical nature of the rhetorical narratives at play. As she notes earlier in the essay, "the imposition of a sentimental, or false, narrative on the disparate and often random experience that constitutes the life of a city or country means, necessarily, that much of what happens in that city or country will be rendered merely illustrative, a series of set pieces, or performance opportunities" (713). In using anadiplosis to refer to the city's turn to a new narrative, Didion underscore her point that this narrative, while "new," is "yet familiar," the tripling of the word *work* emphasizing the repetitive nature of the city's rhetoric. This is a rhetoric in which all the requisite narrative conventions are at play: there is the city as admirable protagonist ("vital") in conflict ("beleaguered") with an unnamed antagonist, a problem needing resolution, and an ending assuring not only victory but an affirmation of the protagonist. Whether the city "would or would not weather" the crisis in this latest iteration, Didion's parenthetical confirms, is not really in question, because the narrative work, renamed through apposition as a "dreamwork," does not really deal with reality in the first place.

The rhetoric of the preferred storyline demands that certain narrative conventions must be met; there must be a central organizing conflict with obvious roles for the key players, roles that emphasize dramatic contrasts and extremes, good guy versus bad guy. In order to work symbolically, such narratives must maximize the distance between perpetrator and victim to ensure the necessary tension that will later be rhetorically resolved. In this case, Didion writes "as a news story, 'Jogger' was understood to turn on the demonstrable 'difference' between the victim and her accused assailants" (687). This difference is established through the selection of details that focus on "perceived refinements of character and of manner and of taste" (697). In so selecting these details, the media, Didion charges, end up suggesting "not the actual victim of an actual crime but a fictional character of a slightly earlier period, the well-brought-up virgin who briefly graces the city with her presence and receives in return a taste of 'real life'" (697).

In the courtroom and in the press, those in control of the narrative, the "good guys," must necessarily be able to cast themselves as victims and their opponents as aggressors in a storyline compelling enough to be invested in. This storyline must also confirm the beliefs of the key players while obscuring whatever is actually going on. For instance, she notes that

> [a]mong the reporters on this case, whose own narrative conventions involved "hero cops" and "brave prosecutors" going hand to hand against "crime" (the "Secret Agony of Jogger DA," we learned in the *Post* a few days after the verdicts in the first trial, was that "Brave Prosecutor's Marriage Failed as She Put Rapists Away"), there seemed an unflagging enthusiasm for the repetition and reinforcement of these elements, and an equally unflagging resistance, even hostility, to exploring the point of view of the defendants' families and friends and personal or political allies (or, as they were called in news reports, the "supporters") who gathered daily at the end of the corridor from the courtroom. (720)

The reporters, who play a large part in setting the agenda for public discourse, are quick, according to Didion, to revert to the conventions of crime reporting, the central organizing principle of which is the setting of the "hero" against the "criminal." Rather than identify any particular reporters for whom these storylines are particularly appealing, Didion begins by noting that such an attitude is more generally to be found "among the reporters on this case, whose own narrative conventions involved 'hero cops' and 'brave prosecutors.'" The quotation marks setting off these words perform a double duty—they both suggest that these were labels actually employed by reporters (though Didion does not explicitly attribute them to any source) and signal, graphically, to readers that these words denote abstractions not to be taken seriously. Lest the quotation marks are not enough to empty these words of their meaning, any positive connotations summoned by their use are quickly undermined by a parenthetical whose inclusions of tabloid headlines lauding the bravery of a woman beset by marital struggles suggest a much-less heroic and far more mundane reality.

Following the parenthetical, this long sentence continues by aurally suggesting, through alliteration and anaphora, how entrenched these preferences for heroic storylines are. Once again relying on the word *seemed* in order to make a claim she has no intention of substantiating with further evidence, she notes that "there seemed an unflagging enthusiasm for the repetition and reinforcement of these elements." The alliteration found in the parallel pairing of "repetition and reinforcement" emphasizes both the repeated use of these elements and their function in focusing the discourse to the point that any viewpoints resistant to the framework established by this discourse are met with "equally unflagging resistance, even hostility." In this way, the "point of view of the defendants' families and friends and personal or political allies (or, as they were called in news reports, the 'supporters')" was simply not acknowledged. Much as these people "gathered daily at the end of the corridor from the courtroom," far removed from the place where the story will unfold within the framework established by those in power, they are placed at the end of Didion's sentence, each preposition further emphasizing their distance from the discourse that dominates. This long list of people, their large numbers suggested by the repeated use of coordinating conjunctions ("families *and* friends *and* personal *or* political allies . . . *or* 'supporters") are "*at* the end *of* the corridor *from* the courtroom."

This courtroom provided a stage upon which the city could work out its problems in a simplistic and cathartic fashion. New York, was, at that time, according to Didion, "rapidly vanishing into the chasm between its actual life and its preferred narratives" (714), her metaphor calling forth a striking image of a city undone by its own rhetoric, a city in need of release. "In a city in which grave and disrupting problems had become general—problems of not having, problems of not making it, problems that demonstrably existed, among the mad and the ill and the under-equipped and the overwhelmed, with decreasing reference to color—the case of the Central Park jogger provided more than just a safe, or structured, setting in which various and sometimes only marginally related rages could be vented" (714). Like so many of Didion's sentences, this one is long and periodic, beginning with a prepositional phrase that foregrounds the city and continuing with a parenthetical interrupted by a second parenthetical before concluding with the main claim being made about the city.

The parentheticals permit her both to modify, through apposition, the "problems" she mentions, as well as amplify the sense that these are omnipresent. Anaphora lends the first part of the parenthetical ("problems of not having, problems of not making it, problems that demonstrably existed") a repetition suggesting the ubiquity of these problems—the lack of coordinating conjunctions quickening the tempo of the sentence as the problems add up. This parenthetical is then itself modified further (though this interruption is not marked by either parenthesis or dashes, so as to ensure the rhythm of the sentence is not further interrupted) when Didion outlines those most afflicted by the "problems." Unlike in the first parenthetical, this time she employs coordinating conjunctions, each "and" making her sound deliberate and emphatic and creating an impression of a multiplying list of unfortunate citizens—they are "the mad *and* the ill *and* the under-equipped *and* the overwhelmed"—whose needs remain unmet by a rhetoric that refuses to address their very real problems.

At the heart of Didion's critique of this rhetoric is her recognition of the transformative ("magical") powers of language, the potency of symbols, especially insofar as those symbols are put in the service of narratives. The writing of "Sentimental Journeys" provides her an opportunity to perform an extended critique of such magical thinking (years before she would deconstruct her own following the death of her husband). She stands outside the framework constructed by those in control of the public myths, a type of "film critic" able to recognize that what she is watching is only so much posturing, a "series of set pieces" (713) that transform any undesirable realities into digestive narrative elements supporting a more palatable and desirable self-image.

For her, in the case of the New York jogger, but also in many other situations, the adherence to the conventions of narrative is frequently neither an innocent nor a harmless act, but one with sometimes significant consequences for the most powerless. In this case, the narrative convention of crime news stories calling for white, attractive, female victims whose lives include attending expensive schools or working at glamorous jobs, women who are easy "to cast . . . as part 'of what makes this city so vibrant and so great'" (699) or whose tragedies occur as "fate's random choice," meant that other victimized New York women—nonwhite, uneducated, poor, or perhaps with a tendency to make unwise decisions—were largely ignored by the prosecutors, the press, and the public.

In this case too, the narrative convention of resolution meant that any "data" that created cognitive dissonance had either to be transformed or ignored. Accordingly, Didion observes, New York's "essential criminality and its related absence of civility," were transformed into "points of pride, evidence of 'energy' "; that New Yorkers were strong and could survive and even thrive within its boundaries was the point of the narrative; the problem was not with the city but those who could not hack it: "provincials, bridge-and-tunnels, out-of-towners" (708). In her one "appearance" in the essay, Didion provides a striking example of how such magical thinking works. After she and her husband step into a computer store to escape muggers, the clerk comments that such criminals "go after poor people like you from out of town, they prey on tourists." In response to Dunne's comment that he and Didion live in New York, she writes: " 'That's why they didn't get you,' the clerk said, effortlessly incorporating this change in the data. 'That's how you could move fast' " (709).

Didion's work has often been described as heavy on detail, invested in the particular and the concrete. In her earliest essays in particular, her practice of summoning up evocative images and emblematic moments imbues her writing with a strong sense of the physical world and creates a palpable sense of her presence in it. However, in this essay, the anecdote above, related in just four brief sentences, provides the sole reference to Didion's actual experiences in the city about which she writes. In choosing to remain largely "outside" the city within the space of this essay, she emphasizes her distance from "the sentimental stories told in defense of its own lazy criminality,"[20] a distance that allows her to see these narratives for what they are: rhetorical "frameworks," or "constructs," or, in Burkean terms, terministic screens that, while they reflect reality to some degree, offer a rhetorical *selection* of reality, one that *deflects* attention from any narrative elements that might undermine the preferred storylines.[21]

In focusing on these rhetorical frameworks rather than on her own lived experiences of New York, she is far less descriptive than in earlier essays and far more blunt in her criticism. Accordingly, her style is less emotional and impressionistic and far more understated, ironic, and assertive. Her long cumulative sentences do not work, as they had in her earliest essays, to create the impression of a writer mentally working through her experiences, "dramatizing her thinking,"[22] and opening up a dialogue with her readers. Rather, these sentences, sometimes whole paragraphs long, allow her, through repetition and apposition, to repeat and rename her claims, their rhythms meant to induce agreement with her arguments, their parenthetical asides an opportunity for her to express, even more directly, her position in regard to politicians, the press, and the public, and their "magical" uses of language.

CHAPTER 3

# Lifting the Curtain

## The Rhetoric of Politics

Published almost ten years after 1992's *After Henry* and written across a decade of immense political upheaval across the globe, as well as during a period of considerable domestic political scandal, *Political Fictions* marks, to a significant degree, a return to familiar territory, a continuation of familiar themes, a demonstration of a familiar style. It is, in many ways, a work that allows Didion to synthesize and solidify lines of argument that had begun to work their way up to the surfaces of earlier pieces and to use, most fully and forcefully, the voice of the nascent rhetorical critic on evidence in those writings. Her arguments are constructed carefully, the evidence collected and presented to the reader through anecdote and quote, through selection, synthesis, and juxtaposition. She positions herself as critic from the outset, conveying an almost total disengagement from political life in order to foreground her utter disenchantment with domestic politics, about which, as she writes on the very first page, there "remained . . . something resistant, recondite, some occult irreconcilability that kept all news of it just below my attention level."[1] In particular, she finds herself resisting the rhetoric of this politics, which is expressed, as she describes it, "in a language I did not recognize" (733).

"Early in 1988," she begins the foreword, "Robert Silvers of *The New York Review of Books* asked me if I would do some pieces or a piece about the presidential campaign just then getting underway in New Hampshire" (733). In introducing a work devoted to analysis of political life by noting that the work was, in fact, only produced upon request (and a vague one

73

at that), Didion makes it clear early on that the reporting on political events to follow results not from any passionate engagement with political life, any particular devotion to any political ideology, or any investment in either of the major political parties, but from mere acquiescence. In so doing, she anticipates and forestalls any appearance of political bias, and, as in her other works, positions herself as a critic who operates outside of the system upon which she focuses her gaze.[2]

Robert Silvers, she writes, "would arrange credentials. All I had to do was show up, see what there was to see, and write something" (733). Her use of indefinite pronouns here (she has to write "something") and in the first line ("some pieces or a piece") is meant to suggest her total disengagement from her subject matter—this disengagement is further established by the fact that the paragraph continues with a description of her failure to show up for months (even as she noted that it was "all she had to do").

Upon receiving "a more urgent call from *The New York Review*" alerting her to the fact that the California primary was mere days away, she ended up going, but, again, she makes clear, not due to any interest in the primary itself. "It so happened," she writes, employing a dependent clause suggesting that mere coincidence rather than any real sense of interest was at work, "that my husband was leaving that day to do some research in Ireland." "It so happened," she repeats, using anaphora to amplify the sense that her subsequent reporting occurred by chance, "that our daughter was leaving that day to spend the summer in Guatemala and Nicaragua." And so, she concludes, "there seemed, finally, no real excuse for me not to watch the California primary (and even to vote in it, since I was still registered in Los Angeles County), and so I went to Newark, and got on the plane" (733–34). In this last line, her use of a double negative emphasizes that she goes in the absence of an excuse not to, and indeed votes for the same reason, her lack of interest in voting made clear by the parenthetical marking of this comment as an aside.

What follows her trip from Newark is described as "her introduction to American politics" (734), though of course, as someone who was raised among "conservative California Republicans" and who "voted, ardently, for Barry Goldwater," and then later "registered as a Democrat" (735), she was hardly unfamiliar with this country's political system. What she claims not to have realized or recognized before her writing of the pieces that compose this collection, however, was "the ways in which the political process did not reflect but increasingly proceeded from a series of fables about American experience" (735). This recognition provides the theme that lends coherence to the work's eight pieces, essays written over a dozen years and meant to unmask political performers, Democratic and Republican alike, and pull the curtains up on the theater that is political life. That this effort is one largely without impact, she concedes, occurs to her quite early in her reporting—no amount of probing and exposition seems enough to prompt widespread disenchantment with a political process that, to her, is deeply problematic. This despite the fact, that, as she writes,

> [i]t was clear for example in 1988 that the political process had already become perilously remote from the electorate it was meant to represent. It was also clear in 1988 that the decision of the two major parties to obscure any possible perceived distinction between themselves, and by so doing to narrow the contested ground to a handful of selected "target" voters, had already imposed considerable strain on the basic principle of the democratic exercise, that of assuring the nation's citizens a voice in its affairs. It was also clear in 1988 that the rhetorical manipulation of resentment and anger designed to attract these target voters had reduced the nation's political dialogue to a level so dispiritingly low that its highest expression had come to be a pernicious nostalgia. (736)

In this passage, in addition to her characteristic use of anaphora to drum her points home, Didion employs expletive constructions ("It was"). Expletive constructions, especially if overused, tend to impede concision and are technically unnecessary for clarity, but their use here permits Didion to place the word *clear* early in each of these sentences, with the result that the word is emphasized both in each individual sentence as well as cumulatively. Because the overall aim of this foreword (and, indeed, the entire collection) is to make clear the realities of a political process to a public for whom "even that which seemed ineluctably clear would again vanish from collective memory, sink traceless into the stream of collapsing news and comment cycles that had become our national River Lethe" (736), it is essential that she return, repeatedly, to what she sees as self-evident. The placing of "clear" early in each sentence—a positioning made possible by the use of expletive constructions—allows her to do just this.

According to Didion, the forgetfulness of the public has less to do with apathy—to which the press commonly attributes low voter turnout—than with its opposite, repulsion. They have, she contends, rightfully rejected a process that does not deliver what it endlessly promises. The essays that follow this foreword explore this process as it is manifested in everything from a presidential campaign heavy on photo ops and pseudo-events to an administration's response to atrocities abroad; from the construction of a political persona to the "running" of a political story by a prominent and revered journalist; from the prosecution and subsequent impeachment of a president for sexual misdeeds to the rhetoric generated by the close margins of the 2000 presidential campaign.

The first essay of the collection, 1988's "Insider Baseball," situates Didion outside of the political process, establishes the themes that carry throughout the whole collection, and showcases some of her key stylistic moves. In this first piece, she focuses on the behind-the-scene workings of the 1988 California primary as well as the Democratic and Republican national conventions. "It occurred to me during the summer of 1988," Didion begins,

> that it had not been by accident that the people with whom I had preferred to spend time in high school had, on the whole, hung out in gas stations. They had not run for student body office. They had not gone to Yale or Swarthmore or DePauw, nor had they even applied. . . . They were never destined to be, in other words, communicants in what we have come to call, when we want to indicate the traditional ways in which power is exchanged and the status quo maintained in the United States, "the process." (743)

All but the most casual reader of Didion knows that she—having graduated from Berkeley and secured a prestigious internship with *Vogue* shortly before publishing her first novel, marrying a writer, and beginning a bicoastal life lived among the literary and cultural elite—is not at all like these people with whom she recalls spending time. Her decision to identify herself with people who "led lives on that social and economic edge referred to, in Washington and among those whose preferred locus is Washington, as 'out there'" (743) is clearly a strategic choice intended to establish her remove from people inside the process, "constituting as they do a self-created and self-referring class, a new kind of managerial elite" (743).

Composing a version of herself seemingly unadulterated by either bias or misconception, she carefully deploys pronouns to convey her sense that the political process is an insiders' game that alienates and estranges voters, coming, as they do, from "outside" the process. At the heart of this argument is an "us versus them" mentality, one dependent on a container metaphor and drawing heavily on allusion to the world of Hollywood scriptwriting and production. The language of politics, the rhetoric of political performances, is the barrier or "obscuring device," which excludes the American people from the political process and makes them audience to the carefully staged and filmed and publicized narratives constituting the political process. That this estrangement is problematic not just to Didion but her readers is assumed by her frequent attempts to identify with them. Third-person plural "they" is used deictically to suggest the distance between politicians and the public, and use of first-person plural "we" or "us" allows her to position herself as an outsider alongside her readers and to suggest that her perceptions are as much theirs as her own.

Of the politicians endlessly fabricating set pieces, writing scripts, and producing pseudo-events, she writes, from her position outside of the process: "*They* tend to prefer the theoretical to the observable, and to dismiss that which might be learned empirically as 'anecdotal.' *They* tend to speak a language common in Washington but not specifically shared by the rest of us" (743–44). Her anaphoric use of "They" reemphasizes her distance from the rhetoric of Washington, and her use of the first-person plural "us," not only aligns her with those outside the process but with her readers, who, it is to be understood, are, as she is, outside the political process she is intent on deconstructing. "They"—the politicians, the public figures, the players behind the scenes—are inside the process, speaking a language that makes sense only to them, engaged in a politics as theater, a politics remote from "the real life of the country." "They" are interested in the theoretical, the illusionary, that which can be manipulated and worked over in service of self-promoting ends, "that which occurs only in order to be reported" (750).

"We" (Didion and the readers) are interested in the "empirical and observable," in reality rather than narrative, in the meaningful rather than the deliberately meaningless. "When *we* talk about the process, then *we* are talking, increasingly, not about 'the democratic process,' or the general mechanism affording the citizens of a state a voice in its affairs, but the reverse," she observes, before describing a political process that operates on a type of closed set, accessible only to those who speak the language, those who "invent, year in and year out, the narrative of public life" (744). "Here *we* had the last true conflict of cultures in America, that between the empirical and the theoretical," she writes of standing, the day before the 1988 California primary, in a crowd in San Jose listening to Dukakis speak generically of wanting to bring "people together," as she watches a confused man in a down vest and camouflage hat elbow his way through the crowd in a futile attempt to "speak to the next president" (746).

And of the 2000 presidential election, when the vote came down to a few hundred votes in Florida, she notes that "*we* had reached the zero-sum point toward which the process had been moving." The Reagan years are the period, for Didion "where *we* reenter the real woo-woo of the period, the insistence on the ineffable that began with the perceived need to front the administration with a 'leader' and ended by transforming the White House into a kind of cargo cult" (799). And of the Dukakis campaign, she writes that "what strikes *one* most vividly about such a campaign is precisely its remoteness from the real life of the country" (745), the all-inclusive yet nonspecific pronoun suggesting a shared recognition of the absurd distance between political and real life.

It is a fine line Didion must walk, working as she is, from inside the process—both a seasoned journalist and a member of the privileged upper class from which politicians often come and to whom they often turn for financial support and political direction—and outside the process as an ostensibly neutral observer. Not many people outside the process have the former governor of California (Jerry Brown) stay overnight in their New York apartment. Not many reporters are given such immediate and ready access to key political players. It is a line Didion has, by this point in her career, become adept at walking. The selection of her content as well as the words within which she composes this material is heavily influenced by her desire to establish her credibility by alluding to her place in the world of privilege and power that give her the opportunity and authority to speak, while appearing to maintaining the authorial distance from this position that legitimizes critiques of it.

In going behind the scenes to report on political campaigns and primaries, which often meant sharing small planes or bus rides with candidates and their entourages, Didion physically collapses the distance between herself and those running the show, but is at pains to demonstrate that her physical proximity to power in no way undermines her ability to recognize "real life" or the empirical. She—with her eye for the concrete, the particular, the banal—still sees that the country is about "two-toned Impalas and people with camouflage hats and a little glitter in their eyes" (746). She, with her preference for the emblematic and the anecdotal, stands with politicians "on the same dusty asphalt, under the same plane trees" (746), and sees the emptiness of their rhetoric, sees how deliberately meaningless these political rallies are.

When Dukakis rolls up his sleeves, as described in "Insider Baseball," for what the television crews referred to as a "'tarmac arrival with ball tossing,'" and tosses a ball back and forth with the traveling press secretary, Didion highlights the artificial and empty nature of the act. "The rest of us had stood in the sun and given this our full attention: some forty adults standing on a tarmac watching a diminutive figure in shirtsleeves and a red tie toss a ball, undeflected even by the arrival of an Alaska Airlines 767, to his press secretary" (752). The parenthetical insertion, a deliberately awkward imposition interrupting the sentence literally mid toss, effectively juxtaposes the image of a descending jumbo jet with the image of a "diminutive figure," a juxtaposition meant to highlight the ludicrous nature of the event. Using apposition to circle back and modify "us," with "forty adults standing on a tarmac," she further highlights the ridiculous and theatrical nature of the event, one played before a captive audience engaged in the surreal act of watching a grown man toss a ball even as jets touch down on the nearby tarmac and the temperature soars over 101 degrees.[3]

It was not, Didion claims, until she read "Joe Klein's version of those days in California" that it occurred to her "that this eerily contrived moment on the tarmac at San Diego could become, at least provisionally, history" (753). In noting that she only came to this realization later, that it was something that "occurred to her," Didion suggests, as she does so often throughout this collection, that her coverage is not colored by bias or preconceived notions. That things "occur" to her suggests the "truth" of those things rather than any subjective interpretation of them. To ensure that her readers experience similar moments of "enlightenment," Didion accumulates evidence through repetition and variation. Descriptions offered from her own experience are often followed by short excerpts from multiple journalistic sources reporting on the same event.

For instance, following her own description of Dukakis's actions, she turns to Klein's piece, in which he writes that "The Duke seemed downright jaunty. . . . He tossed a baseball with aides." She follows his report with an excerpt from Michael Kramer's cover story for the July 25 issue of *U.S. News & World Report* in which he notes that "Michael Dukakis was indulging his truly favorite campaign ritual—a game of catch with his aide Jack Weeks." She then directly segues to what she ironically describes as "a third, and, by virtue of his seniority in the process, perhaps, the official version of the ball tossing," David S. Broder's *Washington Post* account, in which he writes that "the governor loosened up his arm and got the kinks out of his back by tossing a couple hundred 90-foot pegs to Weeks" (753–54).

What all of these journalistic accounts imply, of course, is that the ball tossing was an authentically spontaneous moment of playfulness and athleticism, an unscripted moment of reality that could be reliably interpreted to suggest that Dukakis was a tough (insofar as he played on a broiling hot tarmac with planes touching down around him) and quintessential American male indulging in America's favorite pastime even as he did the serious work of campaigning. In arranging her material in the way she does, beginning first with her own account before moving to journalistic coverage of the same event, Didion acts as film director, her prose a camera directing the attention of her readers. Her account works as the establishing scene: a long shot that includes, within the frame, the entire context for the act—the waiting journalists, the insider dialogue pointing to the fabricated nature of the central action (" 'Ok,' one of the cameramen had said. 'We got the daughter. Nice. That's enough. Nice' " [753]). As in all long shots, any actual figures are minimalized, their human agency presented as insignificant. Through her camera, Dukakis is thus portrayed as a small (both literally and figuratively) man—an insignificant actor on a much larger stage. This scene is then set against the deliberately decontextualized images presented by the close-up accounts of journalists, which take as their focus the man himself and ignore the artificiality of the set outside the frame.

Didion's capacity for manipulating syntax is key to her ability to direct, as with a camera, her readers' attention. As Mark Tredinnick notes, "the cumulative sentence is particularly good for setting a scene or for panning a place or critical moment,"[4] and it is precisely this type of sentence Didion employs time and again to ensure her readers take in the whole scene but also attend to the details of which it is composed. Even as the cumulative sentence moves physically across the page, it pauses "cognitively/ rhetorically"[5] to allow for modifications that redescribe or redefine the initial impression. "What we had in the tarmac arrival with ball tossing," Didion sums up, using the phrase employed by the cameramen to refer to the scripted event, "then, was an understanding: a repeated moment witnessed by many people, all of whom believed it to be a setup and yet most of whom believed that only an outsider, only someone too 'naïve' to know the rules of the game, would so describe it" (754). In disrupting conventional word order and starting the sentence with the nominalization "What we had," Didion both suggests that there is something as yet undefined beyond what the camera has captured and delays defining what it is—her use of "we" offering readers ownership in the conclusion to follow.

The cumulative sentence continues: "What we had . . . then, was an understanding." "Then"—a transitional word suggesting summation—indicates that what follows is Didion's redefining of the act she witnessed. This redefinition occurs through her use of the predicate nominative "understanding," a word she then unpacks further through apposition achieved with a free modifier: "a repeated moment witnessed by many people." The long sentence continues, Didion pausing to modify "people" through further apposition, "all of whom believed it to be a setup and yet most of whom believed that only an outsider . . . would so describe it." Didion then halts the forward motion of the sentence one final time to modify "outsider": "Only someone too 'naïve' to know the rules of the game." The constant interplay between the forward motion created through the accumulation of details and the backward motion initiated by Didion's habit of looping back to modify the statement of her base clause means that the readers are offered both the big picture provided by the long panning shot and the details traditionally captured by the close-up. These details are captured by the use of modifiers, which permit Didion to make concrete the statement being modified.

"The narrative is made up of many such understandings, tacit agreements, small and large, to overlook the observable in the interests of obtaining a dramatic story line" (754), Didion continues, with yet another cumulative sentence, this one working to reinforce the theme that permeates this collection. "It is understood," she notes in the next paragraph—using expletive construction and passive voice to suggest that the filmic conventions of the political process are a given to those on the "inside," who accept such conventions without irony—"that this invented narrative will turn on certain familiar elements." What follows this assertion is a series of sentences arranged through parataxis, each independent clause beginning with the expletive construction "There is." This combination of parataxis and anaphora lends the passage an incantatory rhythm:

> There is the continuing story line of the "horse race," the reliable daily drama of one candidate falling behind as another pulls ahead. There is the surprise of the new poll, the glamour of the one-on-one colloquy on the midnight plane, a plot point (the nation sleeps while the candidate and his confidant hammer out its fate) pioneered by Theodore H. White. There is the abiding if

unexamined faith in the campaign as a personal odyssey, and in the spiritual benefits accruing to those who undertake it. There is, in the presented history of the candidate, the crucible event, the day that "changed the life." (755)

The paratactic structure of this passage is Didion's way of setting descriptions side by side, of accumulating evidence pointing to the prefabricated and predictable nature of the political process. Within these cumulative sentences, the insistently repetitive "There is" returns the readers' attention to the ubiquity of these campaign elements, providing the passage coherence by suggesting a political process that is deceptively seamless and continuous.

This continuity is achieved not by any real connections between political events but rather through the imposition of a narrative line on what would otherwise be disparate events. The mises-en-scène of these events are as carefully composed as those for a cinematic production: "[A]ny traveling campaign, then, was a set, moved at considerable expense from location to location. . . . There was the hierarchy of the set: there were actors, there were directors, there were script supervisors, there were grips. There was the isolation of the set, and the arrogance, the contempt for outsiders" (748). And later, "A final victory, for the staff and the press on a traveling campaign, would mean not a new production but only a new location: the particular setups and shots of the campaign day (the walk on the beach, the meet-and-greet at the housing project) would dissolve imperceptibly, isolation and arrogance and tedium intact, into the South Lawns, the Oval office signings, the arrivals and departures of the administration day" (749).

Later in the same essay, Didion describes a warm June day in 1988 that begins with Dukakis visiting a high school. "This event had been abandoned, and another materialized" (754). Her use of the word *materialized* suggests the lack of logic at work in the process; there is no continuity, no progression, no sequence—one event is as meaningless as the next. One scene "dissolves imperceptibly" into the next, the result a carefully edited montage. As with the shooting of a film, coherence is achieved in pre- and post-production.

By the time these essays were composed, Didion had had decades of writing behind her; she knew her readers, knew how to talk to them, knew how to construct a version (or vision) of herself that appealed. Even as her gaze, arguably, seems to fall more insistently on the political world and less intently on her personal universe than in earlier writings, she maintains her ear for the cadences of the intimate, the personal, and the conversational. As discussed earlier, parataxis, a figure employed more frequently in narrative and explanation, is frequently used to structure her observations, while the hypostatic prose of explicit argument is sometimes avoided. Because they do not involve subordination, paratactic sentences are less complex than hypostatic sentences, and rather than point to precise logical connections, they argue inductively, piling up facts, making them present to the reader. Additive rather than subordinative, they are also more "oral" than "textual,"[6] and hence more memorable.

In "Political Pornography," for example, Didion discusses what is meant by "running the story," in preparation for making the point that Bob Woodward is one of the handful of influential Washingtonians who run the story in D.C. Running the story, means, she writes, employing parataxis, "setting the terms, setting the pace, deciding the agenda, determining when and where the story exists, and shaping what the story will be." She continues, again using parataxis: "There were certain people who ran the story in Vietnam, there were certain people in Central America, there were certain people in Washington" (862). The combination of parataxis with anaphora here is used to rhythmic and, hence, strikingly memorable effect. Additionally, because the phrases and clauses above are coordinated rather than subordinated, their arrangement is flexible—it is not necessary for the reader to suspend comprehension until the sentence has come to its end. Instead, the reader can follow Didion's points as she unpacks them and thus remain "on the same page" as her.

Built through the accumulation and coordination of words, phrases, and clauses—often in the same grammatical form—paratactic sentences also sound more like everyday speech, providing Didion a subtle rapport with her readers. The "running style" produced by her use of parataxis further contributes to the sense that she is discussing things with her readers rather than preaching at them. Conversational in tone, the running style is used by writers to "reflect the mind in the process of thinking," and depends on connectives that add on rather than subordinate.[7] When, for example, she is satirizing Newt Gingrich, by making note, in her typically understated fashion, of his "problematic detours" (i.e., his assertion, in the middle of a nostalgic recollection of spending Christmas recently in a small town, that he is still "a happy four-year-old who gets up every morning hoping to find a cookie that friends or relatives may have left for me somewhere"), she concludes with the following: "This cookie is worrisome: Was it forgotten? Hidden? Why would they hide it Where are they? Are they asleep, out, absentee friends, deadbeat relatives? The cookie was the treat and leaving is the trick?" (852). Her satirical questions, strung together in paratactic form, invite the audience to share in her amused contempt of Gingrich, suggesting, as they do, a mind still working through conclusions and seeking conformation from others.

Her employment of cumulative sentences constructed through apposition and modification also contributes to the running style of her prose, permitting her to move through her points in the same way someone might during a spontaneous conversation, syntactically moving forward and back, so "that the sentence has a flowing and ebbing movement, advancing to a new position and then pausing to consolidate it."[8] In describing, in "Eyes on the Prize," how Governor Jerry Brown began his talk by thanking his absent father rather than sticking to the preferred talking points, she drily notes:

> Referring as it did to a Democratic past, a continuum, a collective memory, this was jarring, off the beat of a party determined to present itself as devoid of all history save that one sunny day in the Rose Garden, preserved on film and repeatedly shown, when President John F. Kennedy shook the hand of the Boy's Nation delegate Bill Clinton, who could be seen on the film elbowing aside less motivated peers to receive the grail: the candidate's first useful photo opportunity. (813)

Here, Didion begins moving "backward," even before she has gotten to the subject of the main clause, renaming, through apposition, "Democratic past" twice, first as "a continuum" and then as "a collective memory," before advancing to the subject, "this," and predicate, "was jarring." This backward movement works because the word *it* is a coherence device linking back to an idea in the previous sentence. After moving forward with the base clause: "this was jarring," she then moves backward again, employing a free (free because it can either go before or after the clause or modifier it modifies) modifier to elaborate on "this." Here in the sentence, although she is still moving backward to elaborate on "this," she is also moving forward to offer more detail about "that one sunny day" mentioned in the free modifier. She employs another two free modifiers ("preserved on film and repeatedly shown" and "when President John F. Kennedy shook the hand of the Boy's Nation delegate Bill Clinton") to modify "one sunny day" and then employs yet another free modifier to say something derogatory about Clinton ("who could be seen on the film elbowing aside less motivated peers to receive the grail").

In a cumulative sentence, the main point—in this case, that Brown's speech was jarring to a party rhetorically focused on the future—is often quite general or abstract; once it is stated, "the forward movement of the sentence stops, the writer shifts down to the lower level of generalization or abstraction or to singular terms, and goes back over the same ground at this lower level. . . . Thus the mere form of the sentence generates ideas."[9] An even more striking example of this occurs in the essay "The West Wing of Oz," when Didion casts Reagan as an inveterate actor, driven far less by political or diplomatic concerns than by his desire to play the archetypal film role of the lone hero fighting against the odds:

> For the "President," a man whose most practiced insights had trained him to find the strongest possible narrative line in the scenes he was given, to clean out those extraneous elements that undermine character clarity, a man for whom historical truth had all his life run twenty-four frames a second, Iran-contra would have been irresistible, a go project from concept, a script with two strong characters, the young marine officer with no aim but to serve his president, the aging president with no aim but to free the tyrannized (whether the tyrants were Nicaraguans or Iranians or some other nationality altogether was just a plot point, a detail to work out later), a story about male bonding, a story about a father who found the son he never (in this "cleaned out" draft of the script) had, a buddy movie, and better still than a buddy movie: a mentor buddy movie, with action. (805)

Didion begins with the phrase "For the 'President'" but does not complete the thought immediately, instead interrupting the flow of the sentence with two appositional phrases providing derogatory commentary on his character before moving to the subject and predicate and completing the main clause ("Iran-contra would have been irresistible"). Although the sentence would have made sense had she stopped here, she moves forward, elaborating on the qualities that would prove irresistible to the "President" by twice renaming "Iran-contra." It is "a go project from concept," and "a script with two strong characters." What follows is a balanced and coordinated pair of phrases ("the young marine officer with no aim but to serve his president, the aging president with no aim but to free the tyrannized") modifying "two strong characters," and thus moving backward through the sentence.

The sentence is then interrupted with a parenthetical aside, a considerably stronger disruption than that caused by her earlier use of apposition and one that brings the ebbing and flowing of the whole sentence to a halt. This is Didion's opportunity, as noted previously, to address her reader in a more direct fashion, to comment on the unfolding argument. Just as one might, in informal conversation, stop and digress, so too does Didion with this parenthetical. She then completes the sentence by continuing to modify and rename "Iran-contra" with a string of resumptive modifiers to suggest a writer still in the process of thinking, of determining how best to characterize her subject. Her use of epanalepsis (repeated use of the words *buddy movie*) moves the sentence gracefully to its end: "a story about male bonding, a story about a father who found the son he never (in this 'cleaned out' draft of the script) had, a buddy movie, and better still than a buddy movie: a mentor buddy movie, with action." In controlling the motion of this sentence, as well as others, through apposition and modification, Didion creates prose that is conversational in tone, rather than declamatory, allowing for an intimacy with her readers that offsets her more strident and sarcastic moments.

She also exhibits a capacity for syntactic gracefulness that saves her from appearing unappealingly dogmatic. The relentless drumming home of points in sentences heavily dependent on anaphora, for instance, is frequently offset by sentences gracefully extended, as the sentence above is, through modifiers (free, summative, and resumptive). These allow her to extend her sentences, to elaborate on, summarize, and reiterate material in a fluid and coherent manner. In "God's Country," for instance, she describes the instantly positive press reaction to George W. Bush's nomination, concluding that "this instant positive judgment was entirely predictable, a phenomenon that occurs on the last night of every convention" (934). Using "phenomenon" to summarize "this instant positive judgment," Didion is able both to loop back and emphasize a key point while adding new information about it and moving the reader forward.

Anadiplosis is also one of her favored methods of ensuring graceful coherence. Later in the same essay, she describes leading Republican and Democratic strategists and pollsters discussing future campaign strategies and observes wryly "that these specialists in opinion research were hearing a certain number of Americans express concern about their own future and about the future of America *seemed clear*. What *seemed less clear* was the source of this concern" (935–36). Sometimes she pairs anadiplosis with epistrophe, further ensuring fluidity, as she does when she notes that Gore's selection of Lieberman as a running mate "was widely construed as Gore's way of transcending this presumed public sentiment, of *'sending a message'* *to the electorate*. The actual *message that got sent*, however, was not *to the electorate* but to its political class." In both of these examples, anadiplosis subtly creates a bridge between two sentences conveying two distinct ideas; it is the literary equivalent of the film dissolve, an editing technique that creates a gradual transition between images or scenes. This is a technique with which Didion would be very familiar, given her screenwriting past. Just as the dissolve stylistically implies a connection rather than explicitly asserting it, so too does anadiplosis.

She similarly achieves a graceful coherence with epistrophe, returning to her main point at the end of successive sentences in order to tie her ideas together rhythmically. There is a striking example of this in a long passage in the foreword, wherein she makes the point that the political system is broken. In order to substantiate this claim, she describes how those in the system evidence a clear understanding of the fact that money and self-interest drive politics. To provide coherence to this lengthy passage and ensure the salience of her claim, she repeats the last clause at the end of several successive sentences. First there is her description of the chairwoman of Dukakis's 1988 New York Finance Council, a woman aware that writing checks is the most effective means of getting heard. This woman, Didion concludes, "had a clear enough understanding of how the contract worked and did not work." This is followed by her description of the only prominent Democrat in West LA to support Jesse Jackson, a man who understands that his support of Jackson means his calls to peers will go unanswered. He, she concludes, "had a clear enough understanding of how the contract worked and did not work." She next describes three more people, none naive about the importance of political connections and deep pockets. Her description of each concludes with "he had a clear understanding of how the contract worked and did not work" (739). In this fashion, she builds her argument inductively, fluidly tying together disparate situations through the repeated final clauses to emphasize that the political process is deeply flawed.

In the same way that these coherence devices offer even her most strident arguments a becoming gracefulness, her use of nominalizations and noncommittal passive voice helps her to avoid sounding shrill. These constructions foreground material implicitly, so that her strongest arguments appear to be based in fact rather than in her own idiosyncratic view of the world. Their construction and employment eliminate the need for Didion to use such subjective phrases as "In my opinion," or "I feel," or

"I believe." The result is a measured and disinterested tone rather than a dogmatic or irrationally bitter one. Although nominalizations are generally frowned upon in nontechnical or nonscientific writing for being, at their best, too abstract and wordy, and, at their worst, pompous-sounding, in her prose their rhetorical function outweighs these concerns. Her voice recedes as these nominalizations allow "facts" to speak for themselves, the result a more ostensibly objective tone. These constructions can be found throughout this book.

For example, she observes of Bob Woodward, a man for whom she has no little disregard: "His preferred approach has been one in which 'issues could be examined before the possible outcome or meaning was at all clear or the possible consequences were weighed'" (854). In nominalizing "prefer," she avoids the more direct assertion "He prefers to examine issues," thus averting the need to back such a claim. Similarly, when she rebuts Representative Tom Foley's assertion that the 1992 Democratic convention was representative of the people it claimed to represent, she writes that "the preferred images of the convention were those of a sun-belt country club" (807). Thus, rather than make the more direct and personal attack "Democratic leaders preferred country-club images," Didion nominalizes "prefer" and more obliquely offers her critique.

One pattern of nominalizations in particular dominates this collection; it involves the use of "*that* clauses" as nouns. The "Foreword" contains a long passage dependent on several of these; here they are joined through the figure of hypozeugma, or the combining of several subjects with one verb phrase, in this case, "had come to be seen":

> That this was not a demographic profile of the country at large, that half the nation's citizens had only a vassal relationship to the government under which they lived, that the democracy we spoke of spreading throughout the world was now in our own country only an ideality, had come to be seen, against the higher priority of keeping the process in the hands of those who already held it, as facts without application. (742)

This long anaphoric series of "that" phrases, composed in the passive voice and employing nominalizations, reads as dry and dispassionate, seeming to speak to foregone conclusions. Such syntactic choices permit her to avoid sounding harsh (i.e. "This was not a demographic") or subjective (i.e. "I do not think this was a demographic profile") while lending her assertions an air of disinterested assurance.

Her stinging critique, in "The West Wing of Oz," of the U.S. government's involvement in atrocities in El Salvador, includes several instances of similar constructions. She defends *New York Times* reporter Raymond Bonner (who had written of a massacre whose existence was officially denied by the U.S. government, and who was subsequently withdrawn from El Salvador by the *Times*) and observes, "that the Times withdrew Bonner was seen, immediately and by larger numbers of people than were actually knowledgeable about El Salvador or administration policy, as 'proof' that he had been wrong about El Mozote." Such construction, combined with passive voice, permits her to make her accusation without pointing to any specific people or groups of people as well as keeps the focus on the supposed state of existing affairs rather than her subjective interpretation of them.

Something similar is at work in "Eyes on the Prize," when she is arguing that Clinton's campaign acted strategically and opportunistically in denouncing controversial black rap star Sister Souljah. "That this opportunity had been seized was precisely what constituted, for the campaign and for its observers, the incident's 'success,' and the candidate's 'strength,'" she writes. And shortly thereafter, referring to the same event, "That Sister Souljah herself was a straw target, was, then, beside the point" (821). She could have written, "The Clinton campaign seized the opportunity" or, "Sister Souljah herself was a straw target," but such syntax ensures these statements become claims, which can be rejected or denied. Rather than confront the reader with such assertions, Didion chooses to write as if the reader is already in agreement with her.

Combined with the noncommittal passive voice, her claims become even less confrontational and more elliptical. The voice created by these stylistic choices is insistent, dry, ironic, and witty—her control of syntax allowing her to avoid a directness that might alienate her readers. For instance, to argue that Democrats use the phrase "middle class" rhetorically and strategically, she writes: "That 'middle class' had been drained of any but this encoded meaning was clear" (823), this construction conveniently allowing her to elide saying specifically to whom it "was clear," and permitting her to suggest that it was clear to everyone. In writing of the Democrats' decision to put Lieberman on the presidential ticket she notes, "That the ticket would otherwise woefully lack this moral compass, and unless shriven by Senator Lieberman would reap the whirlwind of the assumed national yearning to punish Clinton, was accepted as given" (940), again employing passive voice to avoid explicitly saying who accepted this "as given."

Together, nominalizations and passive voice very often lend her arguments an air of objectivity precisely when she makes her most personal criticisms. In, for instance, the sixth essay of the collection, "Political Pornography," which she wrote in 1996 and which takes as its subject Bob Woodward, the well-known and highly esteemed journalist and later editor at *The Washington Post*, Didion employs ironic and biting understatement to make clear that this is no hagiography of the man nor a glowing review of his (at the time) newest book *The Choice*. In lesser hands, criticism of such a revered man might come across as personal and bitter, vindictive even, but Didion's style is so deadpan, so dryly understated, that it is difficult not to be amused by her words even as one might wince in sympathy for their target. She dispatches her arrows with the dispassion of a scientist, the length, complexity, and disinterested tone of her sentences shifting the emphasis from her subjective perspective to the object under dissection. "Mr. Woodward's aversion to engaging the ramifications of what people say to him," she writes, "has been generally understood as an admirable quality, at best a mandarin modesty, at worst a kind of executive big-picture focus, the entirely justifiable oversight of someone with a more important game to play" (854).

Rather than employ the active voice and an active verb (i.e., "Mr. Woodward does not engage"), Didion relies on nominalization and passive voice to make what is actually a direct and personal accusation sound more like established fact. His "aversion to engaging" is "generally understood." She allows, in the last half of the sentence, that people may differ on why this aversion is admirable, but in using apposition twice ("mandarin modesty"; "executive big-picture focus") to rename this "quality" she subtly reinforces it as a given. The construction of the first half of the sentence presents this aversion as fact rather than her opinion, allowing the focus to fall more on his supposed inadequacies than her judgment. Shortly thereafter, she notes that what she finds most remarkable about Woodward's books is that "these are books in which measurable cerebral activity is virtually absent," the scientific-sounding "measurable cerebral activity" combined with the hedge word *virtually* lending the clause an air of carefully qualified impartiality at odds with the harshness of her assessment.

In a subsequent passage criticizing Woodward's tendency to focus more on the process of research than in the resulting product, she writes that "the refusal to consider outcome or meaning or consequence has, as a way of writing a book, a certain Zen purity, but tends toward a process in which no research method is so commonplace as to go unexplained" (854–55). Again, her use of nominalization ("the refusal to consider outcome" rather than "Woodward refuses to"), which is commonplace in technical and scientific writing, and which shifts the focus of a sentence to actions rather than agents, creates the sense that she is merely a neutral observer of an undisputed occurrence.

Understatement also allows her to, in a sense, "recede" from the reader—in expressing an idea by denying its opposite she prompts the reader to do the mental work of unpacking her meaning. "This is not an insignificant time line" (784), she writes in "The West Wing of Oz," when analyzing why Raymond Bonner's report on a massacre was challenged. When she wants to characterize Ronald Reagan as passive and artificial, rather than directly assert this she writes, that it "became apparent to some that the president-elect, without benefit of constructive interpretation, could appear less than fully engaged" (793). This combination of measured wording and stinging criticism creates the dry and ironic tone that permeates much of this essay and the collection as a whole.

Such a tone might be off-putting if Didion were not also witty, but she frequently introduces notes of levity that take the edge off her observations. For example, deep into her unpacking of the many serious issues she has with Reagan's presidency, she begins a sentence about Reagan giving a ceremonial speech by writing: "Not long after the Grenada invasion, for which the number of medals awarded eventually exceeded the number of actual combatants, the president, in his commander-in-chief role, spoke at a ceremony" (795). The parenthetical is, of course, a complete non sequitur, her delivery so dry its humor is easy to miss. But it is just this kind of subtly employed wit that keeps her work from devolving into an undisciplined and unappealing rant. She makes it clear that she, despite her disdain for the ludicrous theater of political life, has kept her sense of humor.

This sense of humor is on full display in the essay "The West Wing of Oz." In it, she describes Bush's visit to Israel and Jordan in 1986 by outlining the many ways his advance team "[improved] visuals for the traveling press." "They had," she writes "asked that Bush be photographed studying, through binoculars, 'enemy territory,' a shot ultimately vetoed by the State Department, since the 'enemy territory' was Israel" (769). Her ironic use of quotation marks and repetition of the words *enemy territory* highlights the absurdity of the request and stands as her only commentary on it. She then writes, "They had also asked, possibly the most arresting detail, that at every stop on the itinerary, camels be present" (769), her understated use of the hedge word "possibly," parenthetically inserted, clearly satiric.

In describing Senator Lieberman, she also interrupts her sentence for a sarcastic aside, observing that "his speech patterns, grounded as they were in the burden he bore for the rest of us and the personal rewards he had received from God for bearing it, tended to self-congratulation" (938). Using understatement, irony, hedge words (i.e., "tended") and humor to compose sly and subtle sentences, and depending far more on third-person or first-person plural ("we") than "I," Didion avoids sounding as if she is indulging in partisan ranting or expressing personal enmity even as she sharply criticizes political players and the political process.

Hedge words (often combined, as in some of the quotes immediately above, with the ironic use of quotation marks and the passive voice) convey the sense that Didion is being deliberately, if deceptively, tentative, almost modest, even as she offers her most forceful points. She spends most of "Insider Baseball," for instance, explicitly making the point that politics is theater, that politics is a game played by insiders, and she offers example after example of how this manifests itself during the political process. Yet, the boldness of this assertion is tempered by diction that suggests a woman who hesitates, refuses to draw explicit conclusions, refuses to impose her views upon her audience. In, for example, commenting on Governor Dukakis's talk at a lunchtime rally in San Diego, one at which the candidate had gone over the same three talking points he had in numerous other speeches, despite the very different crowds he had addressed, she notes that "nothing said in any venue that day had seemed to have much connection with anybody listening ('I want to work with you and with working people all over this country,' the candidate had said in the downtown San Diego office plaza, but people who work in offices in downtown San Diego do not think of themselves as 'working people')" (747).

The parenthetical comment alone clearly indicates that she finds Dukakis's speech to be inauthentic, part of a performance piece, and yet she hedges—his speech "seemed" not to have "much" connection. The evidence she has gathered and presented to the readers is enough, this wording suggests—they can think inductively and draw their own conclusions. She is not going to impose those conclusions on them. These words create a sense of a writer a bit detached, a bit noncommittal, and thus more rational. This is an impression, as discussed earlier in this chapter, created early on, when she first characterizes her attitude toward her subject matter and recognizes that there was "a certain Sisyphean aspect" to her writing efforts.

"Broad patterns could be defined, specific inconsistencies documented, but no amount of definition or documentation seemed sufficient to stop the stone that was our apprehension of politics from hurtling back downhill." There was a "certain" Sisyphean aspect; patterns "could" be defined; but nothing "seemed" sufficient—these qualifiers suggest approximation, probability, doubt.

Didion uses these to limit the scope of her assertions, to avoid appearing unreasonably and offputtingly dogmatic. It is an impression she is at pains to create. In the foreword, she notes that as she began to write the various articles that ended up comprising this collection,

> I was asked with somewhat puzzling frequency about my own politics, what they "were," or "where they had come from," as if they were eccentric, opaque, somehow unreadable. They are not. They are the logical product of a childhood largely spent among conservative California Republicans (this was before the meaning of "conservative" changed) in a postwar boom economy. (735)

Here, she sets her own voice against the voices of readers and critics who find her politics "eccentric, opaque, somehow unreadable." "They are not," she says simply, a brief, declarative assertion. "They are" she repeats a "logical product" of her childhood. Self-aware and poised, she presents her conclusions in this work as the "logical product" of her observations, couching these in the careful language of a scientist. She is never shrill, seldom intemperate. The qualifiers "seem," "tend," "certain," and "apparent" appear regularly throughout the collection, sometimes several times on one page. "There seemed at the time at least two clear reasons that Bonner, not Guillermoprieto, became the target of choice," she offers in explanation for why Raymond Bonner's work on El Salvador was discredited. "Certain parallels were inescapable," she observes, comparing El Salvador and Vietnam. And later in the same essay, writing about Assistant Secretary of State for Inter-American Affairs Thomas O. Enders, she notes that what she finds striking is his "apparent inability" to recognize contradictions between various things he has said.

Other essays contain the same careful hedging, giving the same impression of cautious qualification. "This faith in the laser-like efficacy of Reagan's rhetoric seems undiminished by the fact that it remains largely a priori" (796), she writes of one of her favorite targets. And of his biographer Dinesh D'Souza, she notes that he "seemed to have arrived in this country with preternatural pitch for the exact charged chords . . . that drove its politics of resentment" (791). She characterizes a writer who has profiled Reagan and commented on his willingness to follow a schedule (or "script"), as "betraying a certain queasy wonder at his initial encounter with this apparently cheerful lack of interest" (790). Those reporting on political life fall into a routine that encourages a "certain passivity" (749). Political insiders "tend to speak of the world not necessarily as it is but as they want people out there to believe it is." These same people "tend to prefer the theoretical to the observable, and to dismiss that which might be learned empirically as 'anecdotal.' They tend to speak a language common in Washington but not specifically shared by the rest of us" (743).

Sometimes these hedges pile up in a sentence, leaving Didion many possible avenues of retreat if challenged. "It was," she writes in "Insider Baseball," "by 1988 generally if unspecifically agreed that the United States faced certain social and economic realities that, if not intractable, did not entirely lend themselves to the kinds of policy fixes that people who run for elected office, on whatever ticket, were likely to undertake" (757). Throughout the collection, these hedges, especially in combination with her use of ironic quotation marks, passive voice, and nominalizations introduce an ambiguity, and sometimes passivity, that might seem surprising, given the explicit nature of her assertions and her obvious adherence to her perspective. But such ambiguity and passivity, even as they work against, in some cases, readability and clarity, temper Didion's tone, lending her more aggressive or sarcastic passages some modesty and even levity.

There remains a strong sense, in this essay and the rest of the collection, of a worldly and assertive writer, one unafraid to call it as she sees it yet one practiced in the art of how to do so in sentences that are, like their author, by turns, seemingly spontaneous, fluid, and seamless, but also bold, hard, and precisely crafted. The writing in this collection of essays calls to mind Walter Ong's distinction between the language of oral cultures and literate (or typographic) cultures.[10] Like the former, it is insistently oral: repetitive, copious, formulaic, rhythmic, and potent—prose patterned to be heard, patterned to be appreciated by the ear, to engage the attention. In this sense, it almost seems to replicate the political and media language on which she turns her critical eye—seemingly *all* style, almost poetic in its lyricism, with little of substance to hold the attention once the compelling rhythms of its patterns have faded from the ear.

But like the latter, it is often analytical and complex, full of subordinatives, modifiers, qualifiers, and nominatives that lengthen her sentences and challenge easy parsing. Sophisticated, elegant, and grammatically complicated, many of these sentences are meant for the eye more than the ear, for the intellect more than the emotions. These two characteristics of her prose—its oral nature, its more typographic qualities—are productively put into play against each other. The variety and complexity of her sentences—characteristic of a written text and necessary for the complexity of her arguments—demand the more oral qualities of language without which the sense of her complex arguments might be lost.

The passage below, from the essay "God's Country," demonstrates her facility at composing lengthy, grammatically complex sentences, whose meaning unfolds more slowly and subtly than in more aurally patterned passages. She is discussing, generally, how the press failed to accurately assess how Americans would react to the revelations of Clinton's affair with a White House intern, and, specifically, how Republican pollster Robert Teeter misjudged this reaction, observing:

> That the press and the public might ultimately react in sharply divergent ways seemed not to enter Teeter's analysis, yet we had just lived through a period, that of the events leading up to and following impeachment, during which no political commentator in America failed to express bafflement at the mystery of what was called "the disconnect," which is to say the divergence between what the press thought and what the public thought about President Clinton. (935)

The sheer length of this sentence (seventy-seven words) alone would make it difficult to follow or comprehend were it delivered orally. A declarative, compound sentence, it approaches its conclusion circuitously, the use of a nominalization, a hedge word, apposition, and a double negative delaying the completion of the sentence and demanding the readers' sustained attention.

The nominalization starting the sentences makes an entire initial clause work as a noun: "That the press and the public might ultimately react in sharply divergent ways," is an abstract and indirect way to begin the sentence and one that suspends or delays the completion of the thought until later in the sentence. The inclusion of the hedge "seemed" makes the sentence more tentative, less emphatic, slowing its pace. This is followed by apposition, when "period" is renamed as "events leading up to and following impeachment," which is then further modified with the lengthy (it employs three prepositional phrases) "during which no political commentator in America failed to express bafflement at the mystery of what was called 'the disconnect.'" At this point, "the disconnect," which has already been added to rename "the mystery" is itself renamed as "the divergence," at which time the sentence resolves nicely into the balanced and paralleled pair "what the press thought" and "what the people thought."

This is a sentence that relies on reasoned and analytic subordination; it is subordinative rather than additive, and hence typical of a twentieth-century written text.[11] Such a style provides Didion the syntactic tools to build sophisticated causal arguments. However, the accumulation of phrases that delay meaning could easily overwhelm the reader. The degree to which she modifies, qualifies, and extends her claims could prove taxing. Fortunately, she couples such elaboration with repetition, offsetting the more textual nature of long sentences with more "oral" syntax.

This is, as previously discussed, illustrated in part by her frequent reliance on anaphora, on evidence in much of her nonfiction writing. In, for instance, "God's Country," she repeatedly begins sentences with the expletive "There were/There was," as she paints an unflattering portrait of Senator Lieberman. The description runs across several passages that are complex and richly textured but remain grounded in emphatic statements outlining his most troubling personal tics:

> There were, in those first wobbly steps as a vice-presidential candidate, the frequent references to "private moments of prayer" and to the "miracle" of his nomination. There were the insistent reminders of his own familial devotion; there was the unsettling way in which he seemed to patronize his running mate; there was, the reader of *In Praise of Public Life* learns, "no single reason" for the failure after sixteen years of his first marriage; there were, in the aftermath of Gore's decision to name Lieberman, many dispiriting reiterations of the benefit that would accrue. (937–38)

Such repetition might seem needlessly formulaic, monotonous, or choppy. But Didion's repetitions are purposeful—they ensure that her main points are highlighted and foregrounded and that they are clearly articulated and memorable. Ong notes that those in primarily oral cultures, in order to "solve effectively the problem of retaining and retrieving carefully articulate thoughts" have to think in "mnemonic patterns," their thoughts coming into being in "heavily rhythmic, balanced patterns, in repetitions or antitheses, in alliterations and assonances, in epithetic and other formulary expressions."[12]

Against the backdrop of her carefully composed inductive arguments, where evidence accumulates gradually and exposition unfolds slowly over lengthy and sophisticated sentences, claims composed in more formulaic syntax ensure the salience of her conclusions.

Rhetoricians have long advocated the use of formulas in structuring thought and making it memorable—figures of speech are often formulas outlining how to arrange syntax or pattern sounds to ensure that sound echoes, and thus reinforces, sense. As Ong observes, "Serious thought is intertwined with memory systems. Mnemonic needs determine even syntax."[13] Didion's declarative sentences, whether long and fluid or brief and abrupt, are regularly composed of parts that echo each other in sound, rhythm, and structure so as to provide her main points aural salience. Such sentences depend on accumulation achieved through apposition, parataxis, modification, and repetition. These allow her to display her mounting evidence, to set side by side descriptions that encourage the reader to make the connections she wishes them to make. Oral cultures, Ong points out, favor redundancy, as they lack the ability to loop back through a text the way readers can, and it can be difficult to retain points that are phrased in grammatically complex sentences. Didion's repetitive phrasing, reminiscent of an oral exchange, ensures readers retain the points she makes. Frequently, figures of repetition—anaphora, alliteration, and polysyndeton, to name but a handful—establish the emphasis she needs to foreground arguments and make them memorable and permit her to let her syntax, rather than any possibly unappealing stridency, convey the weight of her ideas.

When she writes, for example, of the reliable patter and patterns of the summer's conventions, in "Insider Baseball," she does so employing anaphora, polysyndeton, and alliteration, her own syntactic patterns replicating those of the political cycle so that the sound of the passage echoes and reinforces the sense. The result reads like a passage from Demosthenes, rhythmic and emphatic. "All the opinions and all the rumors and all the housemaid Spanish spoken in both Atlanta and New Orleans would vanish," she notes, employing both anaphora and polysyndeton. Here the repeated "all"s and "and"s create a rhythmic, rising inflection, each noun emphasized by the slowed pace. "And all that would remain would be the huge arenas themselves," she continues. She uses a resumptive modify to elaborate on the "huge arenas," this modifier creating an emphatic echo as well as creating a seamless transition to the next set of images.

These images are also joined through polysyndeton; "the arenas and the lobbies and the levels and the skywalks to which they were connected," she writes, the chant continuing to rise in inflection. She next employs a summative modifier and apposition to move fluidly to the end of her sentence, "the agora, the symbolic marketplace in which the narrative was not only written but immediately, efficiently, entirely, consumed" (762). Here, this very long (though concise) sentence hurries to its end, the lack of coordinating conjunctions combined with alliteration (*e*fficiently, *e*ntirely) and parallel structure (immediate*ly*, efficient*ly*, entire*ly*) creating a rushed rhythm and falling intonation, together providing a sense of aural finality. Such figured prose features prominently in these essays, but never as mere ornament. Rather, its patterns provide emphasis, coherence, and vivification.

Additionally, the elegance of her syntax (her sentences are often balanced and symmetrical, with parallelism playing a crucial role) often takes the edge off her more blunt observations and harsh assessments. She relies heavily on antithetical pairings, often structured as negative-positive restatements, these allowing her to emphasize her point through repetition. Antithesis, resulting from the yoking of two similarly structured phrases or clauses of roughly the same length expressing opposing sentiment, has a distinctive syntactic and semantic profile that predisposes readers toward seeing two paired terms as opposites.[14] This figure thus creates "tight and predictable" aural patterns "which force semantic opposites,"[15] as when she writes that what dominated the rhetoric of the 1988 campaign "was not . . . awareness of a new and different world but nostalgia for an old one."

This construction forces "awareness" against "nostalgia" within an isocolon and so, through juxtaposition and symmetry, highlights the contrast between the two. Parallel, antithetical, and memorable premises such as this one are effective because they speak to the sense "that opposite things should have opposite qualities."[16] Structurally and iconically, then, they represent the thematic oppositions (i.e., us vs. them, outsiders vs. insiders, audience vs. actors, observable vs. theoretical, real vs. artificial, reality vs. narrative) between her expectations of the political process and the fabrications of politicians and thereby reinforce her arguments subtly rather than explicitly.

Furthermore, given that her sentences are often very long and very complex—more "textual"—these more "oral" constructions foreground key points that might otherwise get "buried," as is evident in the following long, loose, compound-complex sentence: "All stories," she writes, "of course, depend for their popular interest upon the invention of personality, or 'character,' but in the political narrative, designed as it is to maintain the illusion of consensus by obscuring rather than addressing actual issues, this invention served a further purpose" (757). Here, the antithetical pairing found within the second independent clause, as part of a long subordinating clause, sets "obscuring" against "addressing" and offers a distilled but potent and memorable sense of her main criticism of political narratives.

It is a point that can be "heard" against the background of dense text surrounding it. This element of aural persuasiveness is critical as it allows readers to experience "the rhythm of the discourse" in addition to seeing, literally, "the reversal" set up through antithesis. In appealing to readers through sound—through a perceivable pattern built from parallel cola or clauses a pattern reader can anticipate and complete on their own—Didion creates a certain degree of emotional force that is persuasive regardless of the semantic content of the antithesis.

Additionally, she habitually employs ellipsis, an economical way of writing arresting and aesthetically pleasing sentences. For instance, American reporters covering pseudo-events, Didion argues, are willing "to present these images not as a story the campaign wants told but as fact." And someone who would consume these "facts," who digests them as true, was an "outsider," who "was seen as responsive not to actual issues but to their adroit presentation." In both these instances, clauses are balanced and negatively/positively restated in symmetrical clauses: "not as a story" and "but as fact;" "not to actual issues" and "but to their adroit presentation." In these she elides the second "present," and the second "responsive," though their presence is necessary for the logical completion of both thoughts. Her elision of the verb (or nominalization of the verb) in the second half of antithetical pairings prompts the readers to mentally complete the thought themselves by filling in the missing verb. A further, rather striking example of this occurs when she recalls "pink-cheeked young aides on the Dukakis campaign referring to themselves, innocent of irony and so of history, as the 'best and the brightest' " (748). Here she symmetrically and artfully pairs two balanced phrases ("innocent of irony" and "of history"), eliding "innocent" before history to create an economical and arresting sentence.

Examples of these constructions abound in her text. In one passage, she describes the way President George Bush's supporters worked to change the way he was characterized. "What was at first identified as 'the wimp factor," she writes ". . . was replaced not by a more complicated view of the personality but by its reverse." Here "was replaced" is elided after "but." At another point she notes, in regards to the political process: "When we talk about the process, then we are talking, increasingly, not about 'the democratic process,' or the general mechanism affording the citizens of a state a voice in its affairs, but the reverse." In this sentence, she elides "we are talking about" after "but." In omitting these phrases, Didion compels the readers to complete, unconsciously, her arguments, this subtle collaboration increasing the likelihood they will respond favorably to her claims.

And there is this passage regarding the 2000 presidential election, in which she relies on antithesis and elision to represent (and thus suggest) close relationships between ideas as she builds her argument:

> Yet the events in question were in many ways not only entirely predictable but entirely familiar: the reactive angers that drove this post-election period were not different in kind from the reactive angers that had driven American politics since the 1960s. Now as before, the "rule of law" was repeatedly invoked, although how a matter as demonstrably lawyered up as the Florida recount could be seen to threaten the rule of law was unclear. Now as before. (741)

The antithetical pairing comes in the initial clause; events were "not only entirely predictable but entirely familiar," the construction permitting her to reiterate and thus emphasize her point that all was "politics as usual," the elision of "were" leaving space for readers to complete the aural pattern. Her use of epanalepsis further creates aural patterns, lending the passage its rhythm: "reactive angers" is repeated as is "rule of law," and "Now as before"—their echoes reinforcing her point that, over time, nothing has changed. The patterns of political life are, she argues—and the sounds of her sentences imply—familiar and predictable.

The Didion at work in these pages is nobody's fool. Long disenchanted and disillusioned with the narratives spun by the "big names" in politics and the storylines publicized by a complicit and possibly star-struck media, she composes a portrait of a political process absurdly and obviously theatrical. While she appears to play the game—riding along on the buses, waiting on the tarmac, recording the speeches, even hosting Jerry Brown for an overnight—she maintains a critical distance from the proceedings. Her skeptical eye and ear for irony produce prose that cuts, razor-sharp, through the political puffery at work. Despite the crafted hedging, the air of passivity, and the understatement, she is as straight a shooter as ever, her voice on the page giving lie to the prevailing image of her as fragile, neurotic, tentative. In syntax that alternately sings and stings, sentences that accumulate or withhold, Didion lays bare the mechanisms of a process so relentlessly artificial and self-serving it is not possible for even a naive reader to maintain the illusion that it works to serve the interests of those outside of it.

CHAPTER 4

## *Terra Incognita*

## On Loss and Memory

Written in 2005 and 2011 respectively, Didion's memoirs *The Year of Magical Thinking*, which concerns the death of her husband John Dunne and the serious and prolonged illnesses and hospitalization of her daughter Quintana Roo, and *Blue Nights*, dealing with the latter's death only twenty months after Dunne's own, were, for the most part, well received by critics and admired by readers. *The Year of Magical Thinking*, in particular, was critically praised (it received the National Book Award and was later turned into a successful one-act play starring Didion's close friend Vanessa Redgrave) and seen as more typical of her writing in its control and style. *Blue Nights*, often described as "raw" and "fragmented," had a more mixed, though mainly positive, reception, with some readers feeling it failed to adequately focus on its supposed subject matter, Didion's late daughter. As has always been true of Didion's writing, both these books were not without their detractors (with their usual critiques of her "aloofness," "solipsism," "narcissism," and "pretentiousness"), but, on the whole, influential reviewers and writers (e.g., Kakutani, Pinsky) wrote very favorably of these latest works, and many reviews and much internet commentary suggest that their publication was responsible for introducing new readers to her work while reinforcing the devotion her longtime fans had for her writing.

 *The Year of Magical Thinking* is both memoir and meditation and traces a period of time in Didion's life that begins with the sudden (though, as she begins to come to realize toward the end of the book, not entirely unexpected) death of her husband after almost forty years of marriage, and ends a little more than a year later, when she finds "the craziness is receding but no clarity is taking its place."[1] Between these two points in time, she deals not only with Dunne's loss but with Quintana's rapidly failing health. It is a year of unimaginable and disorienting loss—the extraordinary closeness of her marriage is legendary; she and Dunne lived together, worked together, edited one another's work, and were seldom apart.

Quintana is her only daughter, a much-beloved adult child who had only a few months earlier been a "deliriously happy bride" (65), but who is now undergoing a series of traumatic and mystifying heath crises that land her repeatedly in ICUs at the edge of death. As Didion goes through Dunne's personal effects—removing the bills from his wallet, neatly tucking them in place with her own—and crisscrossing the country to remain steadfastly at Quintana's side even as her brain fails and her pupils become dilated and fixed, she filters through the memories that arise unbidden. And she is struck time and again by details (the faint pencil marks of a note Dunne wrote, leis floating in the water in Hawaii, Quintana's bassinet next to wisteria in a box garden) that transfix her even as she tries and fails to read them for signs of how she could have prepared herself for such loss. Traveling seamlessly and repeatedly between past and present, the work traces the trajectory of her thinking as she moves from the shock incurred in the immediate moments of these tragedies to the acknowledgment that she must, as she writes in her hauntingly rhythmic prose style, "relinquish the dead, let them go, keep them dead. Let them become the photograph on the table. Let them become the name on the trust accounts. Let go of them in the water" (223–26). It is not, at the end of *Magical Thinking*, something she is ready to do.

Didion writes this book at a time when death, as she notes, "occurs largely offstage" (60), when the time-honored rituals of mourning are no longer sharply observed, and the act of dying has become "professionalized," occurring largely in hospitals rather than homes (60). She feels keenly the loss of any established etiquette for grieving, for having one's grief validated, recognized, tolerated. Having thought, by her own admission, since childhood "a great deal about meaninglessness" (189), she is someone who looks for signs in the landscape, finds meaning in the Episcopal litany (if not the truths it professes), believes in rituals, imbues them with a significance that transcends the everyday. She writes, in the immediate aftermath of John's death:

Setting the table. Lighting the candles. Building the fire. Cooking. All those soufflés, all that crème caramel, all those daubes and albóndigas and gumbos. Clean sheets, stacks of clean towels, hurricane lamps for storms, enough water and food to see us through whatever geological event came our way. *These fragments I have shored against my ruins,* were the words that came to mind then. These fragments mattered to me. I believed in them. (190–91; emphasis original)

Using fragments to describe fragments, withholding transitions and connections as she pulls together disparate objects from different time periods, she conveys her strong need for the concrete, those things that anchor her in time and place, those actions that have protected her or at least offered the promise of protection. Candles, fires, lamps, and warmth are motifs across the work signifying light, safety, home. Unmoored in the wake of her loss, she casts about for language that will capture her experience and bring sense to the senseless. Immersed in the cold and clinical jargon of the medical professionals who oversee her husband's death and monitor her daughter's fragile life, she searches for the poetic (*These fragments I have shored against my ruins*, she writes, borrowing from T. S. Eliot's *The Waste Land*) and the profound and a world where "mourning is still recognized, allowed, not hidden from view" (60). Her search is captured in language that is both a litany and a lament. She remarks, of those searching for answers about Quintana's health:

> I had no answers.
> I had no prognosis.
> I did not know how this had happened. (99)

These sentences—repetitive, rhythmic, concise—are characteristic of much of her prose in this work, as she struggles with the thin divide separating life and death. "There were no faint traces about dead, no pencil marks,"[2] she observes metaphorically, yet she "still believed that given the right circumstances he would come back. He who left the faint traces before he died, the Number Three pencil" (150).

Marking a sharp departure from her overtly political and argumentative writing of the previous two decades, these memoirs move Didion, always a presence in her writing, front and center, the subject of her own dissection and commentary. Having made a career out of observing and dismantling—coolly, bluntly, and intelligently—the mythologizing impulses of others, she, in these books, turns her unflinching gaze on her own habits of magical thinking, and reexamines her beliefs in patterns, logic, coherence, meaning. In these two works is the same marriage of the personal and the universal, the concrete and the abstract, that so strikingly characterized *The White Album* and *Slouching Towards Bethlehem*; here is the voice of an essayist rather than a critic. When, in *Magical Thinking*, Didion writes of Dunne's death, when she writes of her own grieving, she neither intends to offer a clear-eyed exposition on the nature of death and grieving nor pour out her heart in order to share herself completely with her readers.

Instead, she strikes a middle ground, attempting, as is the nature of the essayist, to make sense of her experiences through the act of composition. An inveterate essayist, still fairly unpracticed at extended memoir,[3] she, as the origins of the word "essay" suggest, "attempts" to explore philosophical questions—questions about life, loss, death, grief, motherhood, illness, and aging, among others—through the prism of her personal experiences. The books speak to her own experience of loss, but she also pulls back from reflecting on these experiences to generalize on historical and cultural experiences of grief. In particular, in *Magical Thinking*, though much content is devoted to self-reflection, these self-reflections often lead "outward," inviting readers to question their own assumptions about life and death and the many moments contained between them. In other words, she writes of her experiences, not solely because they are hers, but because they might also provide "a door through which others may pass."[4] These experiences include the very act of trying to compose (select, arrange, control) in the wake of traumatic events—compose herself and, perhaps more significantly, her words. Ancient Roman rhetoricians believed that the duty of the orator was to teach, to please, and to move,[5] and what is obtained by examining the rhetoric of her highly oratorical style in these latest two books is not as much a sense of how her form rhetorically suggests certain conclusions or secures the assent of her readers but rather how it lends the books their powerful pathos and permits her to make present for her readers the reality of grief in ways deeply moving and instructive.

Although these are of course intensely personal works in many ways, works that expose her and her vulnerabilities to a degree her earlier works do not, she is still characteristically restrained, her dignity maintained. Never effusive, overwrought, melodramatic, nor hysterical, she favors omission and implication, both at the level of content and the level of syntax (through use of figures such as ellipsis and asyndeton). Clear boundaries are never crossed. While her book recognizes that grief is a shared experience, she does not write to invite readers to identify with her (and certainly, for many readers, her characteristic references to friendships with celebrities such as Natasha Richardson, stays at hotels like the Beverly Wilshire, and homes in Malibu and Manhattan act as a barrier to such identification at any rate). She refuses to slip into the easy patois of many essayists of recent years (Lamott and Roiphe come to mind), with their hip, postmodern, self-deprecating irony, and easy humor. She is never silly, never goofy, never exploiting herself or inviting the voyeuristic gaze. In this age of reality TV confessionals, social media self-promotion, and celebrity overexposure, readers might expect a more explicit and sentimental rendering of grief, but Didion's potency lies in her ability to direct attention rather than manipulate emotions. She is a screenwriter by profession, master of the mise-en-scène; she knows how to supply the evocative images, compose the poignant moment, and frame her experiences, the only soundtrack the rhythm of her sentences. As in a Bergman film, much is achieved through stillness and the long take.

In the more overt and explicit works of cultural and political critique discussed earlier in this book, Didion's voice is assertive, emphatic, and insistent. It is her style every bit as much as her content that conveys her confidence. She uses, for instance, anaphora to hammer home her points rhythmically, litotes to emphasize absurdities through understatement, and polysyndeton to enumerate and emphasize the missteps, mistakes, and idiocies of political players and the media. While her writing in those essays remains idiosyncratic and grounded in the personal, it is also both implicitly and explicitly argumentative, and at times, dogmatic, in a way that is atypical of essayistic writing. There is little uncertainty or hesitance expressed, for instance, in her ridiculing of Newt Gingrich or her critique of Bob Woodard. She may pose questions in these writings, but those questions are almost exclusively rhetorical (and often sarcastic) and rarely indicative of indecision or uncertainty on her part. She adopts clear positions and lays out her proof in declarative sentences, moving inductively from instance to instance, utterance to utterance, in order to make her point.

Many sentences are blunt, abrupt, and remarkably concise given the import of their content. She writes from experience rather than an urge to explore or reflect, her years of moving in the same rarefied circles as Hollywood insiders, political players, newsmakers, and the cultural elite providing her with the authority and expertise necessary for understanding, analyzing, and, in many cases, deconstructing their discourses and motivations. She is on sure footing as she mocks the political process from her privileged position on the tarmac with a presidential candidate or likens a presidency to a theatrical production, and the directness of her syntax reflects this confidence. Theirs is a discourse community of which she is a member, their language her own even as she draws clear boundaries between their manipulations of language and her own rhetorical use of it and even professes her inability to penetrate it.

*The Year of Magical Thinking* and *Blue Nights*, however, present readers with a different Joan Didion. This Joan Didion is no longer certain. After the publication of these books, in an interview with her close friend of forty years, Sara Davidson, Didion notes a shift in her own attitude toward life, and recognizes a new weakness in herself. " 'For the first time ever, I feel frail,' Joan said, adding that she no longer 'believes absolutely' in her ability to overcome any obstacle." Davidson continues to probe, pointing to Didion's previous belief in a Western code of independence and self-reliance:

> "So the Western code . . . ?" I said.
> "It's not my code anymore because I'm not self reliant. It would be a useless code."
> I asked if anything has replaced it.
> "Work harder." She laughed. "I think we need to find another code."
> "What might that be?" I asked.
> "I don't know." But after reflecting, she said the code would have to include "acceptance. And surrender." She looked taken aback, as I was, by what she'd just heard herself say. "Surrender was never close to my code before! It did not involve surrender. But I don't mean it in a negative way, like giving up. I mean . . . acceptance."[6]

This Joan Didion has entered a world unfolding with "the nonsequential inexorability of a dream" (136)—a phrase she uses to describe the day Quintana is medically transferred via helicopter). In being forced (unwittingly and unwillingly) into the discourse of grief as well as that of medical professionals, she is confronted with the limits of her experience and knowledge. Her confrontation with these limits, which is, in some sense a confrontation with her own "ignorance" (of, for example, the etiquette of grieving, the psychological and physical impacts of grief, the medical conventions and terminology surrounding death), dislocates her and drives her search for answers and understanding. She describes, for instance, going to the bookstore at the UCLA medical center—while Quintana lays in critical condition facing brain surgery—to find books that might help her understand the terminology the doctors are using to describe areas of the brain. She purchases one entitled *Clinical Neuroanatomy* but finds that as she starts to read the text, "I could think only of a trip to Indonesia during which I had become disoriented by my inability to locate the grammar in Bahasa Indonesia, the official language used on street signs and storefronts and billboards." *Clinical Neuroanatomy*, she concludes "seemed to be one more case in which I would be unable to locate the grammar." She puts it on her bedside where it remains for the duration of their time in California (104).

Here then, within the pages of these powerful memoirs, Didion returns to the essayistic voice so characteristic of her earliest works. She questions far more often than she asserts. She embraces ambiguity and resists certainty; she employs repetition (most frequently in the form of anaphora but also in the form of polysyndeton, epistrophe, and epanalepsis) not to amplify her claims but to emphasize her struggles and represent, through form, the circling and turning over of details, facts, and thoughts that follow the deaths of her husband and her only daughter.

The syntax in these books—the use of fragments, repetition, parenthesis; the frequent avoidance of transitional phrases; her habitual use of parataxis—communicates a wish to avoid imposing a narrative line upon a sequence of events she often finds incomprehensible. Yet, ironically, it is this same style, this same habit, that ensures that the narratives she shares are both clear and coherent, the "truths" in them insistent and memorable. She noted, after the publication of *Magical Thinking*, that she intended the work to be "less polished"; however, when she had finished it she realized, she shares in an interview, "that it was exactly as polished as everything I wrote had always been."[7]

The rhythms created by clauses that echo one another, words and phrases that repeat, and sentences that vary in length according to the meaning they are meant to convey, rather than rendering her experience inaccessible, allow for her beliefs to "penetrate" the readers' minds. She may, in terms of content, circle repeatedly back to the same moment, the same evocative detail, even the same assertions in a way that seems pointlessly repetitive, evidence of a woman unmoored, a writer undisciplined. Her punctuation may be erratic, and her voice may frequently sound doubtful, skeptical, unsure, and even shaky, that of a woman "suddenly spinning into madness." But this is Joan Didion—even while she details the myriad ways in which her life, following her husband's sudden death, falls apart, she maintains strict control over her words.

This control is obvious, for instance, in the following spare passage describing her travel alone through familiar parts of California, after Dunne's death and during Quintana's long hospitalization:

> I could avoid passing the intersection at Sunset and Beverly Glen where for six years I had turned off to the Westlake School for Girls. I could avoid passing any intersection I could not anticipate, control. I could avoid keeping the car radio tuned to the stations I used to drive by, avoid locating KRLA, an AM station that had called itself "the heart and soul of rock and roll" and was still in the early 1990s programing the top hits of 1962. I could avoid punching in the Christian call-in station to which I had switched whenever the top hits of 1962 lost their resonance. (115)

What she describes are the actions of a woman struggling to exert control in an otherwise uncontrollable situation, the repetitive, controlled, and concise wording mirroring her attempts to navigate terra incognita even as she travels through familiar territory. The repeated emphasis on "I" is made more potent by its placement at the beginning of each sentence, this use of anaphora implying that Didion is the subject of each sentence, the agent of the actions. Parataxis, the arrangement of simple sentences in coordinate (rather than subordinate) structure ensures coherence even as the contents of the sentences suggest no inherent linearity to her actions. Such stripped-down prose seems fitting for a woman described, by the social worker with her at the time she receives news of her husband's death, as "a pretty cool customer" (15). And a cool customer she remains; asked, after her daughter's death if she means to alter *Magical Thinking* (which she had completed but which was awaiting publication) to include her daughter's passing, she replied tersely: "It's finished."[8]

## *The Year of Magical Thinking*

As for where it begins, *Magical Thinking* opens not with the scene of her husband's death, not with her subsequent trip to the hospital, nor with the handling of an apartment filled with his personal effects. Rather, it opens with her own typed notes, notes typed up within days ("a day or two or three after the fact") of Dunne's passing:

> *Life changes fast.*
> *Life changes in the instant.*
> *You sit down to dinner and life as you know it ends.*
> *The question of self-pity.*³ (emphasis original)

What follows is this: "Those were the first words I wrote after it happened." These abstract phrases—"after the fact," "after it happened"—not only suggest that Didion is unwilling to face the reality of her husband's death but also that his death is, in many ways, not the focus of the book. On this opening page, it is easy to see why one reviewer refers to her style in this work as "dispassionate," but it is significant that this same reviewer ascribes the success of this book to, in part, the tension between this style and what Didion is describing.⁹ Didion begins a memoir on loss by foregrounding writing itself, this reference to her own notes focusing the reader not on her husband or his death or her grief but on the effect of these on her ability to communicate meaningfully in the medium that has, her entire life, been her primary means of making sense of life and herself.

After these initial notes, she says, "[F]or a long time I wrote nothing else" (3). Her earlier use of polysyndeton ("a day or two or three") coupled with the vague phrase "a long time" suggest that trauma has disrupted her sense of time, or at the very least undermined her belief that to anchor anything in a definite date provides any control over one's fate. Most people are anchored in time—in calendar dates, clock time, times of day, seasons of the year—but Didion's sense of order has been disrupted; when the ordinary instant can end in death, when one minute one's husband can be discussing single malt scotch and the next be falling silently from a chair, his blood to be cleaned up later by the housekeeper, time ceases to be relevant in quite the same way. By the same token, cause and effect, or, in other words, meaning itself, are called into question, a theme Didion returns to repeatedly in this work and its successor.

Thus is one of the central tensions of this book set up, a tension between her writing habits (style is nothing if not habit) and her newfound feeling that it is impossible (even inappropriate) for her to compose this work in a way that will make sense of the senseless. Ironically, in interviews following the book's publication she says that this book "just flew out," and, having written it in just eighty-eight days, she remarks that she "found it amazingly easy to write." She continues, "[I]t was like sitting down and crying. I didn't even have the sense that I was writing it. I'm usually very conscious of the rhythm of sentences and how that's working. I didn't even give that any thought."[10]

Yet, within the text itself, she, time and again, questions (often parenthetically) her own assertions and speaks to the difficulty of interpreting the meaning of events and the impossibility of textually representing a coherence that no longer seems to exist in her life. While her nonfiction writing has always incorporated elements of metadiscourse—moments where she comments on her own attempts to write, to narrate, to represent the subjects on which she turns her gaze—the point of these latter books *is* the metadiscourse. She is not solipsistic—she does not assume that her readers are hungering for a full report on her long list of emotional and physical ailments or a chronological rendering of her husband's demise. Instead, as she asserts early on, in a passage worth quoting in full:

> This is my attempt to make sense of the period that followed, weeks and then months that cut loose any fixed idea I had ever had about death, about illness, about probability and luck, and about good fortune and bad, about marriage and children and memory, about grief, about the ways in which people do and do not deal with the fact that life ends, about the shallowness of sanity, about life itself. (7)

As a lifelong writer, one who, at this point, had been writing professionally for more than fifty years, she has, by her own account been dependent on the act of composition as a means to make sense—of the world, of herself. The act of writing is so essential to who she is and how she sees things that words and sentences, and the rhythms they create and contain, do not merely reflect what she perceives or express what she believes but rather shape who she is and how she understands the world. She observes that "as a writer, even as a child, long before what I wrote began to be published, I developed a sense that meaning itself was resident in the rhythms of words and sentences and paragraphs, a technique for withholding whatever it was I thought or believed behind an increasingly impenetrable polish. The way I write is who I am, or have become" (7).

Yet the events of December 30, 2003, the day her husband died, a day when their only child lay unconscious in the ICU at Beth Israel Medical

Center, challenge, according to this book, her lifelong ability to compose a narrative that makes sense, undermine her faith in words to represent adequately the events she experiences. Whereas writing had once determined who she was or who she was becoming, she finds herself wishing, at this moment that

> I had instead of words and their rhythms a cutting room, equipped with an Avid, a digital editing system on which I could touch a key and collapse the sequence of time, show you simultaneously all the frames of memory that come to me now, let you pick the takes, the marginally different expressions, the variant readings of the same lines. This is a case in which I need more than words to find the meaning. This is a case in which I need whatever it is I think or believe to be penetrable, if only for myself. (7–8)

What follows then, essentially, is a series of montages, images curated from the past mixed in with present moments, the past and present in constant conversation as memories prompt recognitions and reflections recast past events in a different light. While writing must, necessarily, take place sequentially, syntactically—one sentence following the other, one paragraph following the next—such graphic linearity, along with the rhythm it, particularly in the case of her style, imparts, Didion realizes, imposes a false narrative line out of sync with her experience of trauma, whether it be her experience in the moments in which this trauma occurred or in the days, weeks, months, and years that followed.

She wishes to refuse, she indicates in the passage above, the responsibility of composing in a linear fashion, sensing her inadequacy to do so in a way that will accurately represent the multitude of perceptions and perspectives available. This is the same writer who had claimed, very early in her career, that

> to shift the structure of a sentence alters the meaning of that sentence, as definitely and inflexibly as the position of a camera alters the meaning of the object photographed. . . . The arrangement of the words matters, and the arrangement you want can be found in the picture in your mind. . . . The picture tells you how to arrange the words and the arrangement of the words tells you, or tells me, what's going on in the picture.[11]

This is a writer who is now no longer quite sure "what is going on in the picture," and who is questioning whether any meaning can be conveyed "definitely and inflexibly." This, then, is a writer who wishes to put her readers in the editing room with all the available materials—all the images and details—and avoid the act of composition all together. She remembers but has no wish to re-member, to piece together and make a coherent whole, out of the fragments through which she is sorting.

Rather than attempt to do so, she, by her own account, structured the book "so that it replicated the experience of grief—the way in which you obsessively go over the same scenes again and again and again trying to make them end differently."[12] In doing so, she, intentionally or not, ensures that this work's most striking images and ideas stick in the readers' minds long after they have finished the book, repetition being one of the most common ways to amplify material rhetorically and make it memorable. Some of this replication happens at the level of the sentence, some of the fragments from the first pages appearing time and again, italicized for emphasis, set in relief against different time periods, appearing in different contexts, the only link between otherwise disparate moments that stubbornly circle around the same impenetrable questions.

> *You sit down to dinner and life as you know it ends.*
> *The question of self-pity.*

These words appear on the very first page only to resurface, partially, on page 26: *You sit down to dinner* and then in full on page 63: *"You sit down to dinner and life as you know it ends,"* on page 77 and page 98. Other key phrases follow this same pattern, and to track their reappearance is to understand the power of grief to hold one in its centripetal orbit, ever approaching resolution but never arriving at it.

It would be easy to assume that such repetition would lend itself to wordiness, yet every word, every sentence in this memoir is functional and essential. In keeping with Strunk and White's belief that a "sentence should contain no unnecessary words, a paragraph no unnecessary sentences, for the same reason that a drawing should have no unnecessary lines and a machine no unnecessary parts,"[13] Didion's prose is pared down, words selected (and omitted) and arranged for maximum effect. Given the subject matter, she is, in fact, remarkably restrained; her many recollections and recognitions could easily dissolve into self-indulgent, sentimental, rambling, and clichéd prose were it not for her ability to be both precise and concise. "Grief, when it comes, is nothing we expect it to be," she writes, before continuing a page later: "Grief is different. Grief has no distance. Grief comes in waves, paroxysms, sudden apprehensions that weaken the knees and blind the eyes and obliterate the dailiness [sic] of life" (37). Anaphora here keeps the focus on "grief," imbues it with an ontological weight. This repetition of "grief," rather than being superfluous and distracting, works with the hurried rhythm produced by asyndeton in the first part of the final sentence to suggest the overwhelming nature of grief's effects, and the repetition of "and" in the last part slows the rhythm, permitting her to emphasize grief's physical impact.

To say Didion is concise is not to say she shies away from long sentences—her characteristically long and complex sentences are to be found throughout the book, and she employs, as is her habit, frequent parenthetical asides. But none of these sentences are gratuitous, even when they consist of repeated words or phrases. In the opening pages, for instance, as she discusses her early inability to process her husband's death, she writes:

> I could not yet face, for example the blood on the living room floor that stayed there until José came in the next morning and cleaned it up. José. Who was part of our household. Who was supposed to be flying to Las Vegas later that day, December 31, but never went. José was crying that morning as he cleaned up the blood. When I first told him what had happened he had not understood. Clearly I was not the ideal teller of this story, something about my version had been at once too offhand and too elliptical, something in my tone had failed to convey the central fact in the situation (I would encounter the same failure later when I had to tell Quintana), but by the time José saw the blood he understood. (6)

At the start of the passage Didion employs a simple sentence followed by three brief sentence fragments. It would seem, for matters of economy or flow, that she could simply write "I could not yet face, for example the blood on the living room floor that stayed there until José, a part of our household, who was supposed to, but did not, fly to Las Vegas later that day, came in the next morning and cleaned it up." Such a sentence, while still long, would cut down on what might appear, at first glance, to be wordiness and meaningless repetition. But in composing these sentences (and fragments) in the way she does, with José's name repeated twice and set apart, through punctuation, from the sentences around it, and modifiers describing him similarly punctuated,[14] she is able to convey to her readers, through style, her own slowed processing of events, the fragmented nature of her perceptions. The sentences are incomplete and halting, their repetitions a reflection of a mind working its way through the observable in order to approach the incomprehensible. It is frequently the case that Didion reverts to this style when discussing her husband's death and their daughter's illness, and it is also frequently the case that these shorter, more fragmentary sentences are preceded and followed by long and complex ones, as above. "When I first told him what had happened he had not understood," she writes. "Clearly I was not the ideal teller of this story, something about my version had been at once too offhand and too elliptical, something in my tone had failed to convey the central fact in the situation (I would encounter the same failure later when I had to tell Quintana), but by the time José saw the blood he understood" (6). This long, loose, compound/complex sentence marks a shift in time. While in the opening lines of the passage she has placed herself at the scene just hours after Dunne's death, the word *When* indicates that she is reflecting at a remove from the events described. Time has passed; she has already begun to analyze her initial reactions, parsing her own language. As such, this latter sentence has a flow the earlier sentences do not, mirroring her ability to think more coherently and critically once further removed in time from the event.

The parenthetical here does not interrupt so much as it adds information that continues to move the sentence forward to its logical conclusion, and there is an obvious causal relationship laid out within the sentence, the use of the coordinating conjunction "but" indicating, clearly, the relationship between the ideas expressed in the two independent clauses; she was a poor storyteller, but José understood once he saw the blood. This is not to say the sentence represents a moment of complete comprehension—she remains elliptical even as she describes her own tendency to be elliptical: "something in my tone had failed to convey the central fact of the situation," she writes, not bothering to identify the "something" nor to say anything more concrete than "the central fact" and "the situation," the abstract nature of these terms indicating a continuing refusal to confront, directly and explicitly, the events of that day.

When she does first refer to her husband's death in concrete terms, her tone becomes almost clinical, suggesting a continuing desire to maintain some distance from the trauma of the day. She writes: "Nine months and five days ago, at approximately nine o'clock in the evening of December

30, 2003, my husband, John Gregory Dunne, appeared to (or did) experience, at the table where he and I had just sat down to dinner in the living room of our apartment in New York, a sudden massive coronary event that caused his death" (6–7). Within this long complex and periodic sentence, one interrupted and extended by multiple modifiers that slow the pace, as if to suggest that Didion is still processing the central facts of the trauma, she offers a spare but concise portrait of the moment that she will circle around and return to repeatedly throughout the remainder of the work. Because it is a periodic sentence, the full sense of what Didion is conveying is not completed until the final words. This form thus allows her to build up, climatically, to the information she most wants to emphasize, the sudden death of her husband, while juxtaposing the trauma of this moment with the banality of the everyday.

She builds to this climax by employing introductory phrases and clauses that both convey information and suspend understanding. The beginning of the sentence sets the scene; two introductory phrases allow her to delay announcing his death. She next employs apposition both to introduce and rename the subject of the sentence: "my husband, John Gregory Dunne," further slowing the pace of the sentence, before moving to the action of the sentence: "appeared to (or did) experience." The insertion of this parenthetical correction is interesting, suggesting, as it does, that she is still coming to grips with the fact that his death has actually occurred, when of course both she and her readers know it has. The "or" suggests uncertainty even as she concedes a fact. She next delays completing the independent clause by inserting several prepositional phrases that further set the scene: "at the table," "where he and I had just sat down to dinner," "in the living room of our apartment," "in New York." Now situated in her apartment at the proper place and time, the scene set clearly before their eyes, in all its ordinary and everyday nature, the readers are confronted with its horrible disruption.

And then she, refusing the logical linearity of chronological order, jumps back in time, returning to the moments before Dunne's collapse, a passage worth quoting in full, with original formatting intact:

December 30, 2003, a Tuesday.
We had seen Quintana in the sixth-floor ICU at
    Beth Israel North.
We had come home.
We had discussed whether to go out for dinner or eat in.

> I said I would build a fire, we could eat in.
> I built the fire, I started dinner, I asked John if he
> wanted a drink.
> I got him a Scotch and gave it to him in the living
> room, where he was reading in the chair by the fire where
> he habitually sat.
> The book he was reading was by David Fromkin, a
> bound galley of *Europe's Last Summer: Who Started the
> Great War in 1914?*
> I finished getting dinner, I set the table in the living
> room where, when we were home alone, we could eat
> within sight of the fire. I find myself stressing the fire be-
> cause fires were important to us. I grew up in California,
> John and I lived there together for twenty-four years, in
> California we heated our houses by building fires. We
> built fires, even on summer evenings, because the fog
> came in. Fires said we were home, we had drawn the cir-
> cle, we were safe through the night. I lit the candles. John
> asked for a second drink before sitting down. I gave it to
> him. We sat down. My attention was on mixing the salad.
> John was talking, then he wasn't. 9–10

The first half of this passage consists of sentences that are short and declarative, with no transitions to bind them; they read like a list, and, indeed, they are a list, the words of a woman methodically working her way through events, paring them down to their essentials in preparation for analyzing the point at which things stopped being logical and coherent. The result is almost poetic in form, the repetition of "We" and then "I" creating a predictable rhythm that carries the reader along. This first half is both clear and coherent, the ideas in one sentence linked to the ideas in the next through the repetition of key words (e.g., "fire") and the use of pronouns as coherence devices. Further, the use of parallel structure keeps ideas similar in meaning (e.g., "I built . . . I started . . . I asked") in similar grammatical form, ensuring clarity. Thus, form enforces matter; the scene she has described is coherent; it makes sense—there are clear relationships between one moment and the next (she says she will build the fire, she builds the fire, he sits next to fire).

The pace of the passage picks up in the second half; with "I finished getting dinner," her sentences become longer and less choppy, pulled together through transitional words indicating causal relationships, e.g., the word "because" ("I find myself stressing the fire *because* fires were important to us." "We built fires even on summer evenings, *because* the fog came in") [emphasis mine]. The time she reflects on is one in which things make sense, actions follow intentions. Although she is pulling back, in time and place, from the night of Dunne's death in this portion, she is still working her way toward its inevitable appearance, and the knitting together of sentences here quickens the pace of her story. "Fires said we were home, we had drawn the circle, we were safe through the night," she writes, the parallel phrases mixed with asyndeton to hurry the rhythm. Having established, metaphorically (with her reference to prairie wagons encircling a camp fire), a connection between fire and comfort and security, she reenters the scene at the apartment with the brief: "I lit the candles," suggesting, of course, that these candles impart the same sense of safety as the fires of their past.

The next three sentences are brief but fluid. "John asked for a second drink before sitting down," followed by "I gave *it* to *him*" and then: "*We* sat down" [emphasis mine]. The pronouns in these latter two sentences act as coherence devices, linking the three sentences together. This logical sequence of events is then followed immediately by "John was talking, then he wasn't," a concise sentence rendered in two powerfully paralleled and antithetical phrases that illustrate, by virtue of their proximity in space (only three words separate "talking" from "wasn't") her later statement that life can change "In a heartbeat, or the absence of one." Her use of ellipsis (it is understood that she means "wasn't *talking*") allows her to end the sentence abruptly, the words seemingly cut off midsentence.

Profoundly traumatic events often occur in the midst of the most banal circumstances, their disruption of these circumstance so absurd as to prove unfathomable. Yet even as she delivers the news of his death here and reflects on it again later, her prose remains controlled and tightly composed. "*You sit down to dinner and life as you know it ends.* In a heartbeat. Or the absence of one. During the past months I have spent a great deal of time trying to keep track of, and, when that failed, to reconstruct, the exact sequence of events that preceded and followed what happened that night" (63). The italicized phrase, repeated throughout the book, is followed by two abrupt, short fragments, constructed in parallel form to suggest a similarity in meaning even as they contradict one another. The clichéd sentiment "everything can change in a heartbeat" is met with its grim, elliptical opposite: "Or the absence of one."

These fragments are then followed by an elegant long, but simple sentence, pairing balanced and parallel constructions ("to keep track of, and . . . to reconstruct;" "that preceded and followed") and ending "heavily"[15] in a noun, "night," this heaviness providing the last part of the sentence, "what happened that night," with rhetorical emphasis. This is not the sentence of a hysterical women at a loss for words nor even a writer who professes to have a new distrust in the power of language to shape understanding. Rather, it is the sentence of a practiced and graceful writer, one attuned at some level (conscious or not) to the powerful rhythms created by repetitions in structure and sound, one who remains in control of her writing even as that writing traces the trajectory of her grief.

And, in point of fact, it is this very tendency toward control that proves to be central to her inability to come to terms with the death of her husband and the severity of her daughter's illness. Much of the book describes her attempts to decode the language of the medical community, to gain the information that will make clear to her what has happened and is happening and thus provide her with the knowledge she irrationally thinks will allow her to reverse her husband's death and control her daughter's illness. She recalls, for example, buying several sets of scrubs in California while Quintana is being treated at the UCLA medical center, her immediate reason being that she has flown west with only her late-winter clothes she had been wearing in New York. It is not until later that she recognizes that her wearing of the scrubs would represent an inappropriate foray into a discourse community in which she has no real place. "So profound was the isolation in which I was operating," she writes "that it did not immediately occur to me that for the mother of a patient to show up at the hospital wearing blue cotton scrubs could only be viewed as a suspicious violation of boundaries" (106).

This kind of disordered thinking, and, more powerfully the "magical thinking" prompted by Dunne's death, evolves out her inability to accept the evidence set before her and her conviction that certain gestures on her part—sleeping alone in the days after Dunne's death so that he could come back; wanting to delay the obituary in case he was not really dead; keeping his shoes in case he will need them ("how could he come back if he had no shoes?"[41])—will somehow reverse what cannot be redone. Despite her explicit recognition that such thoughts are irrational, she believes she has the power to, after the fact, retroactively prevent his death, or, through denial, render it undone. "I see now that my insistence on spending that first night alone was more complicated than it seemed, a primitive instinct," she reflects, continuing:

Of course I knew John was dead. Of course I had already delivered the definitive news to his brother and to my brother and to Quintana's husband. *The New York Times* knew. The *Los Angeles Times* knew. Yet I was myself in no way prepared to accept this news as final: there was a level on which I believed that what had happened remained reversible. That was why I needed to be alone . . . I needed to be alone so that he could come back. This was the beginning of my year of magical thinking. (33)

Didion employs anaphora, polysyndeton, and epistrophe in this passage, lending it an emphatic tone—*of course* she has not lost it; she knows he is dead as does everyone else. She has told his brother *and* her brother *and* Quintana, so no one need doubt she is in denial. She is aware that the *Los Angeles Times* knew, as did *The New York Times*. "Yet" as she notes, despite all this evidence to the contrary, she does not really believe he is dead.

A woman, a writer, so clearly disturbed by her husband's death, could easily appear pathetic, but Didion is never pathetic. She is, rather, poignant. Given the subject matter it is no small thing that she manages to convey her story with a great deal of elegance. She has managed to do that rare thing: explore, insightfully, intelligently, and in a deeply moving way, grief, without exposing herself in the process and becoming an object of pity. These are not the lazy sentences of informal exchange with a close friend; in these sentences she is direct and communicates to her readers rather than converses with them. What is withheld, what is omitted, is in many ways more powerful than what is present in this work. Her reflections on pivotal moments are inevitably pared down, set in sentences deceptively short and simple given the complexity and weight they are meant to convey, with the result that her illogical thinking is thrown into bas relief. The prose is neither convoluted nor overwrought but syllogistic in form, the better to highlight the absurdity of her thinking. Graphically, the brevity of these reflections often creates a white space interrupting, and sometimes punctuating, the longer, denser text of the paragraphs surrounding them. In, for instance, approving the obituary, she realizes (later) with horror:

I had allowed other people to think he was dead.
I had allowed him to be buried alive. (35)

No transitions connect these two sentences, the first literal, the second figurative. There is no actual causal connection between them—Dunne is dead whether or not she approves the obituary. It is her magical thinking that connects the two thoughts, and in recognition of this she sets the two claims apart in two separate sentences, the better to highlight the illogic of her reasoning.

Similarly, when she approaches the room where he keeps his clothes, she reflects:

> I could not give away the rest of his shoes.
> I stood there for a moment, then realized why: he would need shoes if he was to return.
> The recognition of this thought by no means eradicated the thought.
> I have still not tried to determine (say, by giving away the shoes) if the thought has lost its power. (37)

Again, even as she lays out this chain of events, moving from past to present, she makes no attempt to establish a causal connection between them. And the third line, a short, grammatically simple, perfectly balanced sentence clearly implies that the laws of cause and effect play no part in her grieving. "The recognition of this thought by no means eradicated the thought," she writes, epistrophe doubling the word *thought* and thus highlighting the potency of disturbed thinking. She makes no attempt, as she notes, to test her thinking any further, withholding from her readers the simplistic satisfaction that might be gained through witnessing a situation resolve cleanly.

Such omission is characteristic of her writing; she is, after all, the writer who famously scorned feminists of the '60s and '70s for having "a thrifty capacity for finding the sermon in every stone."[16] "The idea that fiction has certain irreducible ambiguities seemed never to occur to these women,"[17] she notes dryly, and then proves her own willingness to confront and present the "irreducible ambiguities" provoked by Quintana's illness and John's death without recourse to easy answers or pat conclusions. She resists certainty in favor of uncertainty—questioning herself, her perceptions, her handling of grief, her memories, her actions, continuously throughout the book, aside from the last chapter, a point at which she seems to realize that questions will take her no further. In the final chapter there are no questions, but there are also no conclusions. Rather, there is a settled and sad acceptance, if not embrace of, the ambiguities generated by Dunne's death and Quintana's long illness, a resignation in the face of uncontrollable and unimaginable trauma but certainly no argument meant to persuade readers of the "correct" way to grieve. "I look for resolution," she writes in the final pages, "and find none" (225).

What Didion does find, often throughout the book, is information. "Information was control," she writes of her earliest searches for works that will elucidate for her the nature of her experience and thereby impart to her the information necessary to bring John back and keep Quintana with her. "I need to know how and why and when it happened" (22), she writes of her desire not only to see John's autopsy report but actually to attend the autopsy itself. She searches through the available literature, looking to poetry, fiction, and memoir and finding that, as she wryly notes, "given that grief remained the most general of afflictions its literature remained remarkably sparse" (44). Information, she learns, is not control. Her attempts (and failures) to learn the medical terminology that will make Quintana's illness make sense do nothing to actually ensure Quintana's health. Her attempts to reconstruct the moments leading up to John's death and her actions in its immediate aftermath do nothing to bring him back.

Didion concludes the book with a memory of swimming with John at Portuguese Bend in 1979 and 1980:

> I think about swimming with him into the cave at Portuguese Bend, about the swell of clear water, the way it changed, the swiftness and power it gained as it narrowed through the rocks at the base of the point. The tide had to be just right. We had to be in the water at the very moment the tide was right. We could only have done this a half dozen times at most during the two years we lived there but it is what I remember. Each time we did it I was afraid of missing the swell, hanging back, timing it wrong. John never was. You had to feel the swell change. You had to go with the change. He told me that. No eye is on the sparrow, but he did tell me that. (227)

This ending passage begins with a beautifully fluid, loose sentence, one that evokes—with its accumulating modifiers, graceful and climactic parallel structure (changed, gained, narrowed), and rhythmic intensity—the movement of the very water it describes. This sentence is followed by two quick, concise sentences that highlight, through the use of epistrophe (the tide had to be just *right*; the tide *right*), the importance of timing, of being able to read the signs in nature, to seize the right moment. She questions her ability to read the signs, a return to a question that haunts her the entire year. "Each time we did it I was afraid of missing the swell," she writes, employing apposition to elaborate on her fear—"hanging back, timing it wrong"—before offering sharp contrast to her fear in one concise, declarative sentence: "John never was," the absence of the word *afraid* achieved through ellipsis, its absence symbolic of John's fearlessness. "You had to feel the feel the swell change. You had to go with the flow," she notes, slipping uncharacteristically into second person," her words a reminder not only to herself but to her readers, a subtle acknowledgment of their presence in her deeply personal memory, a gentle lesson in a book with very few. "He told me that," she shares, and then, distorting the line of a powerful gospel song, one inspired by a parable in the Gospel of Matthew ("His eye is on the sparrow"): "No eye is on the sparrow, but he did tell me that." These last two sentences trace a circle, moving from the certainty John's directives provide to religious skepticism—a refusal to believe in an attentive and protective God, before returning, hymnlike to the only certainty she has left: "He told me that."

## *Blue Nights*

Following five years after *Magical Thinking* and after the death of Quintana at age thirty-nine, *Blue Nights* finds Didion once again mapping grief's territory, this time, though, as a more seasoned, and wearied, traveler of its terrains. It is tempting, given that both *Magical Thinking* and *Blue Nights* deal with loss and grief and were written only a handful of years apart, to assume that the latter represents only a continuation of the first, the works of the same writer circling around the same issues. But *Blue Nights* marks a seismic shift in how Didion sees the world. While *Magical Thinking* portrays a woman desperate to hold on to the husband and daughter and life she once had—with all its rituals and routines and meaning, *Blue Nights* is the work of a woman disillusioned and disenchanted. Of Quintana's baby teeth, teeth she had once carefully saved in a "satin-lined jeweler's box,"[18] she writes, "I no longer value this kind of memento. I no longer want reminders of what was, what got broken, what got lost, what got wasted" (44). The woman who once kept her deceased husband's shoes so that he could use them when he returned now finds no "satisfactory resolution" (45) in the objects left behind by her late mother and her lost daughter. She has lost her religion: she no longer fetishizes mementos, she distrusts memory, places no faith in medicine, and questions her own ability as a mother. Medicine, she notes in her understated and ironic fashion, is "an imperfect art," (47), the useless advice of a doctor a "catechism" (112) she has been through before.

Little illusion remains for her, and certainly no "magical thinking," with its false promises of return and resolution, graces these pages. Marked by frequent references to "seeing," "understanding," and "realizing," the text is an examination and a lamentation, an exploration and a meditation. *Blue Nights* is Didion's farewell to her daughter but also, and perhaps more so, a confrontation with herself: as a mother, a woman, a writer. It has been criticized by some as being too little about Quintana, too much about Didion herself, and, in point of fact, entire pages go by with a mention of her daughter, and the final portrait one obtains of Quintana from the fragments of her life depicted here is willfully incomplete. Slivers of her childhood are mixed in with details of her wedding (peacocks, leis, red-soled Louboutins) notes from her later hospitalizations, and excerpts of her childhood writing, but in summoning these Didion does not pretend to offer readers a comprehensive account of who Quintana was or how she lived or why she died. Although the passages that discuss her often offer startling accounts of her behavior—her call to a psychiatric hospital at age five for instance; her fear of a "Broken Man" who haunts her dreams and her life—Quintana remains an elusive figure to the reader, her quirks, moods, and medical issues flitting across the pages, present largely through her absence.[19] Surely her premature death is the impetus of the book, but a biographical account of the life cut short is not its end.

Instead, Didion composes a portrait of herself, a woman in her eighth decade surrounded not by those whom she has loved most but by the things they have left behind—notes, photographs, rosaries, clothing, and questions, many questions—a woman all too aware of the blue nights, the nights "in certain latitudes" leading up to and following the summer solstice "when the twilights turn long and blue" (3). "*This book is called 'Blue Nights'*" she writes, "*because at the time I began it I found my mind turning increasingly to illness, to the end of promise, the dwindling of the days, the inevitability of the fading, the dying of the brightness*" (4; emphasis original). That she has been broken by her losses is clear, but equally as clear is her tenacity, her ability to persevere, to, quite literally, compose herself, both in life and in writing.

The self she composes in this book, and the prose in which she does so is both familiar and altered. Anaphora, asyndeton, parallelism, and parataxis are, as in all her other writing, frequently employed to lend her writing its incantatory, rhythmic, elegiac force, as they do in the italicized text above.

She is, as always, both remarkably concise—composing lines of brief fragments that punctuate the text on almost every page—and strikingly fluent, piecing together long, loose sentences that carry the reader fluidly down the page. And she is, as ever, a straight shooter, even when her target is herself, her own perceived failings.

But she is, by her own account, changed, and one of the most troubling signs of this change, for her, is a new inability to compose as effortlessly in the past. In chapter 19, having just discussed a decline in her ability to preserve clear memories of certain places and times or to remember names, she provides a sample of some writing notes from 1995. She offers them, she writes,

> as a representation of how comfortable I used to be when I wrote, how easily I did it, how little thought I gave to what I was saying until I had already said it. In fact, in any real sense, what I was doing then was never writing at all: I was doing no more than sketching in a rhythm and letting that rhythm tell me what it was I was saying. Many of the marks I set down on the page were no more than "xxx," or "xxxx," symbols that meant "copy tk," or "copy to come," but do notice: such symbols were arranged in specific groupings. A single "x" differed from a double "xx," "xxx" from "xxxx." The number of such symbols had a meaning. The arrangement was the meaning. (104)

"The arrangement was the meaning," she writes. A lifelong writer, one so immersed in the patterns of her own writing (and before that the patterns of Hemingway and James, among others) that to generate those patterns is to generate their content, she claims to find herself floundering, unable to summon the rhythms that will write themselves, tell her story. "I had never actually learned the rules of grammar, relying instead only on what sounded right,"[20] Didion observes in *Magical Thinking*, but nothing, in the aftermath of Quintana's death, "sounds right;" no words come easily, she observes.

"All I know," she reflects, "is that I no longer write this way. All I know now is that writing, or whatever it was I was doing when I could proceed on no more than 'xxx' and 'xxxx,' whatever it was I was doing when I imagined myself hearing the music, no longer comes easily to me" (105). While she at first believes that this change in her writing process is due to "a certain weariness" with her own style or evidence of a new wish to be direct, she comes to see it as a sign of frailty, the very frailty Quintana seemed to fear when, as described earlier in the book, she worried how she would take care of her mother if her father were to die. Didion's inability to hear the "music" that generates her sentences is yet one more affliction she finds herself suffering in the aftermath of her losses. "What if," she wonders, "the absence of style I welcomed at one point—the directness I encouraged, even cultivated—what if this absence of style has now taken on a pernicious life of its own? What if my new inability to summon the right word, the apt thought, the connection that enables the words to make sense, the rhythm, the music itself—What if this new inability is systemic? What if I can never again locate the words that work?" (110–11). As in *Magical Thinking*, then, Didion presents herself as so undone by the tragedies of her life as to be unable to do the one thing that has served as her primary means of making sense of the world—write.

That she is more direct in this work than in previous ones, is evident. There are signs throughout of a marked effort to engage more explicitly with her readers than before. "Do note," she frequently implores the reader, "Do notice." "Let me again try to talk to you directly," she writes at the beginning of chapter 25. Her writing here and elsewhere is almost conversational, suggesting a more intimate rapport with her readers than earlier works invited, and encouraging identification in a way she seldom had before. Compared to *Magical Thinking*, for instance, which was almost exclusively written in the first person singular, *Blue Nights* contains several passages in which Didion employs the second person "you" to suggest that her experiences are shared by her readers. In writing, for example, of the signs marking the beginning of the blue nights, she notes, "The initial such notice was sudden, the ringing telephone you wish you had never answered, the news no one wants to get" (18).

And she sets aside an entire chapter (chapter 15) for the purposes of explicitly addressing those of her readers whom she believes to be her critics, anticipating their criticism so as to preempt it, composed enough in her grief to remain aware that she writes for an audience. "There was a reason why I told you about Arcelia and the sixty dresses," she begins, referring to Quintana's Spanish-speaking nanny as well as Quintana's closet full of delicate dresses.

> I was not unaware as I did so that a certain number of readers (more than some of you might think, fewer than the less charitable among you will think) would interpret this apparently causal information (she dressed her baby in clothes that needed

washing and ironing, she had help in the house to do this washing and ironing) as evidence that Quintana did not have an "ordinary" childhood, that she was "privileged." I wanted to lay this on the table. (75)

Directly confronting her readers, Didion is anything but elliptical here, yet despite her assertion that such directness undermines her rhythms or creates an "absence" of style, the pattern and punctuation of these sentences—their parenthetical asides, use of apposition, ironic use of quotation marks—are intimately familiar to her longtime readers. She may have struggled to compose these, and other, lines, but those struggles are not on evidence in the pages of this work.

Rather, for all her loss of faith (in a watchful and protective God, in medicine, in motherhood idealized, in writing), there is no loss in her style. Her writing maintains all the rhythm of religion but none of its false promises; her style repeats its own rituals even as she has lost faith in her ability to compose. Her long lists of details often take on the intonations of a rosary recited, a catechism memorized. Anaphora, alliteration, and asyndeton combine with free modifiers, as below, to lend these passages a biblical quality appropriate to their mediations on life and loss, an oral quality that catches the ear and lingers in the memory long after the chant has fallen silent. "There had been cars, a swimming pool, a garden. There had been agapanthus, lilies of the Nile, intensely blue starbursts that floated on long stalks. There had been guara, clouds of tiny white blossoms that became visible at eye level only as the daylight faded. . . . Time passes. Memory fades, memory adjusts, memory conforms, to what we think we remember" (13).

Throughout the book, aural patterns of rising action followed by a contrasting falling quality stylistically provide the work its undercurrent of lamentation. This is most strikingly observed in her heavy use of anadiplosis and epistrophe, which she employs to a far greater degree in this work than in any of her previous writing. Anadiplosis, created through taking a word or phrase at the end of a sentence and repeating it at the beginning of the next, generates a rising intensity or feeling of climax, and carries the reader rapidly and fluidly forward through a text. "So much for keeping our 'private' life separate from our 'working' life. In fact she was inseparable from *our working life. Our working life was* the very reason she happened to be in these hotels," (90) she writes of Quintana's tendency to navigate the world on adult terms.

And of searching for the point to Jean-Dominique Bauby's book *The Diving Bell and the Butterfly*, a book "extremely meaningful" to Quintana, she reflects:

> Only later, when she was for most purposes locked into her own condition, confined to a wheelchair and afflicted by the detritus of a bleed into her brain and the subsequent neurosurgery, did I *begin to see its point*. *Beginning to see its point* was when I stopped wanting to explore the reasons why it might have been so markedly meaningful to Quintana. (153; emphasis mine)

Epistrophe, the ending of successive sentences or phrases with the same word or phrases, slows rhythm, the heavy emphasis of the repetition marking a falling in tone. "The last time I ever saw her was a few nights after she fell on the bunny slope outside Quebec," she writes of Natasha Richardson, "in a room at Lenox Hill Hospital in New York, lying as if *about to wake*. She was not *about to wake*" (21). And of telling Quintana she was adopted, against the advice of older friends who admonish that "you couldn't possibly *tell her*," she responds, "Of course we could possibly *tell her*. In fact we had already *told her*. . . . There was never any question of not *telling her*. What were the alternatives? Lie to *her*?" (emphasis mine).

Though her meter is not so fixed as to be poetic, the mix of long and short sentences, complete thoughts and fragments, statements and questions approximates the aural effects of an elegy. She writes, of her daughter's wedding:

> After all the words had been said the little girls followed her out the front doors of the cathedral and around past the peacocks (the two iridescent blue-and-green peacocks, the one white peacock) to the Cathedral house. There were cucumber and watercress sandwiches, a peach-colored cake from Payard, pink champagne. Her choices, all. Sentimental choices, things she remembered. I remembered them too. (5–6)

The first sentence is a quiet sentence; in it she takes her time, employing multiple prepositional phrases to lead readers out of the cathedral and to the house, pausing to insert the parenthesis describing the peacocks. The second sentence continues the forward motion suggested in the first, but her use of asyndeton hurries its rhythm slightly even as her listing of sumptuous details suggests a buildup, invites anticipation. The fragment that follows deflates this tone; the mood is changed, reflective. The next fragment extends this mood, and Didion's use of anadiplosis to join it with the final sentence "she remembered. I remembered" creates a melancholic echo at the end of the passage that contrasts sharply with the images and mood suggested by her earlier precise diction with all its connotations of purity and new life: "iridescent," "white," "champagne."

A similar rising and falling tone can be found when she reflects on Quintana's constant "what ifs" regarding her adoption (What if Didion hadn't answered the phone when the doctor called? What if she hadn't been home at the time?). She writes: "Since I had no adequate answer to those questions, I refused to consider them. She considered them. She lived with them. And then she didn't" (63–64). There is an assertiveness, a rising tone in the first, longer, complex, declarative sentence. Immediately the latter part of the sentence is echoed in the next sentence, carrying the reader forward through the passage. "I refused to consider them. She considered them." Then the tone shifts and the lament begins, three short sentences, echoing each other in sound, rhythm, and structure. Epistrophe, the repeated use of "them" at the end of each sentence, lends the whole series its fluidity as well as creates a biblical emphasis, a downshifting in tone at the end of each sentence. "She considered *them*. She lived with *them*. And then she didn't." She uses ellipsis to bring the final sentence to an abrupt and harsh end, the final clipped word "didn't" imparting an emphatic finality that contrasts with the optimism of the word *lived* only five words previous.

Rising and falling aural patterns are also created through antithesis, the brevity of antithetical statements lending an intensity to images, ellipsis lending them their potency. "The aural patterning of the antithesis, its tightness and predictability," Jeanne Fahnestock observes, "are critical to appreciating how the syntax of the figure can be used to force semantic opposites."[21] Thematically, this book explores opposites: past and present, memory and reality, death and life, youth and old age, and it is a particular talent of Didion's to employ antithesis in combination with concision to prompt the reader to mentally "hold disparate images in equilibrium"[22] to see how thin the line between the two can be. Reflecting on the sale of their house in Brentwood to an owner who subsequently killed her flowers to rid the place of termites, she notes wryly: "The termites, I was quite sure, would come back. The pink magnolias, I was also quite sure, would not" (8). Of her realization that adoption necessarily implies rejection: "Doesn't it tell you that, in the end, that there are only two people in the world? The one who 'chose' you? And the other who didn't?" (61). And of the passing of time, "The way in which you live most of your life in California, and then you don't" (17). And in the passage above, in all its finality, "She lived with them. And then she didn't" (64).

"I know that I can no longer reach her," Didion reflects. If she tries to reach her daughter, Quintana will, Didion writes: "Vanish. Pass into nothingness: the Keats line that frightened her. Fade as the blue nights fade, go as the brightness goes" (188). The final line relies on epanalepsis, a figure rarely found in prose and more appropriate to the emotions expressed in poems,[23] the repetition of "fade" at the beginning and end of its first clause and "go" at the beginning and ending of its second transforming it into a refrain. She follows this with the final lines of the book, set off like a stanza, the next line echoing the previous one: "go" and "blue" repeated but this time combined in the same phrase, pulling together ideas already expressed separately. The concluding lines are made coherent and rhythmic through similarity in structure, length, language, and tone. The fluidity is provided by alliteration ("frailty" and "fear" "What" and "wall"), and the emphasis by epistrophe ("lost" is repeated three times). But it is also characteristically raw—the rough edges produced by concision and precision—the blue, the ashes in the wall, the doors locked.

> Go back into the blue.
> I myself placed her ashes in the wall.
> I myself saw the cathedral doors locked at six.
> I know what it is I am now experiencing.
> I know what the frailty is, I know what the fear is.
> The fear is not for what is lost.
> What is lost is already in the wall.
> What is lost is already behind the locked doors.
> The fear is for what is still to be lost.
> You may see nothing still to be lost.
> Yet there is no day in her life on which I do not see her. (188)[24]

# Conclusion

## What Remains

Having turned eighty-five in December 2019, Joan Didion, though frail and frequently ill, still maintains a busy life and public profile at the time of this book's writing. Just weeks after her eightieth birthday she modeled for a Célene print advertisement, looking as assured, composed, and stylish as she did more than forty years ago when she leaned against her Corvette Stingray for a Julian Wasser photo (subsequently displayed in the Smithsonian's National Portrait Gallery's "American Cool" exhibition). The familiar frailty was there, as were the large sunglasses. Kakutani, writing more than three decades ago, observed "a certain sadness in" in Didion's face, visible even behind "oversized sunglasses [meant] to protect her light-sensitive eyes," and it is possible to see this sadness still.[1]

But she has not faded into obscurity as the decades have passed, nor have her keen intelligence or critical eye dulled. In 2011, following the publication of *Blue Nights*, she expressed her desire to continue to write even as family members expressed concern for her health. As she told her friend of forty years, Sara Davidson, "I feel right now as if I can't grab hold of what I want to write. All I have to do is work harder, force myself to ignore the fact that I don't physically feel very good, stop feeling sorry for myself and start another book. I know I can do it."[2] She maintains an active presence on Facebook (with more than 55,000 followers and counting) and collaborated with her nephew Griffin Dunne on a well-received Netflix documentary, *Joan Didion: The Center Will Not Hold* (funded partially through Kickstarter), about *Magical Thinking* and *Blue Nights*. Her popularity has only seemed to increase over the years—as Dunne notes, "At Q&A's with Joan, there are lines around the block. . . . Her readership has gotten younger and younger and those books have opened up whole new audiences to her."[3] A recent piece in *Vogue* echoes Griffin's assertion that Didion's work continues to resonate—titled "Why Joan Didion Matters More than Ever," this article, by her longtime reviewer Nathan Heller, focuses on the compositional control of Didion's style, attributing her enduring popularity and influences to her unique and exquisite prose.[4]

As this book has noted, not all commentary on her work has been positive—there are some who find her style wearisome in its familiarity, her concerns trivial. Harrison's infamous attack—containing her assertion that reading Didion is "is roughly akin to spending several days in the company of Job's comforters—"[5] is legendary for its assault on both Didion's style and her sensibility. The charge that Didion's style is meaninglessly mannered or that it is "fond of repeated phrases" or has "calcified into a set of trademark tics"[6] has been made by several reviewers (some of whom are fans), Martin Amis and Katie Roiphe among them.[7] Those critics who find her sentences mannered, repetitive, and elliptical frequently, though not always, move beyond these syntactical traits, as both Harrison and Bawer do, to criticize her personally, a trend almost certainly motivated by the subjective and personal nature of her essays and the force of her distinctive and idiosyncratic voice. Didion is well aware of these ad hominem attacks, anticipating critics even as she released *Blue Nights* in the wake of her daughter's death. While other writers might have expected sympathy or even a modicum of decency to offset any harsh assessments, Didion was realistic at the time: "I don't think it's critic-proof. Not at all. Not if my daughter's name wasn't critic-proof. Nothing is critic-proof. I'm sure it will enrage some people."[8]

By and large, however, the response to her work has been, from the very start, enthusiastic and positive. Having published only two works by 1968 (her first novel, *Run River*, appeared in 1963 and was followed by *Slouching Towards Bethlehem* in 1968), she was already being recognized as a big talent, her work lauded as significant and unique. In 1968, Wakefield, who socialized with Didion and Dunne in the sixties, hailed her "as one of the least celebrated and most talented writers of my own generation" and proposed that "now that Truman Capote has pronounced that such work[9] may achieve the stature of 'art,' perhaps it is possible for this collection to be recognized as it should be: not as a better or worse example of what some people call 'mere journalism,' but as a rich display of some of the best prose written today in this country."[10] Praise for her work continued to appear in the decades that followed, with, for example, Joyce Carol Oates calling *Slouching* "superb" and noting of Didion's third novel, 1977's *A Book of Common Prayer*, that its language is "spare, sardonic, elliptical, understated"—the work of a woman Oates describes as serious and in control, but also passionate and powerfully ironic.[11]

However one feels about Didion personally, her style, this book argues, does signify. That Didion knows, as Caitlin Flanagan points out, "which woman is wearing a Liberty shift and which one a crepe-de-chine wrapper, who's in a Peck & Peck silk shirtdress with a fallen hem and who's in a navy-blue dress with Irish lace at the collar and cuffs"[12] is proof not of a snob's interest in the rarefied world of luxury goods but of a writer's awareness that style—whether dress, interior design, or words—is substance, that the selection and arrangement of an outfit or a living room or words in a sentence can be a rhetorical act with a powerful impact, especially when it is married with striking and vibrant content. She marries beautiful diction and syntax with vivid, evocative, and concrete detail, all of which should be read semiotically.

When she writes, in *Blue Nights*, of her Brentwood yard, of "beds made of lavender and also mint, a tangle of mint, made lush by a dripping faucet," when she grieves the stephanotis and mint and pink magnolia destroyed by the new owner's wish to drive out termites with poison gas, she is no Martha Stewart; she is assembling and arranging symbols that signify, using her director's eye to create a mise-en-scène that communicates her point. "Here," she is saying, beginning a close-up panning shot, the repeated "and"s mimicking the tracking movement, across her garden—"here is life, and hope, newness, and promise." This is juxtaposed with images of poison and termites, of death and destruction. That the latter prevails is both implied, through style, and made explicit, through assertion. "The termites, I was quite sure, would come back. The pink magnolia, I was quite sure, would not,"[13] she writes, the antithetical pair of clauses verbally and visually highlighting the semantic opposites she sees at work, the epanaleptic repetition emphasizing difference. Decay is forced against growth, the natural order of things captured in the microcosm that is her garden.

That her sentences are frequently beautiful is on evidence across her many works. Gorgeously economical and sophisticated figures abound in, for instance, *Political Fictions*, as when she describes Jesse Jackson's entrance on the political scene by employing the figure of syllepsis. "It was into this sedative fantasy of a fixable imperial America that Jesse Jackson rode, on a Trailways bus,"[14] she writes, the verb *rode* being applied in two ways, one figurative, the other literal. The result is that the sentence slips midway, almost imperceptibly, from the metaphorical into the literal. She also slips seamlessly between the literal and figural shortly afterwards, describing how after the Republican convention she stood, literally, "on Camp Street," on a corner that, metaphorically, "might be construed as one of those occasional accidental intersections where the remote narrative had collided with the actual life of the country." Here she waits, again literally, for "the motorcade itself," which, "entirely and perfectly insulated," is, through her use of synecdoche, to be understood, as "a mechanism dedicated like the process for which it stood only to the maintenance of itself."[15]

This impulse to move seamlessly between the sign and the signified, the literal and the figurative, has been, by her own recollection, present even before she began to write professionally. While still a young coed at Berkeley, she recalls, she

> tried, with a kind of hopeless late-adolescent energy, to buy some temporary visa into the world of ideas, to forge for myself a mind that could deal with the abstract. In short I tried to think. I failed. My attention veered inexorably back to the specific, to the tangible, to what was generally considered, by everyone I knew then and for that matter have known since, the peripheral.[16]

Thus, she writes of lemon groves that are literally peripheral, lining a street upon which a man is burned to death in a Volkswagen Beetle by his own wife. These groves "are sunken, down a three- or four-foot retaining wall, so that one looks directly into their dense foliage, too lush, unsettlingly glossy, the greenery of nightmare,"[17] and she turns her attention to them in order to evoke a sense of the dark brutality they witnessed. When she notes that her attention "was always on the periphery, on what I could see and taste and touch, on the butter, and the Greyhound bus,"[18] she reveals not her superficiality but her sense of the semiotic, of how and what things signify. That she had located, for instance, a Haight-Ashbury quite a bit less innocent, idealistic, or romantic than it was popularly perceived is effectively communicated by her focus, in the final sentences of "Slouching Towards Bethlehem," on the iconic image of the small figure of three-year-old Michael, unnoticed on the floor as he starts a fire in his Haight-Ashbury home (burning his arm before turning to chew on an electrical cord). His actions are ignored by most of the adults around him, engaged as they are in "trying to retrieve some very good Moroccan hash which had dropped down through a floorboard damaged in the fire."[19]

That Haight-Ashbury did not appeal to Didion can most likely be attributed in part to her membership in the "silent generation," born between 1925 and 1945, a generation known for being far more interested in conformity and much more comfortable with authority than the activist generation that followed and populated the streets of that gritty San Francisco neighborhood.[20] She grew up with kids who were, in her words, members of "the last generation to identify with adults."[21] In the '50s, she says, no one on Berkeley's campus "was surprised by anything at all, a *donnée* which tended to render discourse less than spirited, and debate nonexistent" (330). Rather than work against the system or challenge dominant ideologies, those who attended Berkeley with her, according to Didion, avoided politics. "The exhilaration of social action seemed to many of us just one more way of escaping the personal, of masking for a while that dread of the meaningless which was man's fate" (330), she writes.

She got out of Berkeley, but those of her generation who stayed she describes as "survivors of a peculiar and inward time" (331). These peers, like Didion, expected only to focus on the personal, to remain "outside history," to work hard and "make a separate peace" (331). The times she was born in encouraged in her an innate and inchoate focus on the personal. Sitting in a large bare apartment alone in Berkeley, she

> read Camus and Henry James and watched a flowering plum come in and out of blossom and at night, most nights . . . walked outside and looked up to where the cyclotron and the bevatron glowed on the dark hillside, unspeakable mysteries which engaged me, in the style of my time, only personally. (331)

With the dawning of the sixties, however, American culture, of course, underwent a cataclysmic shift, and it is a testament to her passion, drive, and composure that she became not only a significant part of some of the most profound events of the decade but remained apart from them enough to retain her critical eye and write some of the most seminal journalistic pieces of the decade, pieces that married the personal with political. She shared a godchild with Roman Polanski, sat with Joan Baez as she ate cold potato salad with her fingers,[22] drank Pouilly-Fuissé with John Wayne in Mexico,[23] stood in a room where Paul Newman and Jack Lemmon debated the state of the university in America,[24] chatted with Jerry Garcia while he took a break from rehearsing,[25] befriended Linda Kasabian, waited with The

Doors for Jim Morrison to come to a studio session, and hosted Janis Joplin at a party in her house.[26] And these were just some of her acquaintances and experiences.

And for all these connections with some of the biggest names of that decade, and her presence at the scene of some of the most famous events, and for all the accusations that followed of elitist "name-dropping,"[27] she was no sycophant, never one to follow the crowd mindlessly. She did not become a hippie or a Deadhead or write hagiographies of Joplin or Garcia. She did not join the feminist movement or become an apologist for the Black Panthers. Instead, she observed, and she wrote. And she happened to begin writing nonfiction for publication just as a different style of nonfiction writing began to appear, springing forth from writers as diverse as Tom Wolfe, Gay Talese, Truman Capote, Norman Mailer, and Hunter S. Thompson.

And Joan Didion, the only female New Journalist, wrote of her bad nerves, her famous acquaintances, her travels, and her homes and gardens, finding in them evocations and emblems of her times' most compelling issues. Straddling, always, the boundary between the "informal" or exploratory essay and the "formal" or thesis-driven essay, she composed pieces that are, by turns, anecdotal and poetic and formal and persuasive. She observes, reflects, draws conclusions, turns both inward and outwards and her writing process thus is aligned with the methods of the classical essayists, who have traditionally been understood to be "liberally educated person[s] . . . meditative, reflective, clear-headed, unbiased, always seeking to understand experience freshly and to find things of interest in the world."[28]

Didion was no Thompson, with his often drug-fueled and outlandish adventures, nor was she Wolfe, who seemed far less concerned with political and social issues or movements and far more with the rich and the famous.[29] Her material is never crude, grotesque, fabulously outlandish. But her writing, like theirs, makes considerable room for the personal, makes room for the intimate and detailed packing list (*cigarettes, bourbon . . . shampoo, toothbrush and paste, Basis soap, razor, deodorant, aspirin, prescriptions, Tampax, face cream, powder, baby oil*)[30] or for the observation that she is "a thirty-four-year-old woman with long straight hair and an old bikini bathing suit and bad nerves sitting on an island in the middle of the Pacific waiting for a tidal wave that will not come."[31] These personal revelations are never offered gratuitously; careful readers never truly get the sense that she is unhinged, out of control, self-indulgent. As Wakefield notes, her "own personality does not self-indulgently intrude itself on her subjects, it informs and illuminates them.³² Her art, as Oates observes, "has always been one of understatement and indirection, of emotion withheld."³³ She may offer an apparently intimate look at her personal life, a glimpse of her wounded psyche, but she even as she has been, in Oates's words "an articulate witness to the most stubborn and intractable truths of our time, a memorable voice, partly eulogistic, partly despairing," she has remained "always in control."³⁴

Were her writing to remain strictly at the level of the personal and the expressive it could rightly be accused of being solipsistic and trivial, but as with the other New Journalists of the time, and, for that matter, as with classical essayists since Montaigne and Bacon, all these personal revelations function as particulars through which she articulates more universal concerns. Despite all the "domestic details"—the focus on infant dresses hung in a closet, china, and linens—she is a sharply intelligent woman, well educated, well read, well versed on political history. She is capable of drawing on her vast reserves of knowledge, memory, and experience to generate complex, coherent, logical, arguments that steer clear of fallacy and cliché and move far beyond "women's interests" to take on some of the most pressing and pivotal issues of our age, not least the politics of water in California, foreign policies in the Middle East, relations with Cuba, military operations in El Salvador and Grenada, and September 11.

Despite the reviews describing her as fragile, emotional, neurotic, she is not given to sentimentality or pathos, instead viewing with distaste the tendency of others to employ heavy-handed pathos in place of reasoned analysis. Writing a year after 9/11, she observes that "pathetic fallacy was everywhere. The presence of rain at a memorial for fallen firefighters was gravely reported as evidence that 'even the sky cried.' The presence of wind during a memorial at the site was interpreted as another such sign, the spirit of the dead rising up from the dust."³⁵

Her subjects have varied across the decades but all of her nonfiction has, as its common thread, a healthy, sometimes condescending, frequently angry and ironic, skepticism. Born in California, the "golden land,"³⁶ a land settled and sought, throughout American history, by dreamers, opportunists, and those aspiring for fame and fortune, she rejected, early on, rhetoric in favor of reality. She writes, in the sixties of the San Bernardino Valley, that it was a country "in which a belief in the literal interpretation of Genesis has slipped imperceptibly into a belief in the literal interpretation of *Double Indemnity*, the country of the teased hair and the Capris and the girls for whom all life's promise comes down to a waltz-length white wedding dress and the birth of a Kimberly or a Sherry or a Debi and a Tijuana divorce and a return to hairdressers' school."[37]

It was a country she was to leave and return to multiple times, a county about which she wrote with an unflinching eye even as it so evidently remained an obvious object of frequent recollections and her affections. Her ability to balance her affection and nostalgia against the harder truths offers her work its singular flavor. Despite this balance, she is never disinterested; rather, "[S]he writes with a numbed eloquence, and at its best her writing catches with awful immediacy the acrid flavor of an age that has known the Nazis' death camps, Hiroshima, cold war terror, as well as the smaller nastinesses, the riots, the assassinations, the massacres—the mayhem that informs the noisy background of all our lives in a time that seems to have lost its collective mind."

She writes, for instance, about the aftermath of September 11, and brings to her piece her trademark insistence on rejecting the "efficacy of rhetorical gestures" in favor of sustained, serious, and authentic debate. Giving a talk in New York in 2003, she describes her dismay at what she saw on her return to the city shortly after the attacks:

> I came in from Kennedy to find American flags flying all over the Upper East Side, at least as far north as 96th Street, flags that had not been there in the first week after the fact. I say "at least as far north as 96th Street" because a few days later, driving down from Washington Heights past the big projects that would provide at least some of the manpower for the "war on terror" that the President had declared—as if terror were a state and not a technique—I saw very few flags: at most, between 168th Street and 96th Street, perhaps a half-dozen. There were that many flags on my building alone. Three at each of the two entrances. I did not interpret this as an absence of feeling for the country above 96th Street. I interpreted it as an absence of trust in the efficacy of rhetorical gestures.[39]

If, in this passage, the patterns of her sentences are familiar—anaphora, parenthesis, and fragments structure her observations and give them force and resonance—so too is her distrust of jingoism, symbols, slogans, and familiar dramatic conventions. In her rejection of easy resolution, she, like her more vocal contemporary Noam Chomsky, highlights the way events are framed and stories are manufactured by those in power of public narratives. She sees 9/11 as one more troubling instance where a violent and complicated event has become "processed, obscured, systematically leached of history and so of meaning." Rejecting ambiguity and irony, history, politicians, and the public, she charges, transformed, "as if overnight" an "irreconcilable event," so that it was, through rhetoric, "made manageable, reduced to the sentimental, to protective talismans, totems, garlands of garlic, repeated pieties that would come to seem in some ways as destructive as the event itself."[40]

The "flattening" of the event into easily digestible categories—"heroes," "the families," "the loved ones"—is effected through a rhetorical framework that belligerently idealizes historical ignorance and, through calls for "'taste' and 'sensitivity,'" "demand[s] that we not examine what happened."[41] Just as, at the time, it was popularly suggested that there was no room for postmodernist relativism or irony in the wakes of the attacks, so too was there a resolute refusal to look beyond the sociological propaganda[42] generated in its wake. Didion's voice was a lonely one at a time when to dissent from the comforting storylines was viewed as something akin to blasphemy.

That her voice can be both poignantly expressive and powerfully persuasive is evident across her whole body of nonfiction work. It is the paradoxical case that she is, in person and prose, both personal and political, both understated and uncompromising, both elliptical and assertive, both tentative and in control. She once disparagingly said of Doris Lessing that "she comes hard to ideas, and, once she has collared one, worries it with Victorian doggedness,"[43] and it is just this kind of approach she seems to avoid—rejecting didacticism in favor of implication, suggestion, example, repetition. Rather than explicitly set forth a thesis, she often relies on the art of selection and deflection, making salient, through syntactical arrangement, representative moments in longer exchanges in order to highlight the absurdity of the discourse conventions at play.[44]

In place of resolution, she frequently introduces ambiguity, in place of certainty, irony. Her habitual use of hedge words conveys an impression of indecision; she frequently says that things "tend" to happen, and that "certain" people feel a "certain" way or "certain" circumstances exist, and that conclusions are "suggested." Polarizing effects of the New York rape, for instance "tended to reinforce the narrative";[45] a revamping of a newspaper's format "tends inevitably to suggest a perceived problem with the product."[46] There was a "certain dreamland aspect" to the Cotton Club Case;[47] there was a "certain impatience with the way the [the Cotton Club] case was actually playing out."[48] When a *Times* reporter is still employed after insulting his employer, this to her "suggested not only the essentially tolerant nature of the paper but the extent to which Coffey appeared dedicated to the accommodation of dissent."[49] The sensationalistic news coverage of the Central Park rape, "suggesting as it did a city overtaken by animals,"[50] gave way to an idealized narrative.

Her nonfiction writing offers her readers a consistent reminder to look beyond the stories they tell themselves, beyond the stories others tell them, beyond the myths that promise epiphany and resolution. She resists banality, sentimentality, ideology. She does not impose a moral code on her readers or insist they see things her way, but she does warn them away from self-indulgence and self-delusion. Conservative or liberal, religious or atheist, one can believe in something and it is "all right only so long as we remember that the ad hoc committees, all the picket lines, all the brave signatures in *The New York Times*, all the tools of agitprop straight across the spectrum, do not confer upon anyone any ipso facto virtue."[51] A rhetorical critic, she wishes her readers to think for themselves and be skeptical, as she is, of half-truths and palatable phrases, and, above all, to be aware of language as inherently rhetorical. She grapples consistently, from *Slouching* to *Fixed Ideas*, with the means by which language can become, deliberately or not, a tool with which things are obscured, attention is deflected, and attitudes are influenced.

Writing frequently as someone outside of the discourse communities she encounters and resists, she portrays herself as a traveler immersed in foreign languages whose grammar she cannot locate. "We might have been talking in different languages, Brother Theobold and I," she writes of her conversation with a twenty-eight-year-old pastor moving his whole parish out of state, apparently at God's direct prompting: "it was as if I knew all the words but lacked the grammar and so kept questioning him on points that seemed to him ineluctably clear."[52] Ultimately, too, it is the "demands of narrative convention"[53] that she illuminates and which she wishes others to recognize and resist, even as she recognizes the difficulties of stepping outside of the norms of established discourse communities. She is on guard against language "that tends to preclude further discussion" or encourage, as the public life of liberal Hollywood does, to her mind, a "kind of dictatorship of good intentions . . . in which actual and irreconcilable disagreement is as taboo as failure or bad teeth, a climate devoid of irony."[54] Not for her is the language of politics, its demands for filmic conventions, which promises a "strong cause-effect dramatic line," a plot that "will proceed inexorably to an upbeat fade," and a resolution.[55]

Nor, for her, is the discourse of the women's movement of the '60s and '70s with its language of persecution and victimization, but also its romanticized promises of having it all. "Eternal love, romance, fun. The Big Apple. These are relatively rare expectations in the arrangements of consenting adults, although not those of children, and it wrenches the heart to read about these women in their brave new lives,"[56] she writes of young women rejecting convention for a chance to fulfill childhood expectations. Of women all too eager to adopt clichéd statements of oppression and powerlessness, she asks the "obvious." Why did such a woman "not get herself another gynecologist, another job, why she did not get out of bed and turn off the television set," rather than adopt the "half-truths" that have "only the most tenuous and unfortunate relationship to the actual condition of being a woman?" Why, in other words do these women accept the vision of womanhood offered to them in language unexamined? Why do they buy into the rhetoric? "That many women are victims of condescension and exploitation and sex-role stereotyping was scarcely news," Didion allows, "but neither was it news that other women are not: nobody forces women to buy the package."[57]

It is easier, of course, to "buy the package," and Didion recognizes this—her disregard for those too easily given to platitudes and happy endings is tempered by her recognition of her own tendency to distill moments into little stories tracing familiar narrative arcs. This recognition does nothing to dilute her contempt for the ease with which others slip easily into the patois of soap operas with expectations of climactic moments and recognizable conclusions. For instance, she observes a couple engage in a heated argument on a Pan American plane due shortly to depart for Hawaii. The argument intensifies until the man screams "You are driving me to murder" and storms off the plane. She reflects:

> I disliked it because [this incident] had the aspect of a short story, one of those "little epiphany" stories in which the main character glimpses a crisis in a stranger's life—a woman weeping in a tearoom, often, or an accident seen from the window of a train, "tearooms" and "trains" still being fixtures of short stories although not of real life—and is moved to see his or her own life in a new light. I was not going to Honolulu because I wanted to see life reduced to a short story. I was going to Honolulu because I wanted to see life expanded to a novel, and I still do. I wanted room for flowers, and reef fish, and people who may

or may not be driving one another to murder but in any case are not impelled by the demands of narrative convention to say so out loud on the 8:43 a.m. Pan American to Honolulu.[58]

Forty years ago, Didion shared her packing list in *The White Album*, noting that it was composed by someone "who prized control, yearned after momentum, someone determined to play her role as if she had the script, heard her cues, knew the narrative."[59] Positioned, from the beginning, outside of the "script," she would spend the second half of her life selecting and arranging words to counter the narratives that came so easily to so many. Beginning with her time at *Vogue* where "in an eight-line caption everything had to work, every word, every comma,"[60] she evolved into a writer keenly aware of how she composes sentences, revisiting them constantly, retyping her own sentences, finding and refining her rhythm, working with the way ideas and words echo across a text.[61] Her writing method evolved over the years, changing, for instance, with the advent of computers, which had a substantial impact on the trajectory her writing took, encouraging her turn toward longer, more analytical pieces.[62] And she has become, as one reviewer observes, "such a forceful and polished stylist that you sometimes feel as if she's micro-managing your every response."[63]

Others have and will write biographies of Didion, and there is much still to be said about her writing from the perspectives of literary studies, women's studies, trauma studies, and communications studies. This book is not meant either to be a hagiography, a comprehensive account of her life or a survey of her entire oeuvre, but rather the first extended analysis of her style as rhetorical. "Style," writes compositionist W. Ross Winterowd, "is the manner of matter. . . . It is at the level of the sentence that the real generative capacity of language lies . . . in a very real sense manner forces matter."[64] Didion is aware of the boundary between content and style and the ways in which control over the latter influences, informs, and impacts the former, noting once that there "no terrific stories . . . only terrific ways of writing them down."[65]

The rhetorical force of language occurs at the level of the sentence—it is a force of which Didion is distrustful and on which she is dependent. Able to discern the bewitching effects language can have on those all eager for familiar storylines and easy resolution, she frequently employs words such as *spell, occult,* and *chant* to describe political and public rhetoric. The Reagan White House ran, for instance, "on its own superstition, on the reading of bones";[66] the refusal to name the Central Park jogger was a decision she found to rest on certain "doubtful, even magical, assumptions."[67] Magic, with its chants and promises of potency, is ideally suited to political and public discourse that is rhetorical. But, of course, it is also central to the power of Didion's own prose, with its fluent and rhythmic patterns, patterns picked up, in part, by her close copying of literary models. The mechanical act of practicing varied and sophisticated syntactical forms was, she comments, "a great way to get rhythms in your head," and it is these rhythms that seem to carry her through the composition of her striking sentences, giving them their incantatory power.[68] A wordsmith with a lifelong habit of analyzing the "grammar" (rhetoric) of the personal, the political, the cultural, she is herself, this book has tried to demonstrate, a skillful rhetorician whose most powerful tool is her style.

# Notes

## Introduction

1. The most recent monograph on Didion, which focuses on her writing far more than her biography, is *California and the Melancholic American Identity in Joan Didion's Novels: Exiled from Eden*, published in 2019. The author, Katarzyna Nowak McNeice, analyzes Didion's fiction to demonstrate how Didion constructs a "melancholic" identity of California.
2. Katie Roiphe, *Messy Lives*, 105.
3. Bruce Bawer, "Didion's Dreamwork," 88. It should be noted that though the bulk of Didion's reviewers are fans, she has had her detractors—they too read her style as indicative of her character. Bawer reviews Didion's oeuvre and finds her, as he finds her style, repetitive, narcissistic, and snobbish. He writes of her prose in "Goodbye to All That," that it

> exhibits a number of now-trademark Didion elements—the combination of chronic anxiety and stylized world-weariness; the insistent use of the first-person singular pronoun (whose purpose, of course, is to put Didion at center stage); the incessant repetition and parallel structures (which are meant to be incantatory, but which would in later books become so pronounced that they could seem less a rhetorical device than a neurotic tic); and the combination of intimate revelation with a formal tone ("cannot," not "can't"), whereby the author insists upon a certain decorous distance that suggests both (a) that she's not just copying out her personal journals but has serious things to say and (b) that although she's opening up to us, she doesn't want us to warm up to her, doesn't want us to think we're being invited to be (heaven forbid!) her chums.

Barbara Grizzuti Harrison, "Joan Didion: Only Disconnect." Similarly, Barbara Grizzuti Harrison proposes that Didion's subject "is always herself," and that her "style" (quotation marks hers) "is a bag of tricks" that is "pernicious" and only sometimes works but more often serves as padding ("The emperor is actually wearing more clothes, more finery, than his structure will support"). Reading Didion's style as evidence of her character, she finds her superficial, concluding that "For Didion, only surfaces matter."

4. Eugene Scott, "Obama Cautions Against the Politics of Xenophobia and the Rejection of Facts in South Africa Speech."

5. For instance, Kakutani's latest book is entitled *The Death of Truth: Notes on Falsehood in the Age of Trump.*

6. Ava Kofman, "Bruno Latour, the Post-Truth Philosopher, Mounts a Defense of Science."

7. Ibid.

8. Nathaniel Rich, Foreword to *South and West: From a Notebook*, xix.

9. For Didion, "magical thinking" consists in embracing a primitive instinct that suggests one can—in relying on certain gestures, rituals, and words—control fate or even reverse what is final. Like Paolo Freire, who writes briefly about magical thinking in *Pedagogy of the Oppressed* (1–188), she believes such practices should be met with skepticism and critical thinking. Both Didion and Freire believe magical thinking can be deceptive and even dangerous because it is no less potent for being illogical. As William Covino argues in *Magic, Rhetoric, and Literacy: An Eccentric History of the Composing Imagination* (350), both rhetoric and "magic"—communicated through words and symbols—impact people. And, in fact, he sees all successful rhetorical acts as magical, as he sees magic as "the process of inducing belief and creating community with reference to the dynamics of a rhetorical situation." However, while Covino suggests that magical thinking can be positive in a generative sense, as well as open people up to accepting ambiguity and complexity, he also suggests that "understanding magic as a social and discursive process allows us to analyze and critique the powers at work in the 'plain rhetoric' that mesmerizes audiences with its seeming clarity and simplicity." This understanding is in line with Didion's own repeated attempts to unpack the simplistic narratives at work in political and public life, as well as, in her later years, confront the magical thinking she resorts to following the loss of her husband.

10. Chris Anderson, *Style as Argument*, 161.

11. Joan Didion, "Why I Write," 5. Hereafter cited in text.

12. Joan Didion, interview by Susan Stamberg, 23–24.

13. Rachel Donadio, "Every Day Is All There Is."

14. Edward P. J. Corbett and Robert J. Connors, 338. Didion's conception of style is aligned with that of the orators of ancient Greece and Rome, figures such as Isocrates, Aristotle, Cicero and Quintilian, who taught that language is intended to have an effect, and the words chosen for a speech should be chosen to produce that desired effect rather than to merely offer an opportunity for self-expression or representation or literary play. These orators—whose work contributed to the

codification of the discipline of rhetoric more than 2,500 years ago—emphasized impact over expression and "taught there is an integral and reciprocal relationship between matter and form," and that an understanding of this integral relationship "is the basis for any true understanding of the rhetorical function of style."

15. Joan Didion, interview by Linda Kuehl. (Kuehl died shortly after the interview, so Didion actually transcribed the interview for publication and wrote the introduction.)

16. Sara Davidson, "A Visit with Joan Didion," 14.

17. Joan Didion, interview by Hilton Als.

18. Davidson, "A Visit," 14.

19. Ibid.

20. Didion, interview by Hilton Als.

21. Davidson "Visit," 14.

22. Kenneth Burke, *A Rhetoric of Motives*, 57–59. Style is not necessarily rhetorical—it is rhetorical only insofar as it contributes to a writer's argument in a functional rather than embellishing fashion. As Burke argues, style, and figures in particular, can formally induce agreement even when there is resistance to the content of a proposition, (though the stronger the resistance the less likely one is to "surrender" by "collaborating" with the form). Figures such as antithesis and climax have a sort of "universal appeal" that leads to assent and collaboration due to the spontaneous desire of listeners to contribute to the "completion and perfection" of an utterance. Chaim Perelman, "The New Rhetoric: A Theory of Practical Reasoning," 1385. Perelman notes that in functioning to induce adherence or agreement, these formal devices then go beyond bringing a merely aesthetic value to work and instead work argumentatively, bringing about, "a change of perspective." A figure that fails to bring about this change can be considered a mere embellishment or "figure of style," and such a device, insofar as it excites admiration or signals a speaker's originality, works aesthetically rather than rhetorically.

23. Didion, "In the Islands," 277.

24. Ibid.

25. Chaim Perelman, "The New Rhetoric: A Theory of Practical Reasoning," 1385. "It is probable that any of the relegation of style to mere decoration stemmed in part from the 'stylistic tradition of rhetoric,' which resulted when Ramus, in the 1500s, assigned the canons of invention and arrangement to dialectic, leaving to rhetoric only style and delivery, which he considered to be of lesser importance. The result was that many who had no formal exposure persisted in thinking that style, and the figures in particular, were the 'flowers of rhetorics.' But the perception of style as superficial was also perpetuated by the classical use of the word *ornatus* to describe the figures of speech, which seems to connote 'adornment' or 'decoration'" (George Kennedy, *Quintilian*, 81). "However, in Latin, *ornatus* signifies 'equipment or accoutrements,' a soldier's 'gear' or weapons, and has nothing to do with purely ornamental devices." Rather than pointing to the superficiality of style, therefore,

the term actually suggests that style "is a vital and useful quality," which "aids the orator's practical purpose, for by it he compels attention and bends the audience to his will."

26. Michiko Kakutani, "Staking out California."
27. Ibid.
28. Ibid.
29. Michiko Kakutani, "From a Life of Wealth."
30. Michiko Kakutani, "The End of Life as She Knew It."
31. Kakutani, "In Loss, a Mother Explores Dark Questions and Bright Memories."
32. John Leonard, "Books of The Times."
33. John Leonard, "The Black Album." Leonard uses similar language in his 2001 review of *Political Fictions*, writing "to *Political Fictions*, besides her black conceit, her sonar ear, her radar eye and her ice-pick/laser beam/night-scope sniper prose, she brings Tiger Ops assets of temperament" ("Who Stole Democracy").
34. Roiphe, *Messy Lives*, 104.
35. Joan Didion, *Political Fictions*, 736.
36. Michiko Kakutani, "Staking."
37. Caitlin Flanagan, "The Autumn of Joan Didion."
38. John Leonard, introduction to *We Tell Ourselves Stories*, ix.
39. Joan Didion, "A Preface," *Slouching Towards Bethlehem*, 7.
40. Sara Davidson, "Visit," 19.
41. Didion, interview by Susan Stamberg, 26–27.
42. Joan Didion, "A Preface," *Slouching*, 6.
43. Didion, "Goodbye to All That," *Slouching*, 176.
44. Didion, "Georgia O'Keeffe," 272.
45. Didion, interview by Hilton Als.
46. Didion, "The White Album," 210.
47. Barbara Grizzuti Harrison, "Joan Didion: Only Disconnect."
48. Kakutani, "Staking."
49. Flanagan, "Autumn."
50. Didion, "White Album," 185.
51. Didion, interview by Linda Kuehl.
52. Didion, "Notes from a Native Daughter," 131.
53. Ibid., 135.
54. Didion, *Where I Was From*, 962.
55. Didion, "Girl of the Golden West," 584.
56. Didion, "The White Album," 186.
57. Didion, "In the Islands." Didion describes herself as coming "into adult life equipped with an essentially romantic ethic" (278), even though she has, by her early thirties, "misplaced whatever slight faith she ever had in the social contract . . . in the whole grand pattern of human endeavor" (277).

58. Didion, "Comrade Laski, C.P.U.S.A. (M.-L.)," 53.
59. Ibid.
60. Didion, "Good Citizens," 243.
61. Thomas Mallon, "On Second Thought." As Mallon notes, "Didion herself became a writer so famously distrustful of abstraction that the skeptical quotation marks she liked to put around all but the commonest of nouns constituted an important element in one of the most recognizable—and brilliant—literary styles to emerge in America during the past four decades."
62. Didion, "Slouching Towards Bethlehem," 93.
63. Didion, "The Women's Movement," 261.
64. Mark Royden Winchell, 37. Winchell observes that Didion has often remarked on her aversion to politics, and he correctly points out that this does not mean she is indifferent to politics, but, rather that she resists conventional ideology and therefore should be understood as "a partisan not of 'causes' but of the individual human spirit."
65. Didion, *Salvador*, 92.
66. Didion, interview by Hilton Als.
67. Didion, *Political Fictions*, 733–35.
68. Natasha Wimmer, "Telling It Like It Is."
69. Didion, interview by Hilton Als.
70. Didion, "Good Citizens," 244–45.
71. Dennis Rygiel, "On the Neglect," 394. Pointing to "the problematical literary status of nonfiction and especially recent nonfiction," Rygiel argues that because poetry and fiction are considered the "central literary forms," by literary scholars, genres of writing such as the essay are considered secondary forms unworthy of serious critical attention.
72. Katherine Usher Henderson, *Joan Didion*, 136.
73. Muggli, "Poetics," 402–403.
74. Ibid., 403.
75. Anderson, *Style*, x.
76. Muggli, "Poetics," 407.
77. Ibid., 408.
78. Didion, "On the Morning After the Sixties," 330.
79. Muggli, "Poetics," 408.
80. Shortly after Muggli's piece appeared, John Schilb's 1989 "Deconstructing Didion: Poststructuralist Rhetorical Theory in the Composition Classroom" was published. Unlike Muggli, Schilb does not focus on the role Didion's style plays in her rhetoric, but, like Muggli, he explores how her reportage is rhetorical rather than empirical and realistic, yet no less powerful. His analysis is intended less to unpack the poetics of Didion's prose and more to propose how composition instructors might teach a poststructuralist (and, in particular, deconstructive) approach to the rhetoric of nonfiction in order to prompt more self-reflective student writing without

discouraging students from seeing texts as so indeterminate as to frustrate their efforts. He therefore undertakes a deconstructive analysis of the discursive features of Didion's "Some Dreamers of the Golden Dream," the first essay in *Slouching Towards Bethlehem*, which concerns events occurring on October 7, 1969, when Lucille Miller allegedly murdered her husband Cork by setting their car on fire.
 81. Anderson, *Style*, 180.
 82. Ibid., 179.
 83. Ibid., 134–40.
 84. Didion, "On Going Home," 126.
 85. Anderson, *Style*, 138.
 86. Ibid., 172.
 87. Didion, *Salvador*, 14.
 88. Didion, "Goodbye to All That," 172.
 89. Didion, "Sentimental Journeys," 715.
 90. Didion, interview by Hilton Als.
 91. Didion, "A Foreword," *Political Fictions*, 733.
 92. Sara Davidson, *Joan: Forty Years of Life*, Loc 567.
 93. Joan Didion, interview by Charlie Rose.

# Chapter 1

 1. Louis Menand, "Out of Bethlehem."
 2. "The Birth of 'The New Journalism'; Eyewitness Report by Tom Wolfe," 45. It is unclear who coined the term or even when it appeared. Writing in 1972, Wolfe noted that in the mid-1960s, "New Journalism . . . was in the air . . . ; it was not something that anyone took note of in print at the time, so far as I can remember. I have no idea who coined the term the New Journalism or when it was coined. I have never even liked the term. Any movement, group, party, program, philosophy or theory that goes under a name with 'new' in it is just begging for trouble, of course. But it is the term that eventually caught on. At the time, the mid-1960s, one was aware only that there was some sort of new artistic excitement in journalism."
 3. Ibid.
 4. To be clear, the prose in these excerpts represents, as the foreword to the book notes, "an intermediate stage of writing, between shorthand and first drafts. . . . There are sentences that are ideas for sentences, paragraphs that are ideas for scenes" (xii). Some portions of the text are explicitly set off with the subheading "Note:" or "Random notes from the weekend." But the richness of details imbuing these lines—whether in "notes" or narrative passages—is characteristic of all of her nonfiction writing, as is her mixture of long and short sentences, interspersed

with fragments and unconcerned, at times, with proper punctuation. Impacted by variations in phrasing and length, these sentences mix to provide a tonal richness that is highly engaging and redolent of the landscapes she travels.

5. Joan Didion, *South and West: From a Notebook*, 32. Hereafter cited in text.
6. Constance Hale, "The Sentence as a Miniature Narrative."
7. Michael J. Arlen "Notes on the New Journalism."
8. Gay Talese, *Fame and Obscurity*, vii.
9. Menand notes that Silvers was not interviewed by Daugherty and argues that this "leaves a major hole in her biography," as Silvers was, according to Menand, "the key figure in Didion's journalistic transformation."
10. Ellen G. Friedman, "The Didion Sensibility: An Analysis," 82.
11. Jemima Hunt, "The Didion Bible."
12. Didion, interview by Hilton Als.
13. Tracy Daugherty, *The Last Love Song*, 421.
14. Noël Valis, "Fear and Torment in El Salvador," 117–18. "Internally El Salvador's long history of military rule and a powerful landed oligarchy had created by the 1970s an explosive social and economic situation, ideologically translated into an extreme Right and an extreme Left. An archaic social structure had worsened with a declining economy and the influx of peasants into city slums. Social and political activism, in which the Catholic Church and Christian base communities played an increasingly significant role, brought on the wrath of the extreme Right, which seemed incapable of distinguishing between legitimate peaceful dissent and armed opposition. By nearly all accounts, most of the killings, tortures, disappearances were carried out by the armed forces, death squads, and security forces."
15. Ibid.
16. Ibid.
17. Michael McClintock, "A Glimmer of Justice for El Salvador."
18. Mark Falcoff, "Two Weeks."
19. In analyzing "Some Dreamers of the Golden Dream," Schilb focuses on how literal/figural oppositions in Didion's essay are unstable and argues that she presents herself as a recorder of the events described rather a "storyteller," despite the fact that she clearly manipulates the arrangement of the narrative in order to promote certain interpretations of the events detailed. The nonlinear discourse of this particular essay, as he demonstrates in columns, clearly does not match the chronology of the actual events, with the result that readers are led to accept Didion's implication that the principals invite their own fate by choosing to ignore the lessons of history. Additionally, he notes how the first sentence of this essay "This is a story about love and death in the golden land, and begins with the country" (3)—omits references to Didion and so suggests her neutrality and objectivity rather than her role as shaper of the reality reflected in the text. This suggestion of neutrality, this choice of Didion's not to specify "the coordinates of her own role as investigator"

(267), even as she skillfully plots the sequence of her narrative, he argues, is ultimately what makes this a rhetorical piece rather a purely mimetic one. These same strategies are on evidence in *Salvador*.

20. Susan Braudy, "Sisters in Misery."
21. Leonard Wilcox, "Narrative Technique and the Theme of Historical Continuity,"68–80.
22. Didion, "Why I Write," 6.
23. Didion, interview by Hilton Als.
24. Lili Anolik, "How Joan Didion the Writer Became Joan Didion the Legend." "She's cool-eyed and cold-blooded, and that coolness and coldness—chilling, of course, but also bracing—is the source of her fascination as much as her artistry is; the source of her glamour too, and her seductiveness, because she *is* seductive, deeply. What she is is a femme fatale, and irresistible. She's our kiss of death, yet we open our mouths, kiss back."
25. Menand, "Out."
26. Didion, "Fixed Ideas: America Since 9.11," 12–14.
27. Identification, or the act of a rhetorician identifying her cause with an audience's interests, is the one of the most elemental characteristic of rhetoric, and in her other nonfiction Didion frequently employs "we" to suggest that she and the reader share beliefs and habits. This can be seen, for instance, in the opening to "The White Album," when she writes "We look for the sermon in the suicide, for the social or moral lesson in the murder of five. We interpret what we see, select the most workable of the multiple choices. We live entirely, especially if we are writers, by the imposition of a narrative line upon disparate images, by the 'ideas' with which we have learned to freeze the shifting phantasmagoria which is our actual experience" (185).
28. Didion, *Salvador*, 103. Hereafter cited in text.
29. Tom Wolfe, *The New Journalism*, 50.
30. Michael Wood, "The New Journalism."
31. Daugherty, *Last Love Song*, 339.
32. Valis, "Fear and Torment," 120.
33. Didion, interview by Hilton Als.
34. Ibid.
35. Jane Harred, "The Heart of Darkness," 14. As Harred notes "Obviously, though, her insistence that the legitimacy of any view and any discourse must be relative to its social, historical, and discursive contexts puts the authority of all viewpoints, all discourses, at risk, including her own."
36. Valis, "Fear," 121.
37. John McClure, "Writing Off Salvador," 112–113.
38. Ibid., 111.
39. Falcoff, "Two Weeks."
40. Valis, "Fear," 122.
41. Warren Hoge, "A Land Without Solid Ground."

42. Daugherty, *Last Love Song*, 428.

43. Didion, interview by Hilton Als.

44. Nevin Laib, "Conciseness and Amplification," 449. Amplification is essential to explanation insofar as it is "a basic skill of interpretation and inquiry, a means through which we explore and articulate what we perceive and what we mean."

45. Chaim Perelman and Lucie Olbrechts-Tyteca, *The New Rhetoric*, 117. In rhetoric, "the thing that is present to the consciousness assumes . . . an importance" that items not selected do not have.

46. Chris Anderson, *Style*, 139. Anderson describes these efforts as a "rhetoric of process," one through which Didion, in part by modifying initial statements without attempting to synthesize them, makes it appear that it is the process of writing itself that allows her to explore.

47. Carl H. Klaus, "Essayists on the Essay," 155–75. Klaus examines, more comprehensively than I can here, the many ways the essay has been defined, categorized, and understood since its beginnings with Montaigne, in his "Essayists on the Essay." It is worth noting here, however, that one of his main points is that the essayist tends to assign a very important role in the essay to the essayist him or herself with the result that much attention is given over to reflection on the self interacting with the subject as well as the construction of that self in the pursuit of the audience's good will.

48. Laib, "Conciseness," 449.

49. Richard Leahy, "Style Matters: Helping Students Develop Good Style," 7–8. In demonstrating how Didion's style is inventive and impactful, Leahy analyzes the opening passage from Didion's "Many Mansions," and points out how Didion's frequent use of anaphora (sometimes paired with antithesis and isocolon) creates contrast in imagery and ideas, tying "various descriptions together so closely that they comment on each other." Leahy concedes that he cannot determine if Didion is in control of her choices, or if she could name them herself, but argues that they are no less powerful for being unconscious or habitual. His analysis of her prose, albeit it far too brief to constitute a serious consideration of her prose style, is the type of stylistic analysis for which Didion's work calls.

50. Hypotyposis is the figure which permits the rhetor to present things so as to make them seem to happen right before the audience's eyes so that they become present to that audience.

51. Perelman and Olbrechts-Tyteca, *Treatise*, 117.

52. Brian Vickers, *In Defense of Rhetoric*, 320.

53. Edward Corbett and Robert Connors, *Classical Rhetoric for the Modern Student*, 383.

54. Didion, *Salvador*, 14.

55. Daugherty observes that Didion's revisions of *Play It as It Lays* evidence a pattern of moving adverbs from after the verbs and placing them before the verbs, thereby "forc[ing] a greater distance between subject and verb." He brings this up as a reminder to readers that they should be careful not to "dismiss the artist's craft" (288).

56. Didion, *Salvador*, 57: "(*Desaparecer*, or "disappear," is in Spanish both an intransitive and a transitive verb, and this flexibility has been adopted by those speaking English in El Salvador, as in *John Sullivan was disappeared from the Sheraton*; *the government disappeared the students*, there being no equivalent situation, and so no equivalent word, in English-speaking cultures)."

57. Didion, "On Keeping a Notebook," 102.
58. Didion, "Many Mansions," 230.
59. Bawer, "Dreamwork," 94.
60. Eder, "Little World," 830.
61. McClure, "Writing," 110. Hereafter cited in text.
62. Lehmann-Haupt, "Books."
63. Dan Wakefield, "People, Places, and Personalities."
64. Didion, "On Going Home," 125.
65. Braudy, "Sisters."
66. Didion, "Islands," 277, 278.
67. Didion, interview by Frank Rich.
68. Daugherty, 371–72.
69. Christopher Wilson, "The Underwater Narrative, Joan Didion's Miami," 15–23. Wilson argues that reviewers of *Miami*, published four years after *Salvador*, "overlooked Didion's most compelling cultural topic: the relation between contemporary politics and rhetoric," and he proceeds to offer one of the few stylistic analyses of Didion's political critiques. He devotes just under three pages to analyzing what he sees as her "three main stylistic strategies": long and overqualified sentences and paragraphs that act as "spatial analogies" prompting readers to recognize the structure of "rhetorical evasions" generated by politicians; syntax that "asks her readers to experience the 'gaps' and 'angles' within political abstractions and rationalizations when they are imposed upon hemispheric conflicts"; and complicated use of tenses that prompts readers to analyze how the memorialization of past events is rhetorically structured (21–23). While Wilson does not always point to specific passages to make all of these claims, he is precise in his conclusions, as when he argues that her "long and overqualified sentences and paragraphs" (which are familiar to any reader of Didion), do not merely express "an idiosyncratic personal style" or reflect "'tropical' malaise" but rather are constructed in such a way that they mirror and therefore reinforce the content they deliver (15).
70. Didion, "Good Citizens," 241.

# Chapter 2

1. Didion, "In the Realm of the Fisher King," 566.
2. Ibid., 568.
3. Ibid., 576.

4. Didion, "L.A. *Noir*," 650.
5. Didion, "Times Mirror Square," 680.
6. Didion, interview by Hilton Als.
7. Ibid.
8. Didion, "Sentimental Journeys," 704. Hereafter cited in text.
9. Their convictions were vacated in 2002, and the men won a $41 million suit against the city in 2014.
10. Didion, interview by Hilton Als.
11. Jim Buck, who died in 2013, was widely considered to be New York City's first professional dog walker, and he was a highly recognizable and well-known figure in the city for decades.
12. Anderson, *Style*, 142.
13. Ibid., 139.
14. Carl Klaus and Ned Stuckey-French, *Essayists on the Essay*, 169.
15. Muggli, "Poetics," 405. Muggli comments on a similar tendency of Didion's to invent details without explicitly claiming they are real—he calls this tendency, her "generalizing habit of mind," and offers the following example: "Sometimes such detail is obviously invented ('I recall a time when the dogs barked every night and the moon was always full' [WA, p. 41]). And sometimes the detail fits so precisely that it can easily slip by as reported fact. Since the new California governor's mansion, for example, has not been lived in and has no carpets or drapes, the bookshelves are undoubtedly empty. Yet Didion writes, 'In the entire house there are only enough bookshelves for a set of the World Book and some Books of the Month, plus maybe three Royal Doulton figurines and a back file of Connoisseur' (WA, 'Many Mansions,' p. 69). Didion has not seen these books and knick-knacks; she has hypothesized them as the possessions typical of people like the Reagans."
16. Corbett and Connors, *Classical Rhetoric*, 385.
17. Wimmer, "Telling."
18. Mary-Kay Wilmer, "What If You Hadn't Been Home?"
19. Davidson, "A Visit," 14.
20. Didion, "Sentimental," 727.
21. Kenneth Burke, *Language*, 44–62.
22. Anderson, *Style*, 140.

# Chapter 3

1. Didion, *Political Fictions*, 733. Hereafter cited in text.
2. Interview by Sean Hagan. Didion, as has been noted elsewhere in this book, frequently rhetorically positions herself as an outsider, the better to achieve the critical distance necessary to seeing what goes unseen or deliberately ignored by those participating in political and public mythmaking. There is a sense in which

this "outsider" perspective seems to spring from a genuine feeling of being dislocated no matter her physical or intellectual position. In a 2006 interview with Sean O'Hagan for *The Guardian*, the interviewer asks her, as a Californian transplanted to New York, where she feels she most belongs. She responds: "Oh, California. For sure. I'm not really attuned to here. At one level, I feel perfectly comfortable in New York, but I really believe that is because it is one of those cities where people feel comfortable wherever they are from. The only times I felt a deep attachment to the city was in my twenties, and again after 9/11. But I would say for sure that I have a Californian sensibility." When asked to define the Californian sensibility, she explains: "Well. It's an outsider's sensibility. Definitely. On the edge of things. People don't feel at home in Los Angeles if they come from somewhere else. It takes a long time to get it. And people who come from there tend to have an outside point of view. That's certainly true in my case."

3. Wilson points out that Didion's interest lies not only in the "various rhetorical strategies" of politicians and their staff but, more significantly, lies in the "'residues': traces in syntax or the 'accumulation of small particulars' between speakers' intentions and the language they use." He argues her style is deliberate and functional, that her goal is to "mirror, retrace, make us feel the effects of these historical and political residues in her own syntax" (21).

4. Mark Tredinnick, *Writing Well*, Loc 1603.
5. Richard M. Coe, "Generative Rhetoric," 133.
6. Walter Ong, S.J., *Orality and Literacy*.
7. Richard Lanham, *Analyzing Prose*, 65.
8. Francis Christensen and Bonniejean Christensen, *A New Rhetoric*, 22.
9. Ibid., *New Rhetoric*, 23.
10. Walter J. Ong: *Orality and Literacy*. In the third chapter of this work, Ong lays out several characteristics of oral speech. It is, he says, formulaic, aggregative, rhythmic, repetitive, and additive, all features that ensure speeches are emphatic and memorable. These characteristics of language were and are essential in primarily oral cultures, where people cannot depend on texts to recall information.
11. Ibid., 37.
12. Ibid., 34.
13. Ibid.
14. Fahnestock, "Figures of Argument," 119.
15. Fahnestock, *Rhetorical Figures*, 51.
16. Fahnestock, "Figures," 129.

# Chapter 4

1. Joan Didion, *The Year of Magical Thinking*, 225. Hereafter cited in text.
2. Ibid., 148.

3. This book was preceded by her 2003 memoir *Where I Was From*, which, while it includes a great deal of family history and personal meditation, takes as its main focus California.

4. Scott Russell Sanders, "The Singular First Person," 667. In this article Sanders discusses his motivations for writing about his own experiences, arguing that an essay will only find an audience if the essayist moves beyond the merely personal to write about universal experiences and concerns.

5. Cicero, in Book 2 of *De Oratore*, says that the highest duties of the orator are *probare, conciliare, movare* (to teach, to please, to move).

6. Joan Didion, interview by Sara Davidson.

7. Boris Kachka, "I Was No Longer Afraid to Die."

8. Robert Pinsky, "'The Year of Magical Thinking': Goodbye to All That."

9. Emma Brockes, "Joan Didion: Life After Death."

10. Jonathan Van Meter, "When Everything Changes."

11. Didion, "Why I Write," 7.

12. Van Meter, "When Everything."

13. William Strunk Jr. and E. B. White, *The Elements of Style*, 23.

14. John Dawkins, "Teaching Punctuation as a Rhetorical Tool," 534. Dawkins notes that "conventional punctuation is grammar based—marks are prescribed in terms of grammatical structure—but what 'good writers' do, writers like Orwell, is punctuate according to their intended meaning, their intended emphasis." Furthermore, he suggests that punctuation denoting the end of a sentence denotes the maximum degree of separation between ideas contained in adjacent clauses. Didion's use of periods to break up the chain of clauses opening this paragraph graphically represents the shock and disconnect she experiences in processing these memories.

15. Joseph Williams, *Style: Ten Lessons in Clarity and Grace*, 197. Williams explains that words can be classified from heaviest (nominalizations) to lightest (prepositions), and proposes that ending a sentence with a heavy word can provide a "satisfying climactic thump."

16. Didion, "The Women's Movement," 259.

17. Ibid., 258.

18. Joan Didion, *Blue Nights*, 43. Hereafter cited in text.

19. It is particularly ironic, and sad, to compare Didion's present memories of a troubled child with her observations in 1966. Then she wrote, in "On Keeping a Notebook," "Although I have felt compelled to write things down since I was five years old, I doubt that my daughter ever will, for she is a singularly blessed and accepting child, delighted with life exactly as life presents itself to her, unafraid to go to sleep and unafraid to wake up. Keepers of private notebooks are a different breed altogether, lonely and resistant rearrangers of things, anxious malcontents, children afflicted apparently at birth with some presentiment of loss," 102.

20. Didion, *Year*, 140.

21. Jeanne Fahnestock, *Rhetorical Figures*, 51.

22. Constance Hale, "Sentences Crisp, Sassy, Stirring."
23. Corbett and Connors, *Classical Rhetoric*, 392.
24. Jeffrey Berman, *Writing Widowhood*, 166. Berman observes that this last line is particularly easy to misread. It is not the case, he points out, that Didion promises that she will remember her daughter every day, a claim many bereaved people make. Rather, Didion is claiming that she recalls every day of her *daughter's* life, and it is these memories she fears losing. Such a claim speaks to the intense bond Didion had with Quintana and emphasizes, in the very last words of this work, the enormous impact of her loss.

## Conclusion

1. Kakutani, "Staking."
2. Sara Davidson, "'I'm Not Certain Anymore,'" 55.
3. Brett Lang, "Griffin Dunne on Joan Didion Doc's Kickstarter Success."
4. Nathan Heller, "Why Joan Didion Matters More Than Ever."
5. Harrison, "Only Disconnect."
6. Dwight Garner, "The Last Thing He Wanted."
7. Amis, "Didion's Style."
8. Didion here refers to the notorious review of her writing by Barbara Grizzuti Harrison, which she found so wounding she brought it up twenty-six years later in a 2005 interview with *New York Books'* Jonathan Van Meter. "I can still remember the first line," she says, "because it was so far out of left field." She then paraphrases, "Am I expected to admire a woman who would burden her daughter with the name Quintana Roo?" Indeed, Harrison did begin with this line before launching into a full-scale assault on Didion's work, and her style in particular.
9. By which he seems to mean New Journalism, though it is not clear that he might not just be referring to her body of work.
10. Wakefield, "Places, People and Personalities."
11. Joyce Carol Oates, "A Taut Novel of Disorder: A Book of Common Prayer."
12. Flanagan, "Autumn."
13. Didion, *Blue*, 8.
14. Didion, *Fictions*, 763.
15. Ibid., 768.
16. Didion, "Why," 5.
17. Didion, "Some Dreamers of the Golden Dream,"14.
18. Didion, "Why," 6.
19. Didion, "Slouching," 97.
20. There are, of course, many exceptions, perhaps most notably Martin Luther King Jr., born in 1929, and Gloria Steinem, born, like Didion, in 1934.
21. Didion, "On the Morning after the Sixties," 330. Hereafter cited in text.

22. Didion, "Where the Kissing Never Stops," 51.
23. Didion, "John Wayne, A Love Song," 38.
24. Didion, "California Dreaming," 63.
25. Didion, "Slouching," 71.
26. Didion, "White Album," 192–96.
27. Bawer, "Only Disconnect," 88–89. Bawer offers one of the most charged and explicit attacks on Didion's tendency to name drop, "And even when she's describing how her psychological problems incapacitated her, she manages to work in the names of her and Dunne's hoity-toity watering holes."
28. George L Dillon, *Constructing Texts*, 23.
29. Jack Newfield, "Is There a 'New Journalism,'" 45–47. As Newfield wrote, back in 1972, when New Journalism was still gaining steam, "what's called the New Journalism is really a dozen different styles of writing."
30. Didion, "White Album," 202–203.
31. Didion, "In the Islands," 278.
32. Wakefield, "Places."
33. Oates, "Taut."
34. Ibid.
35. Joan Didion, "Fixed Opinions, or The Hinge of History."
36. Didion, "Some Dreamers," 13.
37. Ibid.
38. John Banville, "Joan Didion Mourns Her Daughter."
39. Didion, "Fixed."
40. Ibid.
41. Ibid.
42. Jacques Ellul, *Propaganda: The Formation of Men's Attitudes*, 62–63. Ellul defines sociological propaganda as "the group of manifestations by which any society seeks to integrate the maximum number of individuals into itself, to unify its members' behavior according to a pattern, to spread its style of life abroad, and thus to impose itself on other groups." In labeling such propaganda "sociological," he hopes to demonstrate "that the entire group, consciously or not, expresses itself in this fashion; and to indicate, secondly, that its influence aims much more at an entire style of life than at opinions or even one particular course of behavior."
43. Didion, "Doris Lessing," 265.
44. Didion, "Notes Toward a Dreampolitik," 249. Talking to Brother Theo about his plans to move his church (The Friendly Bible Apostolic Church) from California to Tennessee to avoid an earthquake, she quotes him as saying, "From the natural point of view I didn't care to go to Murfreesboro at all. . . . We just bought this place, it's the nicest place we ever had. But I put it up to the Lord, and the Lord said *put it up for sale*. Care for a Dr. Pepper?"
45. Didion, "Sentimental," 723.
46. Didion, "Times Mirror Square," 674.

47. Didion, "L.A. *Noir*," 653.
48. Ibid., 654.
49. Didion, "Times Mirror," 677.
50. Didion, "Sentimental," 701.
51. Didion, "On Morality,"124.
52. Didion, "Notes," 249.
53. Didion, "Islands," 285.
54. Didion, "Citizens," 241.
55. Ibid., 242–43.
56. Didion, "Women's Movement," 263.
57. Ibid., 261–62.
58. Didion, "Islands," 285.
59. Didion, "White Album," 203.
60. Davidson, "A Visit," 14.
61. Didion, interview by Hilton Als.
62. She credits Silvers for encouraging her to use the computer to compose longer pieces.
63. Amy Wilentz, "Where the Morning Went."
64. Winterowd, "Style: A Matter of Manner," 164.
65. Didion, interview by Stamberg, 22.
66. Didion, "In the Realm of the Fisher King," 577.
67. Didion, "Sentimental," 689–90.
68. Didion, interview by Hilton Als. At various points, Didion has reflected on her practice, as a very young writer, of copying, word-for-word, canonical writers. Such imitation exercises have a long history in both the discipline of Rhetoric and the field of American Composition studies, as I've written about in previous articles and conference papers. Despite, however, my awareness of how "contagious" style can be, I had not anticipated how much my time spent reading, hand-copying, and analyzing Didion's prose over several years would infect my own prose style. As I conclude this work, I must acknowledge that my sentences have become at least partially infected by Didion's style. Even as I have consciously worked against imitation, her rhythms seem to have become lodged in my head, my sentences, for example, becoming longer and more loaded with modifiers and parentheticals. As I worked on editing them, I could only hope they were even partially as effective and graceful as her own.

# Bibliography

Amis, Martin. "Joan Didion's Style." *London Review of Books*, February 7, 1980. http://www.lrb.co.uk/v02/n02/martin-amis/joan-Didions-style.

Anderson, Chris. *Style as Argument: Contemporary American Nonfiction*. Carbondale: Southern Illinois University Press, 1987.

Anolik, Lili. "How Joan Didion the Writer Became Joan Didion the Legend." *Vanity Fair*, 2016. https://www.vanityfair.com/culture/2016/02/joan-Didion-writer-los-angeles.

Arlen, Michael J. "Notes on the New Journalism." *The Atlantic*, May 1972. https://www.theatlantic.com/magazine/archive/1972/05/notes-on-the-new-journalism/376276/.

Banville, John. "Joan Didion Mourns Her Daughter." Review of *Blue Nights*, by Joan Didion. *The New York Times*, November 3, 2011. http://www.nytimes.com/2011/11/06/books/review/blue-nights-by-joan-Didion-book-review.html.

Bawer, Bruce. "Didion's Dreamwork." *The Hudson Review* 60, no. 1 (2007): 85–103. http://www.jstor.org/stable/20464676.

Berman, Jeffrey. *Writing Widowhood: The Landscapes of Bereavement*. Albany: State University of New York Press, 2015.

Braudy, Susan. "'Sisters in Misery': What It Was Like to Interview Joan Didion at Home in 1977." *Jezebel*, March 30, 2017. https://pictorial.jezebel.com/sisters-in-misery-what-it-was-like-to-interview-joan-d-1793791955.

Brockes, Emma. "Joan Didion: Life After Death." Review of *Blue Nights*, by Joan Didion. *The Guardian*, October 21, 2011. http://www.theguardian.com/books/2011/oct/21/joan-Didion-blue-nights.

Burke, Kenneth. *Language as Symbolic Action: Essays on Life, Literature, and Method*. Berkeley: University of California Press, 1966.

———. *A Rhetoric of Motives*. Berkeley: University of California Press, 1969.

Christensen, Francis, and Bonniejean Christensen. *A New Rhetoric*. New York: Harper and Row, 1976.

Cicero. *On the Orator: Books 1-2*. Translated by E. W. Sutton, H. Rackham. Cambridge: Harvard University Press, 1942.

Coe, Richard M. "Generative Rhetoric." In *Theorizing Composition: A Critical Sourcebook of Theory and Scholarship in Contemporary Composition Studies*, edited by Mary Lynch Kennedy, 131–36. Connecticut: Greenwood Press, 1998.

Corbett, Edward P. J., and Robert J. Connors, *Classical Rhetoric for the Modern Student*. Oxford: Oxford University Press, 1994.

Covino, William A. *Magic, Rhetoric, and Literacy: An Eccentric History of the Composing Imagination*. Albany: State University of New York Press, 1994.

Daugherty, Tracy. *The Last Love Song: A Biography of Joan Didion*. New York: St. Martin's, 2015.

Davidson, Sara. *Joan: Forty Years of Life, Loss, and Friendship with Joan Didion*. San Francisco: Byliner, 2011. Kindle.

Dawkins, John. "Teaching Punctuation as a Rhetorical Tool." *College Composition and Communication* 46, no. 4 (December 1995): 533–48.

Didion, Joan. *Blue Nights*. New York: Vintage International, 2011.

———. *We Tell Ourselves Stories in Order to Live: Collected Nonfiction*. Edited by John Leonard. New York: Alfred A. Knopf, 2006.

———. "Cautionary Tales." Interview by Susan Stamberg. In *Joan Didion Essays & Conversations*, edited by Ellen G. Friedman, 22–28. Princeton: Ontario Review Press, 1984.

———. "Fixed Opinions, or The Hinge of History." *The New York Review of Books*, January 16, 2003. http://www.nybooks.com/articles/archives/2003/jan/16/fixed-opinions-or-the-hinge-of-history/.

———. "'I'm Not Certain Anymore': A Conversation with Joan Didion." Interview by Sara Davidson. *Time*, November 7, 2011. http://content.time.com/time/magazine/article/0,9171,2097963,00.html.

———. Interview by Charlie Rose, November 3, 2011. Video, 53:35. http://www.charlierose.com/watch/60000926.

———. "Joan Didion, The Art of Nonfiction No. 1." Interview by Hilton Als. *Paris Review*, no. 176 (Spring 2006). http://www.theparisreview.org/interviews/5601/the-art-of-nonfiction-no-1-joan-Didion.

———. "Joan Didion, The Art of Nonfiction No. 1." Interview by Linda Kuehl. *Paris Review*, no. 74 (Fall–Winter 1978). http://www.theparisreview.org/interviews/3439/the-art-of-fiction-no-71-joan-Didionvs.

———. "Joan Didion Buries the Baby." Interview by Sara Davidson. Blog. http://www.saradavidson.com/blog/2011/10/joan-Didion-buries-the-baby.html.

———. "Political Fictions." Interview by Frank Rich. C-SPAN, November 5, 2001. Video, 57:26. https://www.c-span.org/video/?167370-1/political-fictions.

———. *Salvador*. New York: Vintage, 1983.

———. *South and West: From a Notebook*. New York: Alfred A. Knopf, 2017.

———. "A Visit with Joan Didion." Interview by Sara Davidson in *Joan Didion Essays & Conversations*, edited by Ellen G. Friedman, 13–21. Princeton: Ontario Review Press, 1984.

———. "Why I Write." In *Joan Didion Essays & Conversations*, edited by Ellen G. Friedman, 5–12. Princeton: Ontario Review Press, 1984.
———. *The Year of Magical Thinking*. New York: Alfred A. Knopf, 2005.
———. "The Years of Writing Magically." Interview by Sean O'Hagan. *The Guardian*, August 20, 2006. https://www.theguardian.com/books/2006/aug/20/biography.features.
Dillon, George L. *Constructing Texts*. Bloomington: Indiana University Press, 1981.
Donadio, Rachel. "Every Day Is All There Is." Review of *The Year of Magical Thinking*, by Joan Didion. *The New York Times* Oct. 9, 2005. http://www.nytimes.com/2005/10/09/books/review/09donadio.html?pagewanted=all.
Eder, George Jackson. "The Little World of Joan Didion." *National Review* 35, no. 13 (1983): 829–30. Academic Search Premier.
Ellul, Jacques. *Propaganda: The Formation of Men's Attitudes*. New York: Vintage Books, 1965.
Fahnestock, Jeanne. "Figures of Argument." *Informal Logic* 24, no. 2 (2004): 115–35.
———. *Rhetorical Figures in Science*. Oxford: Oxford University Press, 1999.
Falcoff, Mark. "Two Weeks." *Commentary Magazine*, May 1, 1983, 66–69. https://www.commentarymagazine.com/articles/salvador-by-joan-Didion/.
Flanagan, Caitlin. "The Autumn of Joan Didion," *The Atlantic Monthly*, Dec 20, 2011. http://www.theatlantic.com/magazine/archive/2012/01/the-autumn-of-joan-Didion/308851/.
Frascella, Lawrence. "In 'Blue Nights,' Didion Delivers A Mother's Eulogy." Review of *Blue Nights*, by Joan Didion. *NPR*, October 29, 2011. https://www.npr.org/2011/10/29/141690686/in-blue-nights-Didion-delivers-a-mothers-eulogy.
Freire, Paolo. *Pedagogy of the Oppressed*. New York: Herder and Herder, 1970.
Garner, Dwight. "The Last Thing He Wanted." Review of *The Last Thing He Wanted*, by Joan Didion. *Salon*, August 30, 1996. http://www.salon.com/1996/08/30/sneakpeeks_145/.
Grizzuti Harrison, Barbara. "Joan Didion: Only Disconnect." 1980. http://www.writing.upenn.edu/~afilreis/103/Didion-per-harrison.html.
Hale, Constance. "Sentences Crisp, Sassy, Stirring," *The New York Times*, May 28, 2012. http://opinionator.blogs.nytimes.com/2012/05/28/sentences-crisp-sassy-stirring/?_r=0.
———. "The Sentence as a Miniature Narrative," *The New York Times* March 19, 2012. https://opinionator.blogs.nytimes.com/2012/03/19/the-sentence-as-a-miniature-narrative/.
Harred, Jane. "The Heart of Darkness in Joan Didion's 'Salvador.'" *College Literature* 25, no. 2 (1998): 1–16. http://www.jstor.org.ezproxy.bu.edu/stable/25112374.
Heller, Nathan. "Why Joan Didion Matters More Than Ever." *Vogue*, November 12, 2014. http://www.vogue.com/4109205/joan-Didion-essays-matter/?mbid=social_twitter.
Henderson, Katherine Usher. *Joan Didion*. New York: Frederick Ungar, 1981.

Hoge, Warren. "A Land Without Solid Ground." Review of *Salvador*, by Joan Didion. *The New York Times*, March 13, 1983. http://www.nytimes.com/1983/03/13/books/a-land-without-solid-ground.html?pagewanted=all.

Hunt, Jemima "The Didion Bible." *The Guardian*, January 11, 2003. https://www.theguardian.com/books/2003/jan/12/fiction.society.

Kachka, Boris. "I Was No Longer Afraid to Die. I Was Now Afraid Not to Die." *New York Magazine*, October 16, 2011. http://nymag.com/arts/books/features/joan-Didion-2011-10/.

Kakutani, Michiko. "The End of Life as She Knew It." Review of *The Year of Magical Thinking*, by Joan Didion. *The New York Times*, October 4, 2005. http://www.nytimes.com/2005/10/04/books/the-end-of-life-as-she-knew-it.html.

———. "From a Life of Wealth into a Life of Danger." Review of *The Last Thing He Wanted*, by Joan Didion. *The New York Times*, September 3, 1996. http://www.nytimes.com/1996/09/03/books/from-a-life-of-wealth-into-a-life-of-danger.html.

———. "In Loss, A Mother Explores Dark Questions and Bright Memories." Review of *Blue Nights*, by Joan Didion. *The New York Times*, October 31, 2011. http://www.nytimes.com/2011/11/01/books/blue-nights-by-joan-Didion-review.html.

———. "Joan Didion: Staking out California." Review of *The White Album*, by Joan Didion. *The New York Times*, June 10, 1979. http://www.nytimes.com/1979/06/10/books/Didion-calif.html?pagewanted=all.

Kennedy, George. *Quintilian*. New York: Twayne, 1969.

Klaus, Carl, and Ned Stuckey-French. *Essayists on the Essay: From Montaigne to Our Time*. Iowa City: University of Iowa Press, 2012.

Laib, Nevin. "Conciseness and Amplification." *College Composition and Communication* 41, no. 4 (1990): 443–59.

Lang, Brett. "Griffin Dunne on Joan Didion Doc's Kickstarter Success: 'We Were Flabbergasted.'" *Variety*, Nov 2, 2014.http://variety.com/2014/film/news/joan-Didion-documentary-kickstarter-1201345405/.

Lanham, Richard. *Analyzing Prose*. New York: Charles Scribner's Sons, 1983.

Leahy, Richard. "Style Matters: Helping Students Develop Good Style." *College Teaching* 43, no. 1 (1995): 7–12. http://www.jstor.org/stable/27558689.

Lehmann-Haupt, Christopher. "Books of the Times." Review of *Salvador*, by Joan Didion. *New York Times* March 11, 1983. http://www.nytimes.com/1983/03/11/books/books-of-the-times-025946.html.

Leonard, John. "The Black Album." Review of *The Year of Magical Thinking*, by Joan Didion. *The New York Review of Books*, October 20, 2005. http://www.nybooks.com/articles/archives/2005/oct/20/the-black-album/.

———. "Books of The Times." Review of *The White Album*, by Joan Didion. *The New York Times*, June 5, 1979. http://www.nytimes.com/1979/06/05/archives/books-of-the-times-dread-in-the-sunlight-vietnam-unmentioned.html.

———. Introduction to *We Tell Ourselves Stories in Order to Live*. New York: Alfred A. Knopf, 2006.

———. "Who Stole Democracy?" Review of *Political Fictions*, by Joan Didion. *The New York Times*, September 23, 2001. http://www.nytimes.com/2001/09/23/books/who-stole-democracy.html.

Mallon, Thomas. "On Second Thought." Review of *Where I Was From*, by Joan Didion. *The New York Times*, September 28, 2003. http://www.nytimes.com/2003/09/28/books/on-second-thought.html.

McClintock, Michael. "A Glimmer of Justice for El Salvador." *Amnesty Now* 28, no. 3 (Fall 2002): 12–13.

McClure, John. "Writing Off Salvador." *Minnesota Review* 21, no. 1 (1983): 110–14. https://muse.jhu.edu/.

McNeice, Katarzyna Nowak. *California and the Melancholic American Identity in Joan Didion's Novels: Exiled from Eden*. New York: Routledge, 2019.

Menand, Louis. "Out of Bethlehem: The Radicalization of Joan Didion." *The New Yorker*, August 24, 2015. https://www.newyorker.com/magazine/2015/08/24/out-of-bethlehem.

Muggli, Mark. "The Poetics of Joan Didion's Journalism." *American Literature* 59, no. 3 (1987): 402–21. http://www.jstor.org/stable/2927124.

Newfield, Jack. "Is There A 'New Journalism'?" *Columbia Journalism Review* 11, no. 2 (1972): 45–47.

Oates, Joyce Carol. "A Taut Novel of Disorder: *A Book of Common Prayer*." *The New York Times*, April 3, 1977. http://www.nytimes.com/1977/04/03/books/Didion-prayer.html?_r=0.

Ong, S.J., Walter. *Orality and Literacy: The Technologizing of the Word*. New York: Routledge, 1982.

Perelman, Chaim. "The New Rhetoric: A Theory of Practical Reasoning." In *The Rhetorical Tradition: Readings from Classical Times to the Present*, edited by Patricia Bizzell and Bruce Herzberg, 1384–1409. Boston: Bedford/St. Martin's, 2001.

Perelman, Chaim, and Lucie Olbrechts-Tyteca. *The New Rhetoric: A Treatise on Argumentation*. Indiana: University of Notre Dame Press, 1969.

Pinsky, Robert. " 'The Year of Magical Thinking': Goodbye to All That." Review of *The Year of Magical Thinking*, by Joan Didion. *The New York Times*, October 9, 2005. http://www.nytimes.com/2005/10/09/books/review/09pinsky.html?pagewanted=all&_r=0.

Roiphe, Katie. *In Praise of Messy Lives*: Essays. New York: Random House, 2012.

Rygiel, Dennis. "On the Neglect of Twentieth-Century Nonfiction: A Writing Teacher's View." *College English* 46, no. 4 (1984): 392–400. http://www.jstor.org/stable/376946.

Sanders, Scott Russell. "The Singular First Person," *The Sewanee Review* 45, no. 6 (Fall 1988): 658–72. http://www.jstor.org.ezproxy.bu.edu/stable/27545966.

Schilb, John. "Deconstructing Didion: Poststructuralist Rhetorical Theory in the Composition Classroom." In *Literary Nonfiction: Theory, Criticism, Pedagogy*, edited by Chris Anderson, 262–86. Urbana: Southern Illinois University Press, 1989.

Scott, Eugene. "Obama Cautions Against the Politics of Xenophobia and the Rejection of Facts in South Africa Speech." *The Washington Post*, July 17, 2018. https://www.washingtonpost.com/news/the-fix/wp/2018/07/17/obama-cautions-against-backing-political-leaders-who-embrace-xenophobia-and-reject-objective-truth/?utm_term=.a7f35ee94df9.

Strunk Jr., William, and E. B. White. *The Elements of Style*. Essex: Pearson Education Limited, 2014.

Talese, Gay. *Fame and Obscurity: A Book about New York, a Bridge, and Celebrities on the Edge*. New York: Doubleday, 1970.

Tredinnick, Mark. *Writing Well: The Essential Guide*. New York: Cambridge University Press, 2008. Kindle.

Valis, Noël. "Fear and Torment in El Salvador." *The Massachusetts Review* 48, no. 1 (2007): 117–31. http://www.jstor.org.ezproxy.bu.edu/stable/25091175.

Van Meter, Jonathan. "When Everything Changes," *New York Magazine*, Oct 2, 2005. http://nymag.com/nymetro/arts/books/14633/.

Vickers, Brian. *In Defense of Rhetoric*. Oxford: Clarendon, 1988.

Wakefield, Dan. "People, Places, and Personalities." Review of *Slouching Towards Bethlehem*, by Joan Didion. *The New York Times*, June 21, 1968. http://www.nytimes.com/1968/06/21/books/Didion-bethlehem.html.

Wilentz, Amy. "Where the Morning Went." Review of *Blue Nights*, by Joan Didion. *Los Angeles Review of Books*, October 26, 2011. http://lareviewofbooks.org/review/where-the-morning-went.

Williams, Joseph. *Style: Ten Lessons in Clarity and Grace*. New York: Longman, 2000.

Wilmer, Mary-Kay. "What If You Hadn't Been Home?" Review of *Blue Nights*, by Joan Didion. *London Review of Books*, November 3, 2011. http://www.lrb.co.uk/v33/n21/mary-kay-wilmers/what-if-you-hadnt-been-home.

Wilcox, Leonard. "Narrative Technique and the Theme of Historical Continuity in the Novels of Joan Didion." In *Joan Didion Essays & Conversations*, edited by Ellen G. Friedman, 68–80. Princeton: Ontario Review Press, 1984.

Wilson, Christopher. "The Underwater Narrative: Joan Didion's Miami." *Literary Journalism Studies* 3, no. 2 (2011): 9–29. Communication and Mass Media Complete, EBSCOhost.

Wimmer, Natasha "Telling It Like It Is (or Should Be)." *Publishers Weekly*, Oct 15, 2001. http://www.publishersweekly.com/pw/print/20011015/27425-telling-it-like-it-is-or-should-be.html.

Winchell, Mark Royden. *Joan Didion*. Boston: Twayne, 1980.

Winterowd, W. Ross. "Style: A Matter of Manner." *Quarterly Journal of Speech* 56, no. 2 (1970): 161–67.

Wolfe, Tom. "The Birth of 'The New Journalism'; Eyewitness Report by Tom Wolfe." *New York Magazine*, February 14, 1972. http://nymag.com/news/media/47353/.

———. *The New Journalism*. San Francisco: Harper and Row, 1973.

Wood, Michael. "The New Journalism." *The New York Times,* June 22, 1973. http://www.nytimes.com/books/98/11/08/specials/wolfe-journalism.html.

# Index

Als, Hilton, 34, 35, 36, 39, 41
Anderson, Chris, 4, 21, 22, 24, 59, 155n46

Bawer, Bruce 49, 134, 147n3, 161n27
Berkeley, 1, 22, 51, 76, 136, 137
Brentwood, 9, 130, 135
Brown, Jerry, 78, 84, 100
Burke, Kenneth, 149n22; and terministic screens, 72

California, 11–12, 15–16, 25, 30, 33, 50, 53–54, 60, 74–79, 93, 109, 110, 118, 120, 131, 139, 147n1, 157n15, 158n2, 159n3
camera, 5, 7, 36, 40, 80, 81, 113
Capote, Truman, 8, 22, 30, 134, 138
Carol Oates, Joyce, 134
catharsis, 67
Central Park Jogger, 19, 53, 55, 58, 61, 70, 144
cognitive dissonance, 25, 27, 58, 71
composition, discipline of, 21–22, 162n68
Conrad, Joseph, 6, 7, 48

Daugherty, Tracy, 1, 2, 30, 36, 39, 41, 52

Davidson, Sara, 6, 108, 133
Deconstructive approach, 151–52n80
Democrat, 18, 74, 75, 76, 87, 89; the democratic process, 77, 84, 86, 88, 100
Dickey, Christopher, 34
Dickey, James, 9
diction, and Didion, 4, 5, 7, 21, 22–23, 25, 92, 130, 135
Didion, Joan: and celebrity, 14, 33, 36, 107; dispassionate 35; elitist, 49, 138; enigmatic, 30; frail, 11–13, 29, 108, 133; idiosyncratic 134; narcissistic, 147; neurasthenic, 14, 29; neurotic, 4, 49, 101, 139, 147; privileged, 59, 78, 108, 128; and romantic ethic, 16, 150n57; sarcastic 60, 86, 92, 94, 107; sensitive 12; shy, 4, 6, 12; snob 135, 147; tentative 5, 12–13; witty 7, 89, 91; voice of, 5, 25, 36, 40, 60, 62, 73, 88–89, 93, 100, 106–107, 109; tone of, 38, 88
disappeared, or *desaparecer*, 49, 156n56
discourse, 70, 99, 107, 137, 153n19, 154n35; communities, 108, 120, 142; conventions, 141; political and cultural, 3; political, 69; public, 4, 19, 69; political and public, 145; of the women's movement, 143

domestic: concerns 5, 25; details, 139; focus 52; lives, 43; moments 51; politics, 26, 39; political affairs, 50; political scandal, 73; routines, 9
Doris Lessing, 141
dreamwork, 19, 68, 147n3
Dunne, Dominick (Nick), 29
Dunne, Griffin, 133–34
Dunne, John Gregory, 1, 6–7, 15, 18, 29, 31, 33–35, 47, 50, 72, 103–104, 106, 110–11, 116–17, 119–22, 134, 161n27
Dunne, Quintana Roo, 2, 30, 103–105, 108–109, 110, 115–16, 117, 120–31, 160n24
El Mozote, 34, 89
El Salvador, 18, 25, 33–34, 36–50, 89, 93, 139, n153, n156
essay, the: and essayistic voice, 109; form of, 60; genre of 12, 42, 51n71; and the essayist, 60, 106–107, 139, 155n47, 159n4

Felton, Sharon, 1
feminists, 17, 122, 138
figures of speech, 97, n149; alliteration, 21, 31, 65–66, 69–70, 96, 97–98, 128, 131; anadiplosis, 67–68, 86–87, 128, 130; anaphora, 31, 33, 42, 44, 64–66, 69–70, 74–75, 81, 83, 86, 96–97, 107, 109–10, 115, 121, 125, 128, 140, 155n49; anastrophe, 33, 45; antithesis, 20, 99–100, 130, 149, 155; apposition, 65–66, 70, 72, 79, 81, 84–86, 90, 95, 97–98, 117, 124, 128; asyndeton, 24, 43, 61, 65, 107, 115, 119, 125, 128–29; climax, 66–67, 117, 128, 149; correctio, 66; ellipsis, 99, 107, 119, 124, 130; emblem, 21–23, 35, 64, 138; epanalepsis, 66, 86, 100, 109, 131; epistrophe, 86–87, 109, 121–23, 128–31; exergasia, 67; hypotyposis 44, 155n50; hypozeugma, 88; irony, 5, 21, 33, 35, 41, 61, 81, 92, 99, 100, 107, 141–42; isocolon, 66, 155n49; litotes, 60, 63, 107; metaphor, 7, 21, 23, 31, 33, 43, 45, 56, 70, 77, 105, 119, 135–36; metonymy, 21, 23–24; parallelism, 20, 24, 98, 125; parallel structure, 65, 98, 118; parataxis, 81, 83, 97, 109–10, 125; parenthesis, 7, 24, 27, 33, 42, 46, 56, 60, 62, 68–70, 72, 74, 79, 86, 91–92, 116–17, 128–29, 140, 162n68; personification, 56; polysyndeton, 24, 42, 46, 97, 107, 109, 111, 121 synecdoche, 24, 42, 45, 136; tricolon, 61
Flanagan, Caitlin, 12, 14, 135
Ford, Harrison, 30
form: and content, 5–7; poetic, 31; as rhetorical, 106; of the sentence 85; as style, 22, 47, 50

Garcia, Jerry, 137–38
Gingrich, Newt, 83–84, 107
grammar, 5, 23, 109, 126, 142, 145, 159n14; action verbs, 35; active voice, 38, 90; adverbs, 155n55; antecedent, 59, 61; base clause, 81, 84; cohesive device, 64; coordinating conjunctions, 31, 61, 66, 70–71, 98, 116; deictic terms, 37–38, 77; dependent clause, 74, 81; double negative, 74, 95; dummy pronoun, 60; expletive, 33, 60, 63, 75, 81, 96; first person, 38, 45, 58, 127, 159n4; indefinite pronoun, 74; independent clause, 81, 99, 116–17; nominalizations 35, 80, 87–91, 94–95, 99, 159n15; passive voice,

38, 60–62, 64, 66, 81, 87–90, 92, 94; predicates, 24; prepositional phrase, 31, 70, 95, 117, 129; pronouns, 38, 58–60, 74, 76, 78, 118–19, n147; subordination, 49, 83, 96; third-person plural, 77, 92; transitional words/phrases, 14, 23, 109, 119
grief, 104, 106–108, 111–12, 114–15, 120–24; and magical thinking, 15, 19, 55–56, 71
Grizzuti Harrison, Barbara, 13, 147n3, 160n8

Haight-Ashbury, 11, 17, 136–37
Hemingway, Ernest, 6, 13, 126
Henderson, Katherine Usher, 1, 20, 21
Hollywood, 15, 17, 29, 52, 77, 142

ideology, 17, 25, 35, 43, 74, 142, 151

James, Henry, 6–7, 126, 137

Kakutani, Michiko, 8, 9, 11, 14, 47, 103, 133, 148n5
Kasabian, Linda, 13–14, 137
Kuehl, Linda, 149n15
Latour, Bruno, 3–4
Leonard, John, 10, 12, 150n33
literature: and literary analysis 21; literary approach to, 30–33; criticism of, 21; and literary device 51; and literary effect 12; and literary elite 76; genre of, 22; and literary journalists, 21–22; and literary modelsm 145; and literary nonfiction 21; and literary play, 148n14; and literary scene, 1; and literary style, 151n61; and literary studies, 144
Los Angeles, 2, 30, 55, 74, 158n2
*Los Angeles Times*, 55, 121

Malibu, 30, 107
Manhattan, 63, 107
McPhee, John, 30
media, the, 3–4, 26, 55, 58–59, 68, 107
memoir, 1, 5, 15, 18, 26, 59, 103, 105–106, 111, 114, 123, 159n3
memory, 6, 15, 75, 84, 97, 112–13, 123–24, 128, 130, 139
modifiers, 94, 116–17, 123, 162n68; free, 81, 84, 86, 128; resumptive, 86, 97; summative, 86, 98
Muggli, Mark, 1, 21–23, 151n80, 157n15
myth, 16, 57–58, 71, 142; and mythologies, 4, 15–16, 25–26, 53, 66; and mythologizing, 54–55, 58, 106

Nancy Reagan, 20, 54
New Journalism, 1, 20, 32, 37, 152n2, 160n8, 161n29
New Journalists, 8, 24, 30, 32, 37, 50
New York City, 25, 55, 57, 58
*New York Review of Books*, 18, 74

Ong, Walter J., 94, 96–97
O Keeffe, Georgia, 13

*Paris Review*, 15, 18
Perelman, Chaim, 149n22, 155n45
persuasive, style as, 7, 22, 25, 35, 61, 62; and force of, 99, 138
platitudes, 16–17, 143
Polanski, Roman, 13–14, 137
political process, 26, 74–77, 81–82, 87, 92, 98–100, 108
Poststructuralist, n151
preferred storylines, 68
prose style: bewitching, 144; chant-like, 65; and cadence, 10, 21, 82; enchanting, 10; elegiac, 125;

prose style *(continued)*
  as elliptical, 5, 8–10, 26, 47, 89, 115–16, 119, 128, 134–35, 141; mannered, 2, 10, 134; fluidity of, 4, 49, 86, 130, 131; fragmented nature of, 103, 116; incantatory, 8, 11, 81, 125, 145, 147n3; as lament, 105, 130, 125, 128; as litany, 104–105; lyrical, 31; and phrasing, 97, 153n4; spare, 8, 26, 48, 110, 117, 135
prose stylist, Didion as: 9, 14, 44
pseudo-events, 54, 76–77, 99
punctuation, Didion's use of, 6–7, 25, 109, 116, 128, 153n4, 159n14; commas, 6–7, 31, 144; quotation marks, 17, 39, 60, 62–64, 69, 91, 92, 94, 128, 148n3, 151n61

Republican, 18, 74–76, 86, 93, 95, 136
rhetoric, 4, 15, 17–19, 21, 22–24; and abstractions, 3, 15, 17, 23, 69, 156n69; and agenda setting 69, 83; and amplification, 42, 46, 155n44; and anecdote, 23–24, 54, 72, 73; and collaboration, 24, 65, 149n22; and ethos, 58, 60; and frameworks, 70–72; of gaps, 23; and identification, 5, 20, 26, 36, 39, 56, 107, 127, 154n27; and insider status, 17, 51, 58, 76, 80, 92, 94, 98; and juxtaposition, 45, 61, 73, 79, 98; and narrative convention, 71, 142, 144; and omission, 9, 20, 26, 45, 61, 106, 122; and outsider status, 16–17, 19, 26, 33, 59, 77, 80–82, 98–99, 157–58n2; of particularity, 23; of process, 23 24, 59 ; and pathos, 40, 106, 139; and understatement, 20, 33, 62–64, 90–92, 100, 107, 139

running the story, 83
Rich, Nathaniel, 3
Robbins, Henry, 53
Roiphe, Katie, 2, 11, 107, 134

Sacramento, 1, 15, 51 (Sacramento Valley 15)
scapegoat, 57, 67
Schilb, John, 151n80, 153n19
sentences: balanced 85, 96, 99, 120, 122; coordinated, 21, 83, 85; cumulative 24, 33, 42, 66, 72, 80–82, 84–85; declarative 14, 31, 66, 93, 97, 107, 118, 130; fragments, 32, 105, 109, 115, 119–20, 129, 130, 140, n153; loose, 98, 116, 123, 126; paratactic, 82–84; periodic, 70, 117; rhythmic, 8, 65, 83, 94, 96–97, 104–105; repetitive, 52, 82, 105, 134; simple, 110, 115, 120, 122; running style, 84
"Sentimental Journeys," 25, 53, 55, 71
silent generation, 137
Silvers, Robert (Bob), 11, 18–19, 33–34, 73–74, 153n9, 162n62
style, as rhetorical: 4–5, 7, 11, 12–14, 20–22, 25, 42, 53–55, 57–63, 65, 68, 72–73, 75, 88, 107–108, 120, 135, 140–42, 144–45, 147n3, 148n9, 149n14, 151n80, 154n19, 156n69, 158n3, 159n14
subject matter, 3, 21, 30, 92, 103, 114, 121
symbols, 22, 23, 56, 64; and symbolic language, 15–16, 22, 56–57, 68 98, 124
syntax, 5–7, 11, 22, 46, 62, 80, 89, 96–98, 101, 106, 108–109, 130, 135, 156n18, 158n3

Talese, Gay, 30, 32, 138

# Index

Thompson, Hunter S., 30, 138

Vogue, 1, 5, 14, 76, 134, 144

Wakefield, Dan, 50, 134, 138
Washington D.C., 19, 37, 53, 76, 77, 83, 94
Washington Post, 34, 80, 90
Wasser, Julian, 133
western code, 108
Winchell, Mark Royden, 1, 151n64
Wolfe, Tom 8, 22, 30, 37, 138, 152n2
Woodward, Bob, 83, 88, 90, 91
works, Didion: After Henry, 18, 24, 25, 53, 73; Blue Nights, 10, 24, 26, 103, 124, 125, 127, 133–34, 135; A Book of Common Prayer, 7, 9, 11, 20, 29, 39, 50, 135; "Good Citizens," 20, 52; "Insider Baseball," 76, 79, 92, 97; The Last Thing He Wanted, 9; Miami, 18, 53, 58, 156n69; "On Going Home," 23; "On Morality," 23; Play It as It Lays, 9–10, 20, 155n55; Run River, 11, 29, 134; Year of Magical Thinking, the, 10, 24, 26, 50, 103, 108, 110; "On the Morning After the Sixties," 22; Political Fictions, 12, 18–19, 25, 73, 135, 150n33; Salvador, 5, 18, 22, 24–25, 29, 33; Slouching Towards Bethlehem, 12, 23, 27, 60, 106, 134; South and West: From a Notebook, 24, 35; Stories We Tell Ourselves in Order to Live, 12; Where I Was From, 15, 18, 159n3; The White Album, 8, 10, 20, 22, 27, 29, 30, 33, 53, 60, 106, 144; "White Album, The," 13, 22, 33, 154n27; "Why I Write," 5–6

writing: and copying, 145, 147n3, 162n68; as figurative, 15, 26, 32, 43, 65, 80, 121, 135, 136; as literal 15–16, 32, 43, 79–80, 99, 121, 125, 135–36 153n19; as metadiscursive, 112

www.ingramcontent.com/pod-product-compliance
Lightning Source LLC
Chambersburg PA
CBHW032256150426
43195CB00008BA/479